Graphical Simulation Modeling and Analysis

Using SIGMA for Windows

Lee W. Schruben
Cornell University

The Scientific Press Series
boyd & fraser publishing company

Acquisitions Editor: DeVilla Williams
Technical Editor: Donna Schruben
Production Services: Elm Street Publishing Services, Inc.
Manufacturing Director: Gordon Woodside

One Corporate Place • Ferncroft Village
Danvers, MA 01923

The Scientific Press Series

International Thomson Publishing
boyd & fraser publishing company is an ITP Company.
The ITP trademark is used under license.

Manufactured in the United States of America

ISBN 0-87709-782-8

Library of Congress Cataloging-in-Publication Data

Schruben, Lee W.
Graphical simulation modeling and analysis : using SIGMA for Windows / Lee W. Schruben.
p. cm.—(The Scientific Press series)
Includes index.
ISBN 0-87709-782-8
1. Computer simulation. 2. Computer graphics. 3. SIGMA for Windows. I. Title. II. Series.
QA76.9.C65S3845 1995
003'.35369—dc20 94-14076

2 3 4 5 6 7 8 9 10 MT 8 7 6 5

for Donna

CONTENTS

LIST OF FIGURES

ACKNOWLEDGMENTS

In this book, graphical representations of fundamental concepts are used extensively. An appreciation for "using pictures" as well as mathematics in designing and analyzing simulation experiments was given to me by Professor Russell Barton. For model building—the graphical simulation environment—SIGMA is used. This is the third release of SIGMA. Like its predecessors, this enhanced version of SIGMA was developed without research funding. Special thanks go to Quint King, Frank Chance, and Kevin Healy for their talent, enthusiasm, and support. My continuing thanks go to those who helped with the first two releases of SIGMA, as well as the students in my simulation courses.

PREFACE

The theme of this book is to represent ideas graphically where possible. Pictures are used extensively to explain fundamental concepts. Mathematics and statistics play an important supporting role. Computer code is used sparingly and then only as a last resort.

This book is about the simulation of systems that experience discrete changes at particular instants of time. Applications of discrete event models can be found in a variety of areas such as manufacturing, communication, agriculture, transportation, and health care. Most serious studies of modern production or service systems involve discrete event simulation. Indeed, simulation is often the only reasonable technique for the design and analysis of these systems. Decisions based on simulation models touch almost all aspects of daily life, making it perhaps the most important computer application in science and engineering.

The motivation for this book is to make discrete event simulation models easier to build and use correctly. Courses based on the material in this book are taught primarily in engineering colleges and business schools. A university course can use this book to provide the foundation for an in-depth study of any number of commercial simulation languages during the later part of the course. While the presentations are intended to be straightforward and intuitive, some of the concepts are quite advanced. Previous editions of this book have been used effectively in freshmen courses as well as in courses for advanced Ph.D. students.

An introductory course on simulation fundamentals can be based on Chapter 2 (concepts and terminology), Chapter 5 (graphical modeling), Chapter 9 (input processes), and Chapter 10 (output analysis). Chapters 12 and 13 cover more advanced modeling techniques. These chapters (with the exception of Section 12.5) are more or less software independent.

The basic simulation building block used in this book is the event. Models are developed using the simple and intuitive notion of an *event graph.*

The fundamental concepts of event graphs can be learned in a matter of minutes; however, the event graph paradigm is completely general. Any simulation including continuous time, process interaction, event scheduling, and activity scanning models, indeed any computer program, can be represented using an event graph. The previous lack of a unifying graphical structure for discrete event simulations may account in part for the apparent *ad-hoc* and complex reputation of these models. Without a graphical foundation, discrete event simulations are typically difficult to program and analyze.

This book contains complete documentation for the SIGMA for Windows graphical simulation environment. However, the modeling and analysis concepts presented are universal and apply regardless of the particular software used. Specific material on SIGMA is interspersed among the above chapters with the intent of giving the reader "hands-on" experience as soon as possible. Even if different simulation software is used, the brief tutorials in Chapters 3 and 4 should be taken to reinforce basic modeling and analysis ideas.

Lee W. Schruben
Cornell University

SIGMA FOR WINDOWS

SIGMA for Windows is based on the simple and intuitive event graph approach to simulation modeling. The SIGMA project began in 1983 as an effort to implement the notion of event graphs on personal computers and has evolved into a powerful and practical method for simulation modeling. SIGMA, the Simulation Graphical Modeling and Analysis system, is an integrated, interactive approach to building, testing, animating, and experimenting with discrete event simulations on personal computers while they are running. SIGMA is specifically designed to make learning the fundamentals of simulation modeling easy. SIGMA is able to automatically translate a simulation model into portable source code that can be compiled and run on a wide variety of computers. Unlike other modeling tools, the complete source code for SIGMA-generated simulations, including code for the simulation utility library, is provided. SIGMA can even write a description of a model in English.

All the functionality of the previous versions has been incorporated into this latest version of SIGMA for Windows. However, significantly more powerful modeling capabilities and increased analytical power have been added. This is totally reengineered and recoded software.

HARDWARE RECOMMENDATIONS

SIGMA for Windows requires Microsoft Windows (Version 3.1 or later). Windows runs best on more powerful computers. A fast 486-class computer or higher is recommended; however, any computer capable of running Windows will do. Persons have reported running SIGMA (with DOS emulators) on many computers, including those made by Apple, DEC, IBM (or work-a-likes), NeXT, and Sun.

To take advantage of SIGMA for Windows' ability to paste data, pictures, and text into other Windows applications, it is suggested that you also have a Windows spreadsheet program and word processor. Finally, to take full advantage of the power of SIGMA for Windows, you might want to obtain a C compiler to permit you to easily port and run simulation models on other computers. There are free C compilers in the public domain that are sufficient; however, even the best commercial compilers with source-level debuggers are quite inexpensive.

Disk Contents

Your SIGMA disks contain several different types of files. The function of a SIGMA file is identified by the extension to the file's name. The following table gives the specific file types.

File Name Extension	*File Type Indicated*
`.BAK`	Backup copy of the last saved model
`.BAT`	Batch files
`.BMP`	Bitmaps used for animations
`.C`	Source code in C
`.DAT`	Data files for SIGMA models
`.EXE`	Executable programs
`.H`	Source code in C

`.INP`	Input response files for batched runs
`.MOD`	Sample SIGMA models
`.OUT`	SIGMA output files (if any)
`.PAS`	Source code in Pascal
`.PIX`	Sets of bitmaps for animating a particular model
`.PLT`	Plots from previous simulation runs (if any)
`.SLM`	FORTRAN code for SLAM
`.SMN`	FORTRAN code for SIMAN

➢ **Important:** *Any documentation updates and new features that may have been added to* SIGMA *since the printing of this book would be found in a file called* `READTHIS.TXT` *on your* SIGMA *disk. Double-click on this file to see these updates.*

1

SIGMA: Overview & Installation

Chapter 1 begins with an overview of the new SIGMA for Windows software system. Next, instructions for installing SIGMA under Windows and under OS/2 are given. Following this, a brief tour of SIGMA is presented to acquaint you with some of its basic features.

1.1 The SIGMA Modeling Environment

SIGMA for Windows is a new approach to discrete event simulation modeling and analysis with several unique and powerful simulation modeling features. The most striking feature in SIGMA for Windows is the fact that general simulation models can be created, enriched, and edited *while they are running*. Events can be added, altered, or even deleted during a simulation run. Logic can be changed and errors corrected without stopping a run to change code and recompile. You can even pause and "replay" interesting events. Using SIGMA for Windows, a simulation model can be developed and verified in a fraction of the time it would take using conventional simulation languages.

Animation support is fundamentally different in SIGMA for Windows than in other simulation modeling environments. Animations are not created from simulation models using conventional add-on software; in SIGMA for Windows, *the animation and the simulation model are identical.*

In addition to graphical modeling, analysis, and animation, SIGMA for Windows also includes state-of-the-art graphical data tracking tools and allows pictures, graphs, plots, and data to be pasted into spreadsheets and word processors. For speed and portability, SIGMA models can be automatically translated (with a mouse click) into a variety of languages, including C, Pascal, and FORTRAN (SLAM or SIMAN prototypes). A SIGMA model will even write a description of itself in English.

Figure 1.1: Run Dialog Box

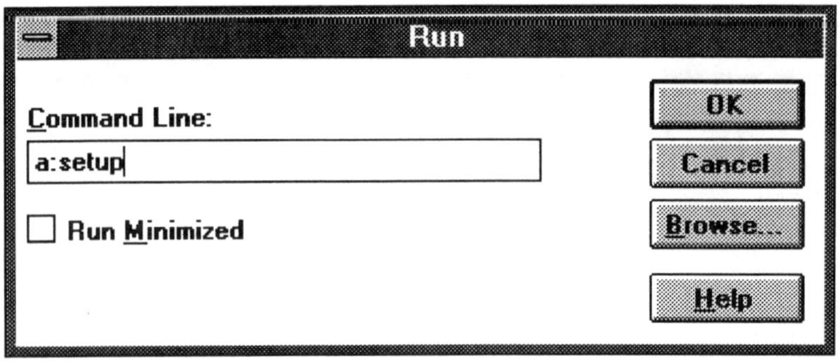

Multiple SIGMA sessions can be run concurrently. You can copy and paste objects from one modeling session to another. In fact, models can be developed in one SIGMA session and then graphically integrated into another simulation model while that model is executing.

SIGMA for Windows supports the full simulation model life cycle: from model building and testing to output analysis, animation, documentation, and report writing. Discrete event simulation model building has never been easier, and the results from simulations have never before been so easy to observe and understand.

1.2 Installing SIGMA under Windows

Installing SIGMA under Windows is a straightforward process.

1. Get into Windows 3.1 and insert Disk 1 in drive a: (or b:).
2. Click on the **Run** command under the **File** menu. A dialog box will appear similar to the one in Figure 1.1.
3. Enter [a:setup] (or [b:setup]) and press the **OK** button.
4. Follow the setup instructions. You will be asked which directory on your hard disk you wish to use for SIGMA. (The default is [c:sigma].) You may choose to use different directories or drives if you already have a DOS version of SIGMA installed since the two versions should be in *different* directories.
5. When setup is complete, copy (drag and drop) any other distribution disk(s) into the directory you chose for SIGMA using the Windows **File Manager**.

There will be three program icons in the SIGMA for Windows group: **SIGMA**, **SIGPLOT**, and **TRANSLAT**. Most users will want to use only **SIGMA**. **SIGPLOT** is a DOS output analysis package for persons who do not have a spreadsheet and want to use the DOS output analysis routines to plot large data sets. **TRANSLAT** is a DOS utility for generating prototype FORTRAN code (using SLAM or SIMAN) from SIGMA models.

> ➢ **Warning:** *You should have at least 100K of free space in your hard drive after installing* SIGMA *in order to save your models.*

(Optional) Click on the **Arrange Icons** command under the **Window** menu in the **Program Manager**. Choose the **Save Settings on Exit** command under the **Options** menu in the **File Manager**. You can make the new SIGMA group box smaller by dragging your mouse on the corners of the box.

1.3 Using OS/2

Installing SIGMA for Windows under OS/2 is also straightforward. Simply copy the contents of the distribution disks into a separate directory and add program icons for `SIGMA.EXE`, `SIGPLOT.EXE`, and `TRANSLAT.EXE`.

1.4 A Quick Tour of SIGMA for Windows

> ➢ *Throughout this book, entries on the monitor, file or directory names, mouse commands, and key strokes or key names are shown in a distinctive typeface (e.g.,* `monitor display`, `FILENAME.MOD`, **Tool Name** *or* **Command Button***, and* [key strokes] *or* [←Enter]*).*

Chapter 3 of this book contains a detailed tutorial. To get a quick flavor of the software try the following steps:

1. *Start a* SIGMA *session.* If you are not already in SIGMA, double-click the mouse button on the **SIGMA** icon in the Windows **Program Manager.** The window that appears is the *simulation graph* window. You are now in SIGMA.
2. *Get into* **Select or Edit** *mode.* Your mouse pointer will look like a plus sign enclosed by a circle, ⊕, when it is in the *simulation graph* window.

Figure 1.2: A Simulation Model of a Carwash, `CARWASH.MOD`

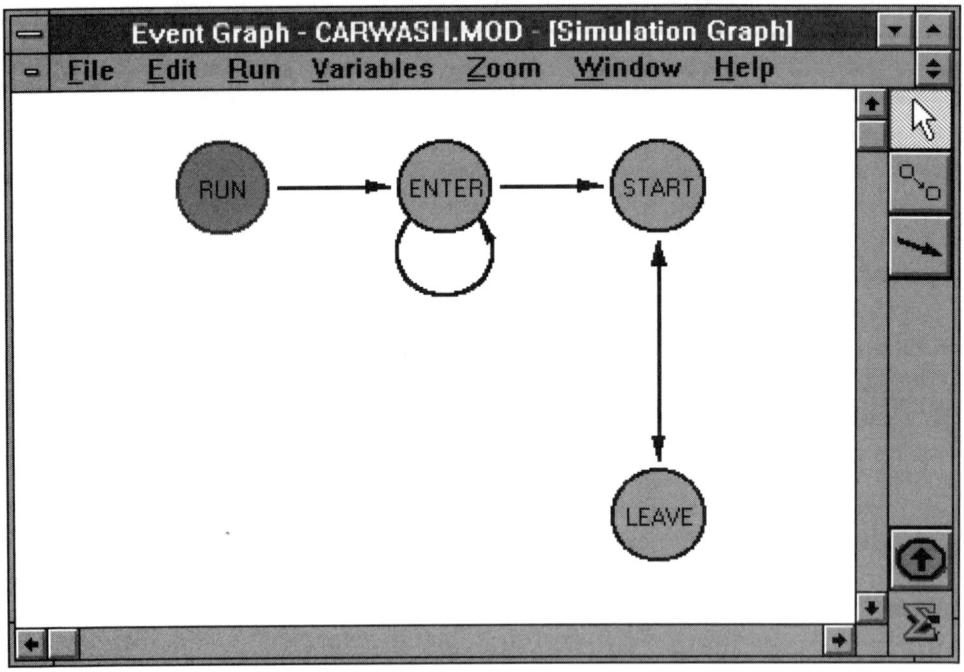

This shape indicates the **Create Process** mode. If you click the right mouse button, the mouse pointer will assume an arrow shape, ↖, which indicates **Select or Edit** mode. Click the right mouse button and get into **Select or Edit** mode.

3. *Read in a model.* Using the arrow-shaped mouse pointer, click on the **File** menu. Click once on the **Open** command. A dialog box will appear. Scroll through the list of file names until you see `CARWASH.MOD.` Double-click on this model, which is a simple simulation of an automatic carwash with only two state variables: `QUEUE`, the number of cars waiting in line, and `SERVER`, the status of the machine, `0=BUSY` and `1=IDLE`. This model is represented in Figure 1.2.

   NETWORK USERS: If you are running SIGMA from a network server, your default drive is probably write-protected. Thus, you will get a system error message if you run the simulation. You must add a drive letter before the output file name in the **Run Options** dialog box. For example, you should change `CARWASH.OUT` to `C:\CARWASH.OUT` so you can write the output to your c: drive. (Click on the **Options** command under the **Run** menu. In the **Run Options** dialog box, add the drive letter to the name of the file in the **Output File** text box. Next, click on the **OK** button and pro-

Figure 1.3: The Run Options Dialog Box

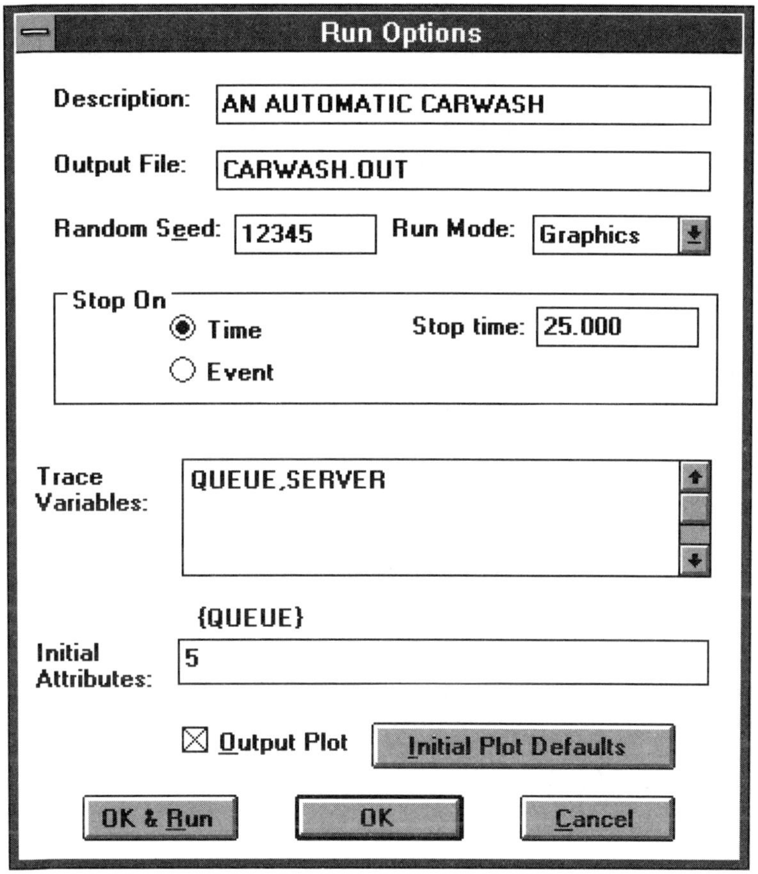

ceed to Step 4.) You should not use a floppy drive as your default drive as this will slow the running of your simulation considerably.

> ➢ **Warning:** *You should not use a floppy drive or a write-protected network drive as your default drive.*

4. *Run the simulation.* Click once on the **Options** command in the **Run** menu. The **Run Options** dialog box will appear (see Figure 1.3). Click the **OK & Run** button at the bottom of this dialog box. (Respond **OK** if a dialog box appears with the question "Replace existing `CARWASH.OUT`?") As

Figure 1.4: The View Output Trace Dialog Box

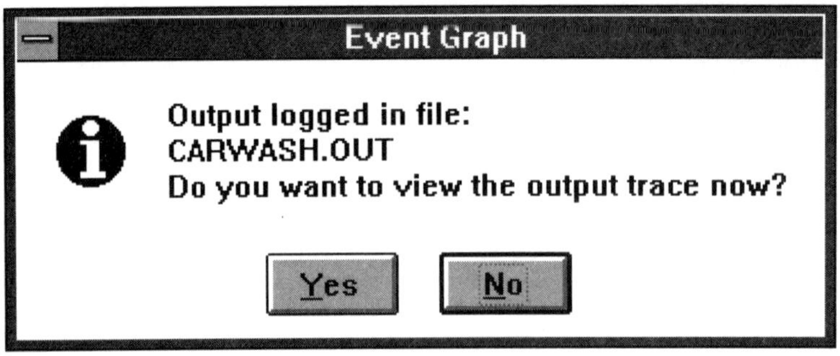

the model executes, you will see a logical animation of the simulation graph. (Notice that the value of the variable `QUEUE` is displayed above the `ENTER` vertex.) A simulation plot showing the graphical output for `CARWASH.MOD` will also appear. The numerical output will be written on your disk in a file called `CARWASH.OUT`.

5. *View the output file.* After the simulation run is complete, a dialog box (like the one in Figure 1.4) will appear asking if you want to view the output trace. Respond by clicking the **Yes** button.

   The output from the simulation will appear in a third window titled `CARWASH.OUT`. You should maximize this window by clicking on the **Maximize** button to see the full screen (click on the up arrow at the far right of the output window title bar—see Figure 1.5).

Figure 1.5: Maximize Button

After viewing the output, hold the [↑Shift] key and press [F4] to tile the three windows again and click on the **Minimize** button for the `CARWASH.OUT` window (click on the down arrow at the right of the title bar—see Figure 1.6).

Figure 1.6: Minimize Button

Hold [↑Shift] and press [F4] to tile the other two windows. You should now see a simulation graph window and a simulation plot window similar to those in Figure 1.7.

Figure 1.7: SIGMA Model with Simulation Graph and Simulation Plot Windows

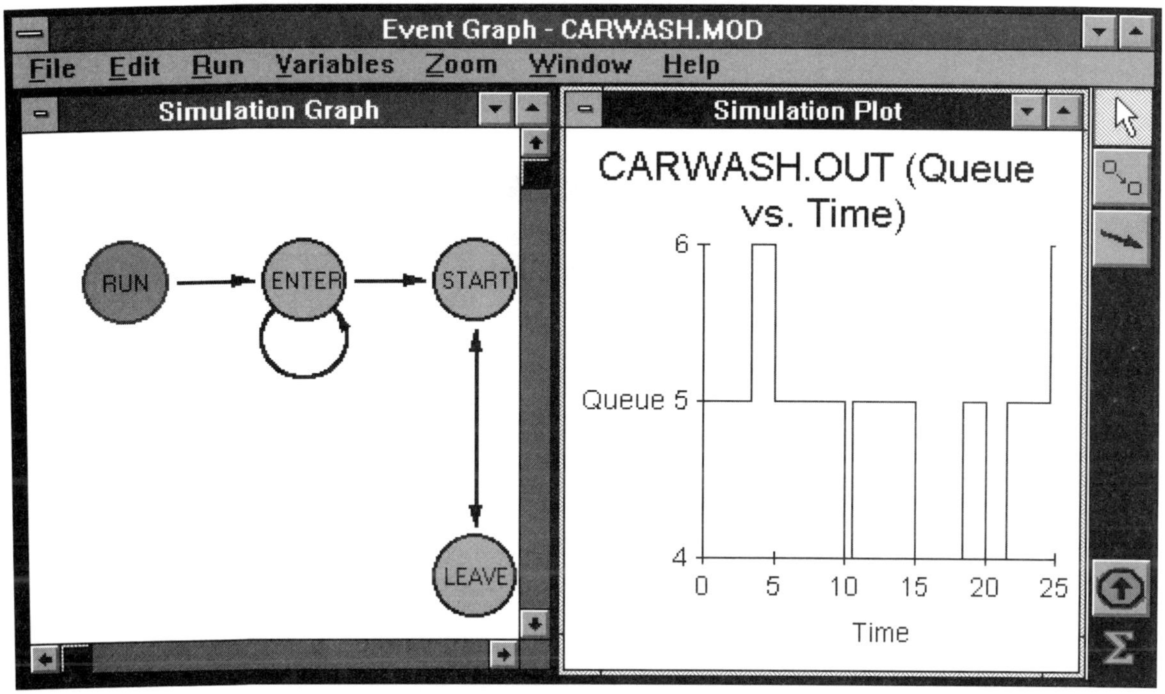

6. *Change the type of output plot.* Double-click anywhere within the area of the *simulation plot* window. An **Output Plots** dialog box will appear. Click the down arrow at the right of the **Plot Type** drop-down list to see the various plot types available to you; click on **Histogram** (see Figure 1.8). Next, click on the **OK** button at the bottom of the dialog box. The output will be graphically represented as a histogram. Open the **Output Plots** dialog box again by double-clicking on the histogram and change the plot type back to **Step Plot.**

7. *Translate model to source code.* Activate the *simulation graph* window by clicking anywhere within that window. Next, click on the **Translate** command in the **File** menu. Three translation choices will appear: **C**, **Pascal**, and **English**. You can translate this model into C, Pascal, and/or English by clicking on the language of your choice. Click on an option; a dialog box will appear with the file name highlighted (with the appropriate file type—i.e., `CARWASH.ENG`, `CARWASH.C`, `CARWASH.PAS`). Click the **OK** button to confirm the file name. Respond **Yes** if you are asked to replace an existing file and **Yes** when asked to see the translation now. Use the scroll bars to view the entire file. Again, minimize the

Figure 1.8: Dialog Box for Changing Plot Type

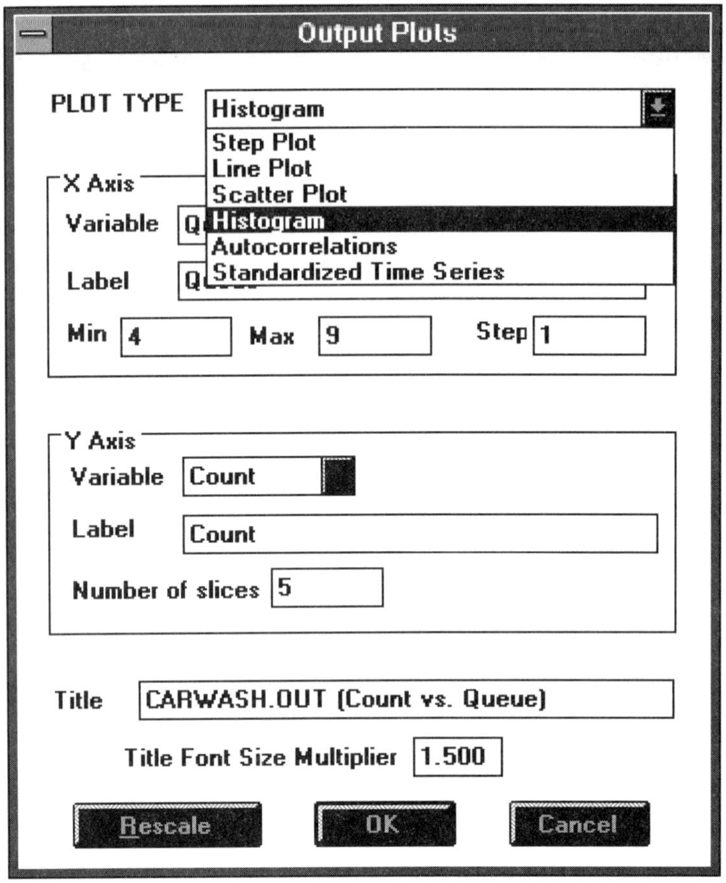

translated file window and press the **Tile** command under the **Window** menu to view all the windows or press [↑Shift-F4].

8. *Examine the event graph.* To see the details of the carwash event graph, double-click on the vertices (balls) and edges (arrows) in the *simulation graph* window. Click the **Cancel** button at the bottom of each **Edit Vertex** or **Edit Edge** dialog box, or click **Exit** in the multiple edge dialog box you see after clicking on the double edge between the `START` and `LEAVE` vertices.

9. *Create another vertex while the model is running.* With the *simulation graph* window active, open the **Run Options** dialog box under the **Run** menu. Increase the **Stop Time** to 10000 by dragging the mouse across the **Stop Time** text box and entering 10000. Click the **OK & Run** button to start the simulation. Click **OK** if asked to replace an existing `CARWASH.OUT`. Move or close the **Trace Window**, if it is active, to get a

better view of the plot window. Look at the value of `QUEUE` in the *simulation plot* window. Click anywhere within the *simulation graph* window to activate it, and then click the right mouse button to get into **Create Process** mode. Click the left mouse button once to add a vertex. Click the right mouse button to get back into **Select or Edit** mode. Double-click on the newly created vertex to open the **Edit Vertex** dialog box. In the **State Change(s)** text box, enter `QUEUE=80;` then press **Execute**. The `QUEUE` in the simulation plot window will increase dramatically. Click on the red **End Run** tool at the lower right of the screen or press [F5] to stop the run. Press [←Enter] several times to confirm ending the run and decline when asked to view output.

10. *Run an animation.* Click the **Maximize** button in the far upper-right corner of the *simulation graph* window. Click **Open** under the **File** menu. Press **No** when asked to save changes to `CARWASH.MOD`. Locate the model called `ANIMATE.MOD` and double-click on it to open it. Press [F5] to start the run. If asked to replace an existing `ANIMATE.OUT`, press **OK**. Press **Yes** if a warning message appears. If you have a fast machine, you may want to slow down the animation by pressing [F2]. You also may want to move the **Trace Window** if it is in the way. Press [F5] to stop the run. Press [←Enter] in response to the messages that appear at the end of the simulation.
11. *Exit* SIGMA. Exit by clicking on the **Close** command in the SIGMA **Control** menu (on the left side of the *title bar* of the *simulation graph* window). Do *not* save your model! Make sure to click the **No** button, when asked to save changes to the model.

You are now ready to learn how to build your own simulations with SIGMA for Windows. This can be a great deal of fun. Enjoy!

2

Discrete Event System Modeling

A process cannot be understood by stopping it. Understanding must move with the flow of the process, must join it and flow with it.
FIRST LAW OF MENTAT*

Chapter 2 contains an introduction to the key concepts and terminology of discrete event simulation. The event graph, a method of concisely organizing the elements of a discrete event simulation, is introduced. Using a simple waiting line as an example, an elementary event graph is developed and explained. The future events list, which is the master scheduler of events in a discrete event simulation, is examined in detail. A verbal description of an event graph is introduced as a first step in developing a formal event graph.

2.1 Background and Terminology for Systems Modeling

In this book we will use computer simulation to study the dynamic behavior of systems—i.e., how systems change over time. Our focus will be on those systems where the status of a system changes at a particular instant of time; such systems are called discrete event systems. Discrete event systems can be found in areas as diverse as manufacturing, transportation, computing, communications, finance, medicine, and agriculture. Engineers, scientists, managers, and planners use simulation methodologies to design and test new systems and to evaluate existing ones, thus avoiding the expense and risks of physical prototypes and pilot studies.

**Dune*, by Frank Herbert. Chilton Book Company: Radnor, PA. 1965.

Simulation is arguably the most important analytical computer application. Wagner (1988), in a review of operations research modeling techniques, conjectured that simulation applications outnumber the application of mathematical programming techniques by a ratio of 10 to 1.

2.1.1 Systems

It will be sufficient for our purposes to define a system as

> *a collection of entities that interact with a common purpose according to sets of laws and policies.*

The system may already exist, or it may be proposed. Using simulation, even theoretical systems can be studied. We intentionally do not define a system by the specific entities in it. Rather, we define a system by its purpose. Thus, we speak of a communications system, a health care system, a production system, etc. Using a *functional* definition of a system helps us avoid thinking of a system as having a fixed structure. Consequently, we view a system in terms of how it ought to function rather than how it has traditionally worked in the past. To design a new system it is necessary to free our thinking from the status quo.

The entities making up the system may be either physical or mathematical. A physical entity might be a patient in a hospital or a part in a factory; a mathematical entity might be a variable in an equation.

When developing simulation models of systems, it is useful to classify entities as being either *resident* entities or *transient* entities. Resident entities remain part of the system for long intervals of time, whereas transient entities enter into and depart from the system with relative frequency. In a factory, a resident entity might be a machine; a transient entity might be a part. Depending on the level of detail desired, a factory worker might be regarded as a transient entity in one model and a resident entity in another.

In describing a particular aspect of the dynamic behavior of a system, it is often useful to focus on the *cycles* of the resident entities. For example, we might describe the busy-idle cycles of machines or workers. Alternatively, we might focus on the *paths* along which transient entities flow as they pass through the system (e.g., parts moving through a factory). Transient entity system descriptions tend to be more detailed (and more informative) than resident entity descriptions. Each type of modeling has advantages: modeling resident entity cycles tends to be easy and efficient, while modeling the details of transient entity flow gives more information. Typically, a mixture of both viewpoints is used, but one or the other predominates.

In systems where there are relatively few resident entities and a great many transient entities, it is usually most efficient to study the cycles of the resident entities. Examples include semiconductor factories with thousands of wafers, communication systems with millions of messages, and transportation systems with tens of thousands of vehicles. In simulating such systems, the cycles of resident entities might be described by the values of only a few variables, while the flow of transient entities might require a great many variables to describe. On the other hand, systems where there are only a few transient entities and many resident entities (a power line inspection system or an airline maintenance facility) may be efficiently studied by examining the flow of transient entities.

It will often be the case that an initial model consisting only of resident entities is appropriate. Thus, first-cut system experiments can be done with a simple and efficient model. After a design has been roughed out and more details are desired, the model can be enriched into a transient entity flow model. Enriching the model to explicitly include transient entities generally makes the model larger, more complex, more prone to errors, and slower to execute. It may be wiser to use detailed transient entity models only for final refinements of a design. A well-designed simulation may have some sections that model only resident entity cycles and other sections that model the detailed flow of transient entities.

Entities are described by their characteristics (referred to as *attributes*). Attributes can be quantitative or qualitative. Moreover, they can be static and never change (the speed of a machine), or they can be dynamic and change over time (the length of a waiting line). Dynamic attributes can further be classified as deterministic or stochastic depending on whether or not the changes in their values can be predicted with certainty. It is sometimes useful to think of entities as belonging in sets owned by other entities. For example, in a factory a set of parts might be waiting in a line (queue) for a particular machine. Also, a set of machines (routing) might be required to process each part. Thus, each machine owns a set of parts, and each part owns a set of machines.

The level of detail with which we choose to describe a system determines whether a particular system component is thought of as an entity or an attribute of some entity. In Figure 2.1, we examine various levels of detail in a regional health care system.

We might think of the number of hospitals in the region as an attribute of the region. For greater detail, we might want to consider each hospital as a separate entity with the clinics offered as attributes. At an even finer level of detail, we might think of the clinics in the hospitals as distinct entities, with the physicians and patients as attributes of each clinic. Still greater detail is obtained by thinking of individual physicians and patients as entities described by their attributes of specialty, schedule, affliction, etc. The level of detail desired depends on our reasons for studying the system. It would not make sense to model a nationwide health care system at the level of individual patients; likewise, it would not be meaningful to model the laundry at a particular hospital from a national viewpoint.

Figure 2.1: The Entity/Attribute Hierarchy for a Health Care System

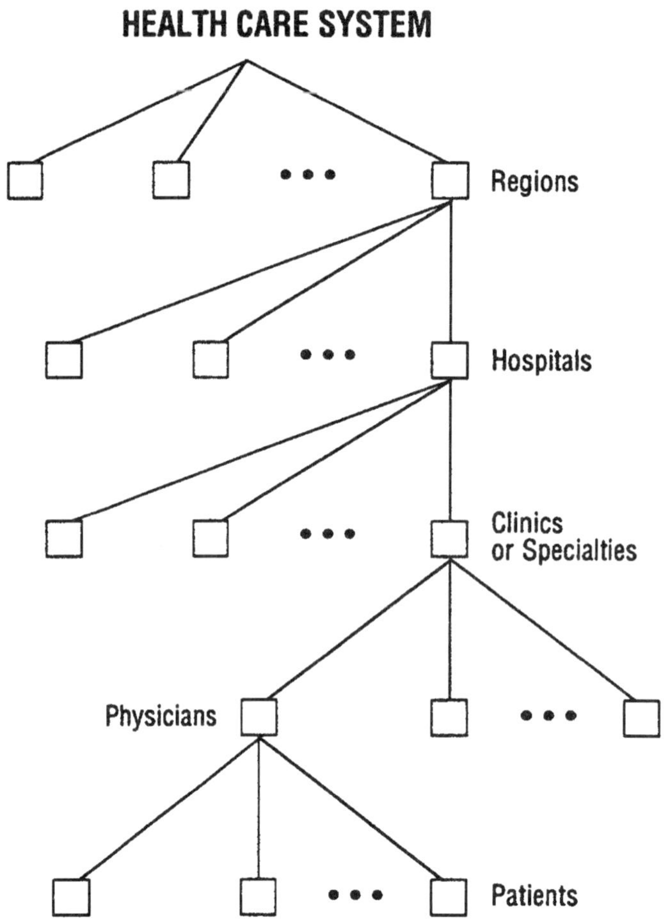

The rules that govern the interaction of entities in a system that are not under our control are called *laws.* Similar laws are grouped in families, members of which are distinguished by *parameters.* Rules that are under our control are called *policies;* a family of similar policies may be distinguished by the values of their *factors.* When we experiment to determine the effects of changes in parameters, we are doing sensitivity analysis. When we experiment with changes in factors, we are doing optimization or design. Sensitivity analysis might examine changes in the rate of patient demand for an emergency room. Optimization in the same setting might focus on adjusting nurses' schedules to provide adequate coverage during peak periods. Unlike the real world, in simulation studies both types of experiments are conducted in much the same manner.

Often throughout this book we will use examples of simple, random systems consisting of a waiting line with one or more servers. (Notable exceptions are the financial risk analysis model in Section 5.5, the critical path model in Section 5.6, and the continuous time simulation of an aquatic ecosystem in Section 5.10.) These stochastic, dynamic queues are found in many of the systems we are interested in studying: parts waiting for a machine, patients waiting for a doctor, jobs waiting for a computer, messages waiting for transmission, etc. The resident entities in the system are the machines, doctors, computers, data busses, . . . generically referred to as servers. The transient entities are the parts, patients, jobs, messages, . . . generically referred to as customers. Although not as obvious, the waiting lines, buffers, and queues are also resident entities in a queueing system. Laws describing the system might include the probability distribution of the time between successive customer arrivals. Policies might include the number of servers, the amount of waiting space, and the priority level different types of customers receive for service.

The *state* of a system is a complete description of the system and includes values of all attributes of entities, parameters of laws, factors for its policies, time, and what might be known about the future. The *state space* is the set of all possible system states. A *process* is an indexed sequence of system states; typically the index is time, but it might be a count of customers or some other system characteristic.

2.1.2 Models

We will define a *model* simply as

a system used as a surrogate for another system.

In typical computer simulation models, a system with mathematical entities is used as a surrogate for a system with physical entities. In this book when we use the word *system,* without qualification, we are referring to a real or hypothetical system that is the subject of the simulation study.

Mathematical models are conceptual abstractions of a particular aspect of a system. The mathematics we will be using include probability, statistics, and graphs. When we use the word *model,* without qualification, we will be referring to a graphical description of a system called an event graph. Finally, *simulations* will refer to computer programs developed from event graph models. Simulations will be our methodology for studying the model. A model serves as the interface between a system and a methodology for studying the system.

When evaluating a simulation, it is important to differentiate modeling a system from coding a model. Whether or not a simulation is "good" is more or less objective. A good simulation is a completely faithful rendition of a good model; nothing in the model is lost in the code. The process of testing if the simulation is good is called simulation verification, which is discussed in more detail in the next section. This is often much more complicated than verification of other types of computer programs. However, there is no conceptual difficulty in defining a good program as being error free.

Defining what constitutes a "good" model is much more subjective. A good model is based on good assumptions. Good assumptions make the simulation more efficient or the system easier to understand while costing little in terms of validity. Driving a good bargain between model simplicity and model validity is the essence of the art of modeling.

A purist view of validity is that a model will be valid as long as it is based on explicit assumptions and the implications of the assumptions are well understood. From this academic viewpoint, a modeling error is not correctly stating and applying all model assumptions. If we take the pragmatist's view of a good model as contributing to correct decisions, it is possible to test the effects of including a particular detail or making a certain assumption by comparing the behavior of the simulation with and without the detail or assumption. Simulation is one of the few methodologies that allows testing the robustness of models with different assumptions. Perhaps the biggest danger in simulation modeling is including too much detail in the model. An experienced consultant in the field once remarked that he could tell a novice at simulation by the excessive amount of detail in his or her models.

A technique for keeping model details at a reasonable level is to focus on the *similarities* among the entities in the system rather than the *differences.* If transient entities (customers, jobs, messages, etc.) can be treated as identical, you can develop a valid model that merely keeps track of the numbers of transient entities at various stages of their progress through a system. This makes it unnecessary to have a detailed record for each individual entity. Such a model would require updating relatively few integers (the counts) instead of creating and maintaining separate records for every transient entity in the system. Similarly, treating resident entities (servers, machines, buffers, etc.) as identical allows you to maintain counts of the numbers of resident entities in the various states of their process cycles rather than keeping a record of the status of each entity. In situations where there are a great many transient entities in the system at one time, it might be necessary to treat transient entities as identical. It is certainly more efficient to have a single integer variable that counts transient entities than it is to create and maintain thousands of complete records.

It is natural to notice differences between entities in a system. However, a valuable modeling skill is the ability to recognize similarities. Differences are modeled only when they are essential to the validity of the study results. It is also natural to include detail unless there are solid reasons for assuming that it can be omitted. When building simulation models of complicated systems, it is good practice to require justification for including detail. Even when the differences in entities are thought to be important, a skilled modeler will be able to define groups of entities that can be treated as identical.

Sometimes the activity of developing a simulation model has as much value as the model itself. Building a model forces us to identify our objectives, determine constraints, quantify our knowledge, and expose our misconceptions. It could be argued that a study has merit even if its recommendations are never implemented and that a simulation model has value even if it never runs. Of course, this is of little comfort to the student who fails a homework assignment or an engineer who must try to find another job. It is vastly more satisfying to professors and employers if the simulation model runs and the recommendations from the study are adopted. The motivation for the development of event graphs was to make simulation models easier to build and verify. With event graphs, it is much easier to verify that your simulation program reflects the way you have modeled the system than it is to validate that the model actually can be used to imitate the relevant behavior of the real system.

2.1.3 Model Verification

An absolutely *valid* simulation model with all the detail and behavior of real life is probably not attainable, or even desirable. However, every simulation model should do what its creator intended. Ensuring that the computer code for the simulation model does what you think it is doing is referred to as the process of model *verification.*

There is a trade-off involved between validation and verification of a simulation model. Adding detail to a model makes the code more complicated. If correctly implemented, this detail will perhaps improve model validity. However, adding complex details can make code verification more difficult if not impossible. Identifying only the substantive details that are important to include in a simulation model is important and often subject to negotiation.

Really gross errors in a simulation code can be detected using standard statistical testing. For example, a classical paired t-test between the means of samples from the real world and those from simulation runs might be conducted. (A description of a t-test can be found in any introductory statistics textbook.) However, there may not be enough real-world data to reject a hypothesis that the model and real world data have nearly the same parameters. Moreover, the data itself may not be valid. (See the "Five Dastardly D's of Data" in Section 9.7.)

Translating a model from computer code into clear language is a good exercise. It is interesting to contrast what two different people think a model is doing. You can also compare what you think your model is doing with what *it* thinks it is doing using the English translations generated by SIGMA.

An excellent tool for helping to verify a simulation model is an informal exercise called a "Turing test," named after a man who conjectured on the possibility of not being able to distinguish computing machines from real people. For a Turing test, actual blank forms used in the day-to-day management of a system are filled in with either simulated or real data. Only the blanks that are *relevant* for the purposes of the study are different. Managers and other people familiar with the system are then asked to identify the real and simulated documents and *tell how each form was identified.* It is vital that everyone know in advance that this exercise is likely to be repeated several times.

People familiar with these forms are usually more comfortable doing this exercise than they are in reviewing a computer code, evaluating a statistical analysis, or even observing an animation. Just the process of determining what data on each form are relevant to the study can make this exercise worthwhile.

A typical experience with a Turing test has been that the manager can immediately identify most, if not all, of the bogus forms! This is actually a good outcome; it indicates that the manager is paying attention, and it can lay the foundation for effective communication. A nontechnical manager "winning" the first round may also help diffuse any antagonism that they may have developed toward the simulation project. What happens next is critical: when the manager tells how the simulated data were identified, changes to the simulation model should be made and the exercise repeated. It is the *repetition* of the exercise that is important, not the outcome of each iteration.

Statistical analysis to assess whether or not the outcome of the exercise is likely to result from guessing is presented in Schruben (1980). However, such formal analysis can actually be detrimental. It could easily inhibit communication and alienate the manager by moving the discussion to the unfamiliar ground of mathematical statistics.

2.2 Discrete Event Systems and Simulations

As stated earlier, systems in which changes occur at particular instants of time are called discrete event systems. In a simulation of a discrete event system, time is advanced in discrete (variable and often random length) steps to the next interesting state change. A discrete event simulation skips over uninteresting time intervals rather than tracking detailed system dynamics. This coarse level of detail permits us to model very large systems such as airports, factories, hospitals, and farms.

A description of the *state* of a discrete event system will include values for all of its numerical attributes as well as any schedule it might have for the future. Changes in the state are called *events.* In a production system, events might include the completion of a machining operation (the state of a machine would change from "busy" to "idle"), the failure of a machine (the machine state would change to "broken"), the arrival of a repair crew (the machine state would change to "under repair"), the arrival of a part at a machining center (the machine might again become "busy"), etc.

The ability to identify the events in a discrete event system is an important skill, one that takes practice to acquire. Initially, you might use the following simple steps as a guide to identify system events:

1. State the purpose of your system. Be aware that there might be several (conflicting) purposes.
2. State the objectives of your study.
3. Design, at least qualitatively, the experiments you might want to run with your simulation.
4. Identify the resident and transient entities in your system and their important attributes; assign names to the attributes.
5. Identify the dynamic attributes and the circumstances that cause their values to change . . . these will be the events.

The building blocks of a discrete event simulation program are *event procedures.* Each event procedure makes appropriate changes in the state of the system and, perhaps, may trigger a sequence of other events to be scheduled in the future. Event procedures might also cancel previously scheduled events. An example of event cancelling might occur when a busy computer breaks down. End-of-job events that might have been scheduled to occur in the future must now be cancelled (these jobs will not end in the normal manner as originally expected).

The event procedures describing a discrete event system are executed by a main control program that operates on a master appointment list of scheduled events. This list is called the *future events list* and contains all of the events that are scheduled to occur in the future. The main control program will advance the simulated time to the next scheduled event. The corresponding event procedure is executed, typically changing the system state and perhaps scheduling or cancelling further events. Once this event procedure has finished executing, the event is removed from the future events list. Then the control program will again advance time to the next scheduled event and execute the corresponding event procedure. The simulation operates in this way, successively calling and executing the next scheduled event procedure until some condition for stopping the simulation run is met.

The operation of the main simulation event scheduling and execution loop is illustrated in Figure 2.2.

Figure 2.2: Main Event-Scheduling Algorithm

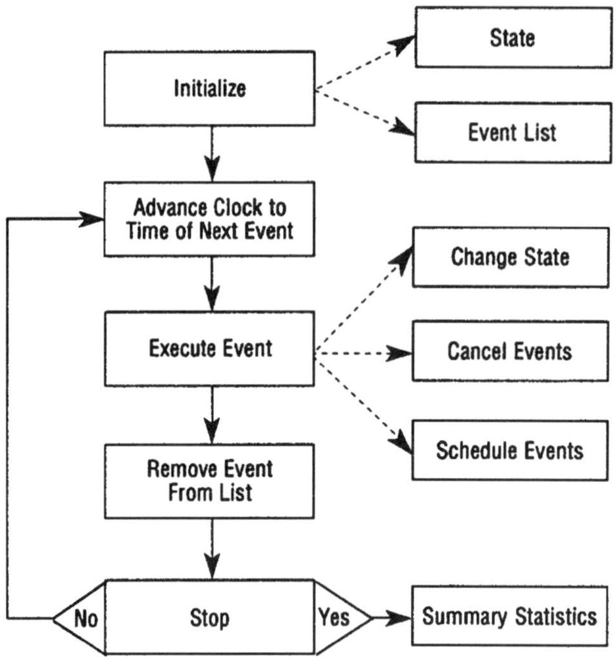

Extended Example: We will follow the changes in a typical future events list by examining a simulation of a machine center with three identical machines (numbered 0, 1, and 2) and two workers (worker 0 and worker 1).

The types of events that might occur in this example are the `ARRIVAL` of the next part at the machining center, a machine "`START`ing" or "`FINISH`ing" work on a part, a `BREAKDOWN` of a machine, and a broken machine being `REPAIRED`. An actual simulation model would, of course, have other types of events.

For each event that pertains to a specific machine and/or operator, the machine number followed by the operator number (if appropriate) are listed as event attributes. At a particular time during a simulation run, the future events list might look like the one pictured in Table 2.1. The future events are logically sorted according to times that events are scheduled to occur. Here time will be measured in minutes.

The current time in this example is 3.00, and the `ARRIVAL` of a part has just occurred at the center. This `ARRIVAL` event has

Table 2.1: Future Events List for a System with Three Machines (Time = 3.00)

	Time	Event Type	Event Attributes
(current time)	3.00	ARRIVAL	
	3.20	FINISH	0,1
	3.35	BREAKDOWN	1
	3.37	ARRIVAL	
	3.40	FINISH	1,0
	3.43	REPAIRED	2
	9.01	BREAKDOWN	0

"scheduled" the next ARRIVAL event to occur at time 3.37. We can determine the status of each machine by scanning down the future events list and checking what lies in the future for each machine. (Recall that the machine number is designated by the first event attribute.) Machine 0 is due to FINISH processing the part it is currently working on at time 3.20, so machine 0 must be busy. Likewise, machine 1 is busy and due to FINISH working on a part at time 3.40. Finally, machine 2 will be REPAIRED at time 3.43, so it is currently being fixed by the repair crew. We can see from the future events list in Table 2.1 that when the part arrived at time 3.00 none of the machines were available to start working on it. Thus, the part will join other parts in a queue waiting to be processed.

Note that machine 0 is due to experience its next BREAKDOWN at time 9.01 and machine 1 is due for a BREAKDOWN at time 3.35—before it can FINISH its current operation. Therefore, when machine 1 breaks down at time 3.35, the FINISH event for this machine at time 3.40 will have to be cancelled.

To see how this machining center simulation might proceed, we will now advance the current time to 3.20 and execute the FINISH event on machine 0. Looking at the second attribute of this FINISH event, we see that operator 1 becomes idle. Since we know that there is at least one part waiting, we can immediately START processing the next part. A new START event for machine 0 has been scheduled to occur at the current time of 3.20 with operator 1. The future events list is now like Table 2.2.

We next execute the START event for machine 0 at time 3.20 with operator 1. Suppose that a stored (or randomly generated) machine processing time for machine 0 is 1.20 minutes, then the FINISH event for this machine will be scheduled to occur 1.20

Table 2.2: Future Events List for a System with Three Machines (Time = 3.20)

	Time	Event Type	Event Attributes
(current time)	3.20	FINISH	0,1
	3.20	START	0,1
	3.35	BREAKDOWN	1
	3.37	ARRIVAL	
	3.40	FINISH	1,0
	3.43	REPAIRED	2
	9.01	BREAKDOWN	0

Table 2.3: Future Events List for a System with Three Machines (Time = 3.20)

	Time	Event Type	Event Attributes
(current time)	3.20	START	0,1
	3.35	BREAKDOWN	1
	3.37	ARRIVAL	
	3.40	FINISH	1,0
	3.43	REPAIRED	2
	4.40	FINISH	0,1
	9.01	BREAKDOWN	0

minutes from the current time of 3.20 or at time 3.20 + 1.20 = 4.40. The future events list after executing the START event at time 3.20 is shown in Table 2.3.

Next, we advance the time to 3.35 and execute the BREAKDOWN event for machine 1. This BREAKDOWN event will cause the FINISH event for machine 1 scheduled at time 3.40 to be cancelled. We will assume here that the part is destroyed when the machine breaks down and that the worker becomes available for other work. If it takes five minutes for a repair crew to repair machine 1, the future events list after the BREAKDOWN occurs is like that in Table 2.4. (Note the REPAIRED event for machine 1 has been scheduled at 8.35, five minutes beyond the current time of 3.35.) The simulation will now advance to time 3.37 when the next ARRIVAL event will occur.

Do not worry if this all seems a bit mysterious for now. Discrete event simulation modeling is more than a simple exercise in computer programming. It is initially somewhat confusing for everyone. You will soon

Table 2.4: Future Events List for a System with Three Machines (Time = 3.35)

	Time	Event Type	Event Attributes
(current time)	3.35	BREAKDOWN	1
	3.37	ARRIVAL	
	3.43	REPAIRED	2
	4.40	FINISH	0,1
	8.35	REPAIRED	1
	9.01	BREAKDOWN	0

discover that it is relatively straightforward once you grasp the concept of an event and understand the relationships between events. For this, we will use event graphs.

2.3 Event Graphs

The three elements of a discrete event system model are the state variables, the events that change the values of these state variables, and the relationships between the events (one event causing another to occur). An event graph organizes sets of these three objects into a simulation model. In the graph, events are represented as vertices (nodes) and the relationships between events are represented as edges (arrows) connecting pairs of event vertices. Time sometimes elapses between the occurrence of events.

The basic unit of an event graph is an edge connecting two vertices. Suppose the edge represented in Figure 2.3 is part of an event graph. We interpret the edge between A and B as follows:

whenever event A *occurs, it might cause event* B *to occur.*

Basically, edges represent the conditions under which one event will cause another event to occur, perhaps after a time delay.

Figure 2.3: Simple Event Graph Edge

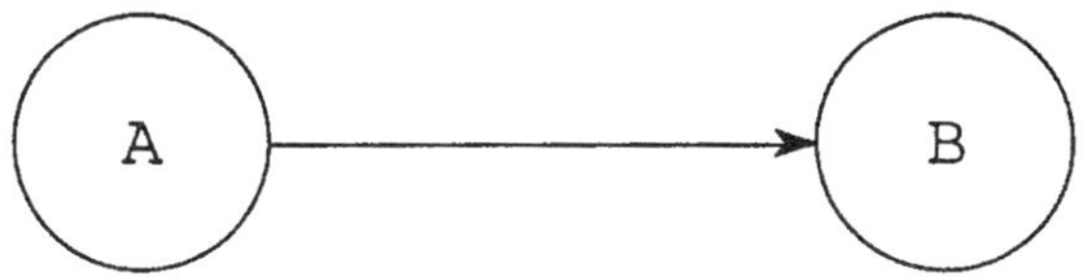

Figure 2.4: Simple Event Graph of a Carwash

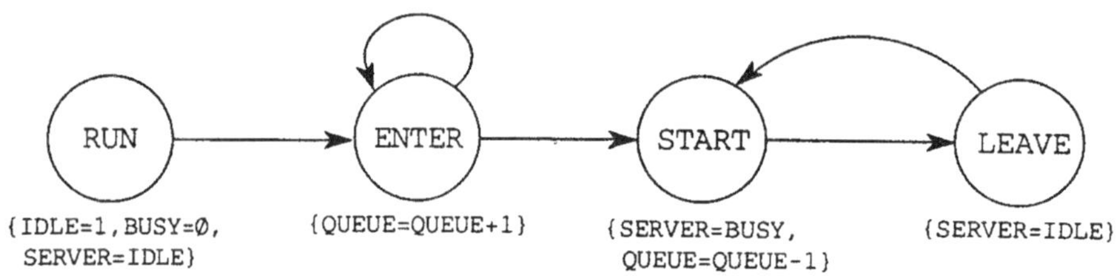

Using this notation, we can build a model that simulates a simple waiting line with one server (e.g., a ticket booth at a theater, the drive-in window at a fast-food restaurant, etc.). For our example, we will model an automatic carwash with one washing bay. The event graph of our carwash is represented in Figure 2.4.

We will begin our examination of this graph by discussing each vertex. The RUN vertex models the initialization of the simulation, the ENTER vertex models a car entering the carwash line, the START vertex models the start of service, and the LEAVE vertex models the end of service.

The state variables chosen to describe this system are:

SERVER = the status of the washing bay (busy, idle), initially set idle.
QUEUE = the number of cars waiting in line, initially set equal to zero.

To make our model more readable, we also define the constants, IDLE=1 and BUSY=0.

Next, we will focus on the changes in the state variables, shown in braces. The simulation RUN is started by making the washing bay at the carwash available for use {IDLE=1,BUSY=0,SERVER=IDLE}. Each time a car ENTERs the line, the length of the waiting line is incremented {QUEUE=QUEUE+1}. When service STARTs, the washing bay is made busy {SERVER=BUSY} and the length of the line is decremented {QUEUE=QUEUE-1}. Whenever a car has been washed and LEAVEs the washing bay, the washing bay is again made available {SERVER=IDLE} to wash other cars.

The dynamics of an event graph model are expressed in the edges of the graph. We read an event graph simply by describing the edges *exiting* each vertex (out-edges). In-edges take care of themselves. Continuing with our example, we look at each edge in Figure 2.4.

The simulation RUN is started by having the first car ENTER the carwash (edge from RUN to ENTER). If the ENTERing car finds the

Figure 2.5: Conditional Event Graph Edge with a Time Delay

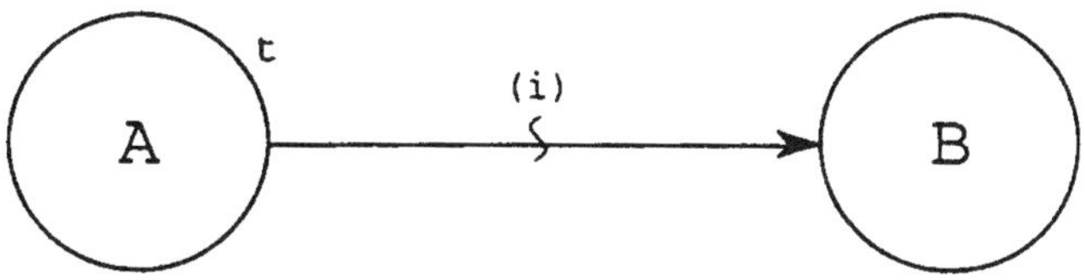

washing bay idle, service will START immediately (edge from ENTER to START). Each time a car ENTERs the carwash, the next car will be scheduled to ENTER sometime in the future (edge from ENTER to ENTER). The START service event will always schedule a car to LEAVE after that car has been washed (edge from START to LEAVE). Finally, if there are cars waiting in line when a car LEAVEs, the washing bay will START servicing the next car right away (edge from LEAVE to START).

The self-scheduling edge (the loop) on the ENTER event is the conventional way of perpetuating successive customer arrivals to the system. There will typically be some random time delay between customer arrivals.

After looking at the carwash model, you may have guessed that the state changes for an event vertex are typically very simple. Most of the action occurs on the edges of the graph. The conditions and delays associated with the edges of the simulation event graph are very important; it is on the graph edges that the logical flow and dynamic behavior of the model are defined. For each edge in the graph we will need to define under what conditions and after how long one event might schedule another event to occur.

We will associate with each edge a set of conditions that must be true in order for an event to be scheduled. Also associated with each edge will be a delay time equal to the interval until the scheduled event occurs. Time will be measured in minutes for our examples. We have enriched the basic event graph to include edge conditions and edge delay times (see Figure 2.5). This edge is interpreted as follows:

> *if condition* (i) *is true at the instant event* A *occurs, then event* B *will be scheduled to occur* t *minutes later.*

If the condition is not true, nothing will happen, and the edge can be ignored until the next time event A occurs. You can think of an edge as nonexistent unless its edge condition is true. If the condition for an edge is always true (denoted as 1==1), the condition is left off the graph. We will call edges with

Figure 2.6: Carwash Model with Edge Conditions and Delay Times

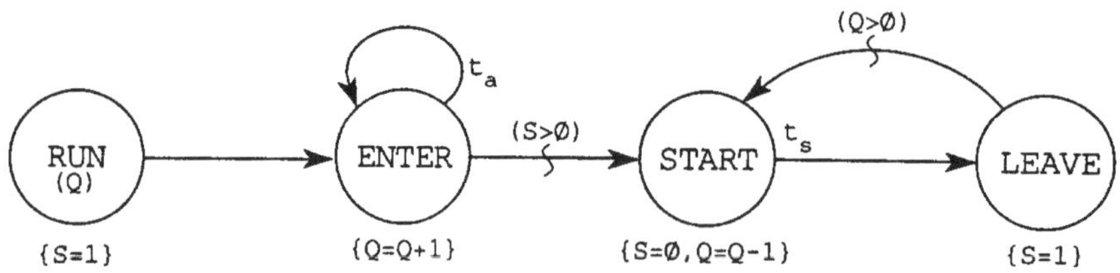

conditions that are always true *unconditional* edges. Zero time delays for edges are not shown on the graph.

While you are learning to read event graphs, it might be a good idea to use the edge interpretation in the previous paragraph as a template for describing each edge. Once the edges in the graph are correct, the state changes associated with each vertex are typically easy to check.

Our carwash model with edge conditions and delay times is shown in Figure 2.6. The state variables SERVER and QUEUE are now denoted by S and Q, respectively, and the status of S is indicated by 1 or 0 (IDLE=1, BUSY=0). In addition, the time between successive car arrivals (probably random) is denoted by t_a and the service time required to wash a car is denoted by t_s. When values of t_a are actually needed, they might be obtained from a data file or generated by algorithms like those in Chapter 9.

In Figure 2.6, state changes associated with each vertex are enclosed in braces and edge conditions in parentheses. As you read the following description of the graph in Figure 2.6, identify a single edge with each sentence.

> At the start of the simulation RUN, the first car will ENTER the system. Successive cars ENTER the system every t_a minutes. If ENTERing cars find that the server is available (S>0), they can START service. Once cars START service, t_s minutes later they can LEAVE. Whenever a car LEAVEs, if the queue is not empty (Q>0), the server will START with the next car.

Now reread the above paragraph without looking at Figure 2.6. You will see that it is a concise description of the behavior of a queueing system. With practice, a system description can be read easily from the edges of a simulation event graph. This is an excellent way to communicate the essential features of a simulation model and a good first step in model validation. With experience in reading event graphs, it becomes easier to detect modeling errors. This graph represents a completely defined simulation model. To run this model, only the starting and ending conditions for the run need to be specified.

Figure 2.7: Verbal Event Graph of a Single Server Queue

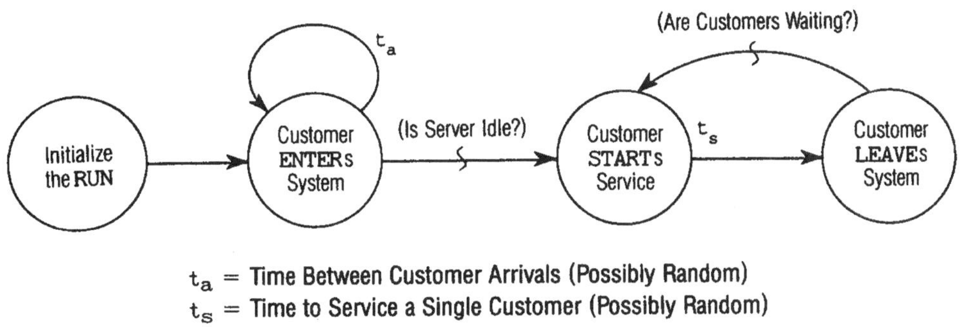

2.4 Verbal Event Graphs

Before designing your own event graph model, it is a good idea to develop a verbal description of your system. This description would include state changes associated with each vertex along with a verbal description of each edge condition and delay time on the graph. A verbal event graph for a generic single server queueing system is shown in Figure 2.7.

Developing a verbal description of your system is a good first step toward building a realistic and accurate simulation model. It will help you conceptualize the major components in the system, determine the key events and their interrelationships, and identify the state variables, edge conditions, and time delays necessary for the model. Note that state variables will need to be defined that permit testing of all edge conditions in your verbal event graph. Once you have constructed a detailed verbal description, the event graph model will be much easier to build.

2.5 Visual Power of Event Graphs

The visual modeling power of event graphs is most appreciated after one recognizes the complicated details involved in a discrete event simulation. The fundamental concept in event graph modeling is to use a directed graph as a picture of the relationships among the *elements* in sets of expressions characterizing the dynamics of the system. Each vertex of the graph is identified with a set of expressions for the state changes that result when the corresponding event occurs. Each edge in the graph identifies sets of logical and temporal relationships between a pair of events.

2.6 SIGMA

SIGMA is a general event graph modeling environment that facilitates the development of correct simulation code. Reading an event graph facilitates model validation, and, since with SIGMA the model is the language, code verification is much easier using SIGMA than using traditional discrete event simulation coding methods.

Using modern simulation languages, it is quite possible to create complicated models of systems without the user having any idea how the simulation program actually works. Indeed a prime objective of some special-purpose simulators is to isolate the user completely from the simulation code. This is an advantage as long as the application does not extend beyond the domain of the simulator. However, once a certain level of skill in simulation modeling has been reached, many feel constrained by the inflexibility of high-level simulators.

The objective of event graph modeling using SIGMA is to provide a user-friendly environment in which to build, verify, and experiment with discrete event simulation models. Unlike most simulation software, SIGMA is designed to remove *all* of the mystery in discrete event simulation. You will have access to the full source code of all SIGMA-generated simulation models. However, you can still choose to remain oblivious to the workings of the simulation program. With SIGMA the choice is yours. Initially event graph modeling may seem a bit abstract, but you will soon find it to be a simple yet powerful approach. SIGMA is suitable for both the beginner and the seasoned professional. While SIGMA is easy to learn and easy to use, it is powerful enough to allow for real growth as modeling skills evolve. Without learning any additional modeling tools, you will be able to model any discrete event system using event graphs.

Programming in the two dimensions of a graph has several advantages over traditional (line at a time) linear coding. Loops, conditional branching, function calls, and even notorious goto's are all easily represented as edges on a graph. In fact once you become familiar with SIGMA, you might consider using it as a general programming tool to create code that has nothing to do with simulation modeling. You might find that graphically programming in a plane makes more sense than writing code in the traditional linear method.

A practical simulation source code generator is included in SIGMA. The generated source code is created with an emphasis on clarity. SIGMA-generated code can execute fast enough to be competitive with most commercial simulation languages; in many cases, it is faster.

Like commercial languages, SIGMA makes simulation modeling much easier than directly writing code. With SIGMA, you interact with a simple graph like that in Figure 2.4. Details on edges (arrows) and event vertices (nodes) are available at the click of a mouse.

SIGMA also has instant input checking. Unlike simple syntax checkers, SIGMA checks your computation by actually executing expressions when they are entered. This helps to ensure that while running your model you will not encounter frustrating spelling, syntax, or computation errors.

Computer programs used for discrete event simulation are distinguished from other types of computer programs by two fundamental characteristics. Discrete event simulation programs will have both logic for representing the passage of time (they are dynamic as opposed to static) and logic for representing randomness (they are stochastic as opposed to deterministic). Reflecting these two fundamental features of a discrete event simulation program, SIGMA does two computations automatically; one computation models time while the other models randomness. In SIGMA, there are only two variables you should not change: `CLK`, which represents the current value of simulated time, and `RND`, which represents a randomly chosen number between zero and one.

A program that has randomness but is static might be used to generate artificial data samples to study the behavior of a statistical procedure; such a program is commonly referred to as a Monte Carlo simulation. Systems that are modeled as continuously changing, such as chemical reactions, electrical pulses, and mechanical linkages, fall into the realm of continuous simulations, which model the progression of change using differential or difference equations. Continuous time simulations are typically dynamic but deterministic. An example of a stochastic continuous time simulation is given in Section 5.10.

2.7 Exercises

2.7.1 Model Evaluation

Read a recent article where discrete event simulation models are used to solve real-world problems. Some of the publications you might look at are *Management Science, Interfaces, Industrial Engineering, Operations Research, Material Handling, Medical Care, Computer Performance Evaluation, Expert Systems,* and *Simulation.* Conference proceedings in various fields of engineering also have articles about simulation; in particular, the *Winter Simulation Conference Proceedings* is a good source.

Collect or create the following:

(a) Photocopies of the title page and abstract of the article (explicitly give the source).

(b) A brief statement of the objective of the simulation project (in your own words).

(c) What programming language was used? Did they justify their choice?

(d) A paragraph describing what real-world data was needed for the model and how it was collected.

(e) A paragraph describing what experiments were run with the model. What factors were varied? What system performance measurements were taken? What analysis was done with these measurements?

(f) Give a one-page critique of the article and project. What would you have done differently?

2.7.2 Short Answers

(a) Give the most important advantage as well as the greatest disadvantage to having a simulation model with very few events as opposed to an equivalent model with many events.

(b) What two features generally distinguish a discrete event simulation program from other types of programs?

(c) What are the two broad classifications of entities in a discrete event system?

(d) Give one advantage and one disadvantage to modeling the flow of transient entities in a system.

(e) Does a model with few entities each having many attributes have more or less detail than a model with many entities each having fewer attributes? Which will generally take more memory to run? Why?

2.7.3 Identifying Discrete Event Systems

For a real system of your choice, describe the system in less than a page and give a one-sentence objective for studying this system with a simulation model. Identify the dynamic attributes of entities in the system and the events where these attributes change values. Give a rough event graph for the system. (Pick something that you personally find interesting but keep it simple.)

2.7.4 Simultaneous Events

In the carwash model, if `Q=5` and there is a time tie between an `ENTER` event and a `LEAVE` event, which event should be executed next? Why?

2.7.5 Events List

In the event graph of Figure 2.6, what is the maximum number of events that might be scheduled on the events list at one time?

2.7.6 Edge Interpretation

For Figure 2.5, which of the following statements are true?

Whenever event `A` occurs: if `t` time units later, condition `(i)` is true, then event `B` will be scheduled to occur immediately.

Whenever event `A` occurs: if condition `(i)` is true, then event `B` will be scheduled to occur `t` time units later.

Whenever event `A` occurs and condition `(i)` is false, event `B` will be scheduled to occur `t` time units after condition `(i)` becomes true.

2.7.7 Future Events List

Assume for the example in Table 2.4 that the times between the next three part arrivals are 2, 1.5, and 3.2 (each `ARRIVAL` event schedules the next `ARRIVAL` event in this model). Furthermore, assume that the processing time for each machine is 0.5 minutes and that there are currently 6 parts waiting in the queue for processing. Finally, assume that once machine 2 is repaired it will be 10 minutes before it breaks again. What does the future events list look like at time 8.00? What is the status of each machine? How many parts are waiting in the parts queue?

2.7.8 Simultaneous Event Errors

Assume that for the model corresponding to the future events list in Table 2.4 that the `FINISH` event made a machine idle and scheduled a `START` event if there were parts waiting in the queue. Also assume that an `ARRIVAL` event will schedule a `START` event if it finds an idle machine. What would happen if a part arrived at time 4.40, just as machine 0 finishes processing? What would happen if the `FINISH` event occurred before the `ARRIVAL` events?

2.7.9 Future Events List

A trace of the events in the first 40 minutes of a simulated multiple machine manufacturing cell contains the following event times.

Job Arrival Times

1, 2, 3, 5, 6, 7, 9, 10, 11, 12, 13, 14, 15, 16, 17, 18, 19, 20, 21, 22, 24, 25, 27, 28, 32, 33, 37, 38, 39, 40

Job Completion Times

5, 6, 7, 9, 10, 11, 13, 14, 15, 17, 18, 19, 21, 22, 23, 25, 26, 27, 29, 30, 31, 33, 34, 35, 37, 38

How many parts are in the system at time 30? If no further arrivals occur after time 40, when will all the remaining parts be finished?

3

Getting Acquainted with SIGMA: A Tutorial

A detailed tutorial of the SIGMA software is presented in this chapter, and all primary elements of an event graph model are explained. Following the tutorial are discussions on using text files, printing graphs and output, using SIGMA graphs and output in spreadsheets and word processors, and automatically translating SIGMA code into C, Pascal, and English.

3.1 Exiting from SIGMA

Before using any new software, it is important to know how to exit and return to your operating system. There are four methods to exit from SIGMA:

1. Click the **Exit** command under the **File** menu.
2. Click the **Close** command in the SIGMA **Control** menu to the left of the title bar.
3. Hold down the Alt key and press the F4 key [Alt-F4].
4. (If all else fails) reboot your system, simultaneously pressing the Control, Alt, and Delete keys [Ctrl-Alt-Delete].

Using the first three methods will cause you to leave SIGMA and return to the **Program Manager**. But before exiting, a dialog box will appear if you made any changes to the model. Clicking on the **Yes** button will save your changes, clicking **No** will not save your changes, and clicking **Cancel** will void the command. To return to SIGMA after exiting, double-click the mouse on the SIGMA icon. *The fourth option, rebooting, will cause your changes to be lost.*

3.2 Help Menu

The **Help** menu consists of three commands. The first, **Contents**, provides basic information on event graphs, definitions of important terms, and explanations of special features. The second, **Using Help**, is an overview of how to use the **Help** program. The third, **About SIGMA**, indicates the current version of your event graph modeling system. The on-line **Help** menu is not intended to serve as a substitute for the information in this book.

3.3 An Introduction to the SIGMA for Windows Environment

As mentioned earlier, you start SIGMA from the **Program Manager** by double-clicking on the **SIGMA** icon. The *simulation graph* window, depicted in Figure 3.1, should appear. This window is the primary window for a SIGMA modeling session. There are two other kinds of windows in SIGMA: *simulation plot* windows and *output* windows. These windows are created when a SIGMA model is executed and are linked to the model. When a simulation graph window for a particular model is closed, the plot window and output window associated with the model will remain on the screen but they no longer will be dynamic. Note: Several SIGMA modeling sessions may run simultaneously; thus, several simulation graph windows representing different models may be open at one time.

Figure 3.1: SIGMA's Simulation Graph Window

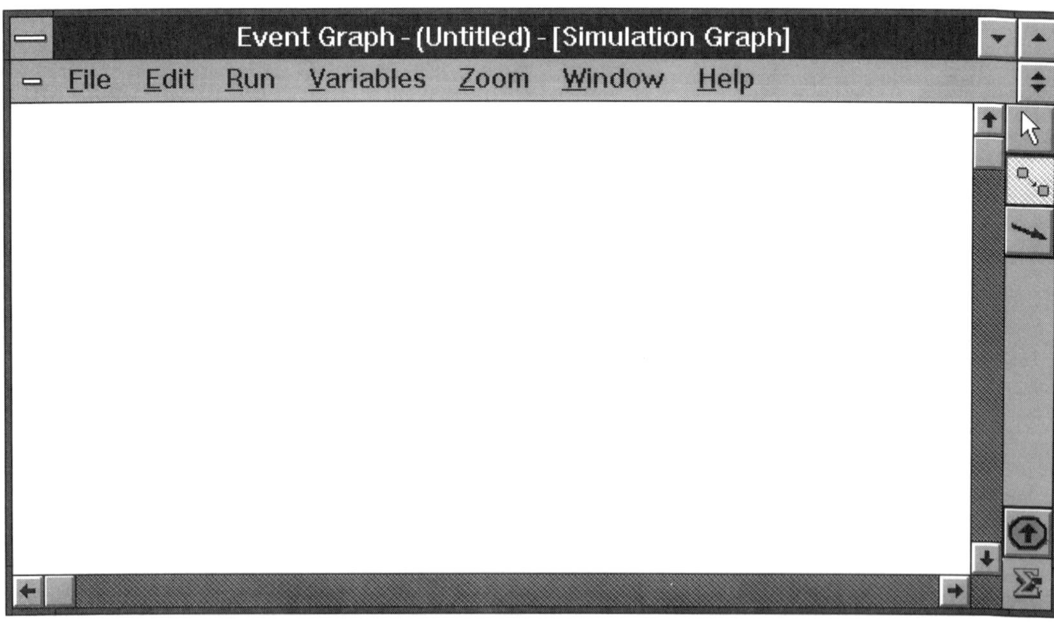

Figure 3.2: SIGMA Toolbar

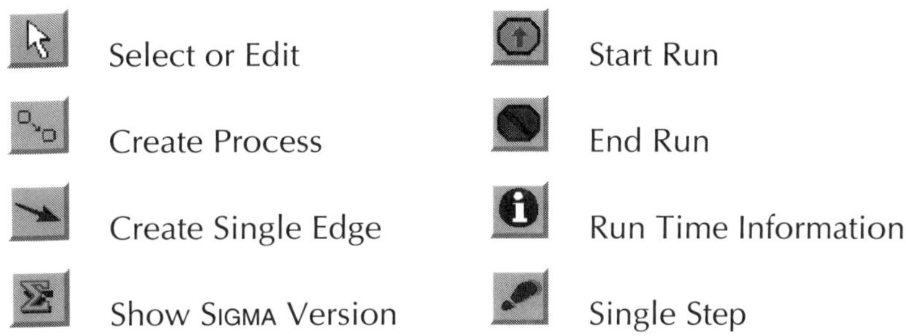

Looking at the simulation graph window, a toolbar can be seen along the right side of the window and a menu bar across the top of the window under the title bar. The toolbar contains a number of useful tools that will facilitate your use of this system (see Figure 3.2). The **Start Run** and **End Run** tools allow you to start or stop a simulation run; the **Select or Edit**, **Create Process**, and **Create Single Edge** tools let you quickly create a model; the **Single Step** tool allows you to watch the simulation as each event is executed; and the **Run Time Information** and **Show SIGMA Version** tools provide you with additional information. To activate a tool, simply click the mouse on it.

A window is activated when the mouse pointer is clicked anywhere on it. As each window is activated, the menu bar changes. The menu bar for the simulation graph window contains the following menus: **File, Edit, Run, Variables**, **Zoom**, **Window**, and **Help**. The simulation plot window contains the **File**, **Edit**, **Options**, **Window**, and **Help** menus; the output window contains the **File**, **Edit**, **Search**, **Window**, and **Help** menus.

The commands in the menus will appear on the screen after you click on a particular menu or after you press [Alt] and the letter underlined in the menu name—e.g., [Alt-F] will open the **File** menu. The commands in the menus can be executed by clicking the mouse on the appropriate command, using [↑] and [↓] to highlight the command and pressing [←Enter] to select the highlighted entry, or pressing the underlined letter in the command name. Some of the commands will produce dialog boxes in which to record additional information. Use the mouse pointer or use [Tab] and [↑Shift-Tab] to move through the various options in the dialog boxes; exit the boxes by clicking on an appropriate command button. The **Cancel** command button is used to close a dialog box where no changes are desired.

3.4 Conventions Used in This Book

The next few sections of this book are in tutorial format. The various typefaces in this book indicate the kind of response to provide.

Typeface Example	Indicates
[sigma]	Characters that you are to type at the keyboard. (Do not type brackets.)
[Ctrl-Alt-Del]	Hold down Control key and Alt key while pressing the Delete key.
`edit`	Characters displayed on the monitor screen.
`FILENAME.MOD`	The name of a file.
Create Process	Special SIGMA tools or command buttons.
Click the mouse	Directions you should follow.

3.5 Exploring Our Carwash Model: A Tutorial

This section explores the model of a carwash. To begin, start a SIGMA session and open `CARWASH.MOD`.

Click the mouse on the **File** *menu in the simulation graph menu bar.*

Click the mouse on the **Open** *command in the* **File** *menu.*

A dialog box will appear with a list box of alphabetized file names. Use the scroll bar to view model names that are not visible. Locate `CARWASH.MOD` and open this file.

Scroll down until `CARWASH.MOD` *is located and double-click on it.*

This will retrieve a model of the carwash discussed in Chapter 2. This model represents a simple waiting line with a single server. Your screen should look like the one in Figure 3.3.

There are four events represented by the four vertices in this model. The `RUN` vertex starts the simulation, the `ENTER` vertex models customers entering the carwash, the `START` vertex occurs when a car starts service in the washing bay, and the `LEAVE` vertex occurs when a car finishes service and leaves the washing bay. The time intervals between successive customer arrivals to the carwash are independent and random.

Next, click the mouse on the **Create/Edit Variables** command in the **Variables** menu to see the list of state variables for this model in the **State Variable Editor** dialog box. Any state variables you define can be used anywhere in your SIGMA model. We refer to them as state variables to emphasize that they are accessible to all parts of the model.

Click the mouse on the **Create/Edit Variables** *command in the* **Variables** *menu.*

Your screen should be similar to the one in Figure 3.4. Clicking on one of the state variables in this dialog box will cause the details associated with that state variable to be displayed in the input boxes above. Now changes can be made to the variable.

Figure 3.3: Event Graph for a Single Server Queue, `CARWASH.MOD`

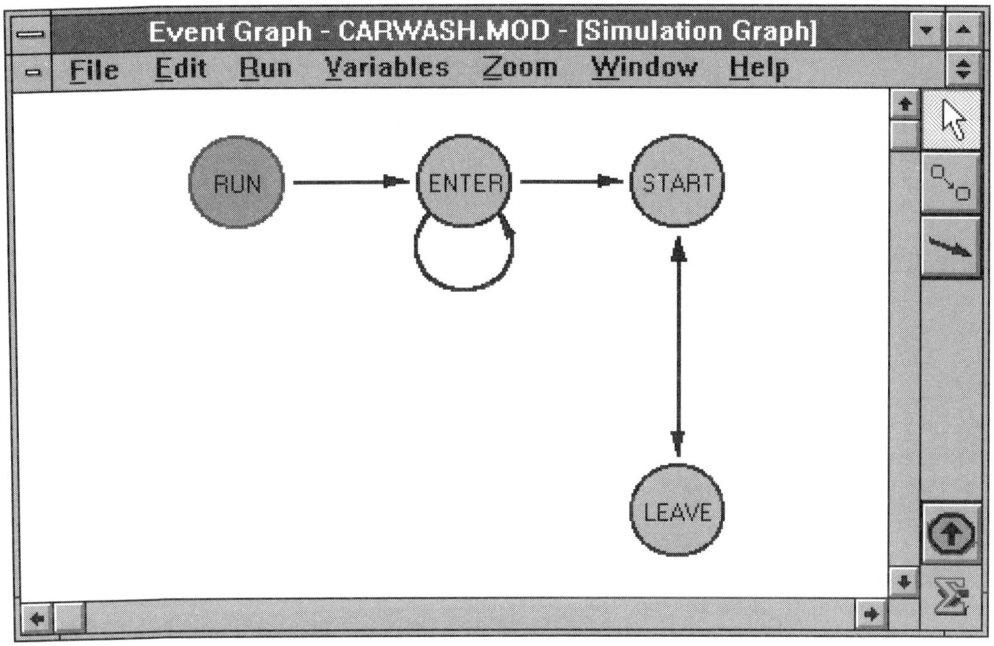

Click once on one of the state variable names in the dialog box.

If you clicked the mouse on the variable named `QUEUE`, you should see the screen in Figure 3.4. If you clicked on the state variable named `SERVER`,

Figure 3.4: The State Variable Editor Dialog Box

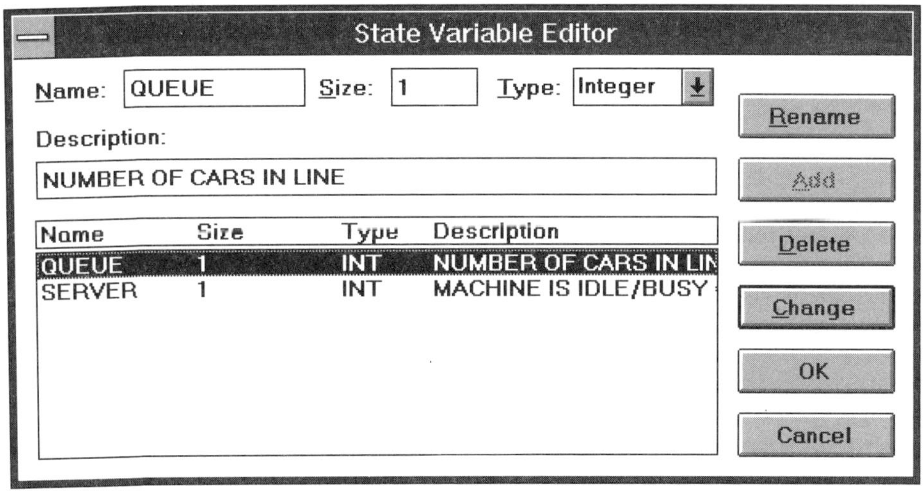

Figure 3.5: The Dialog Box for the RUN Vertex

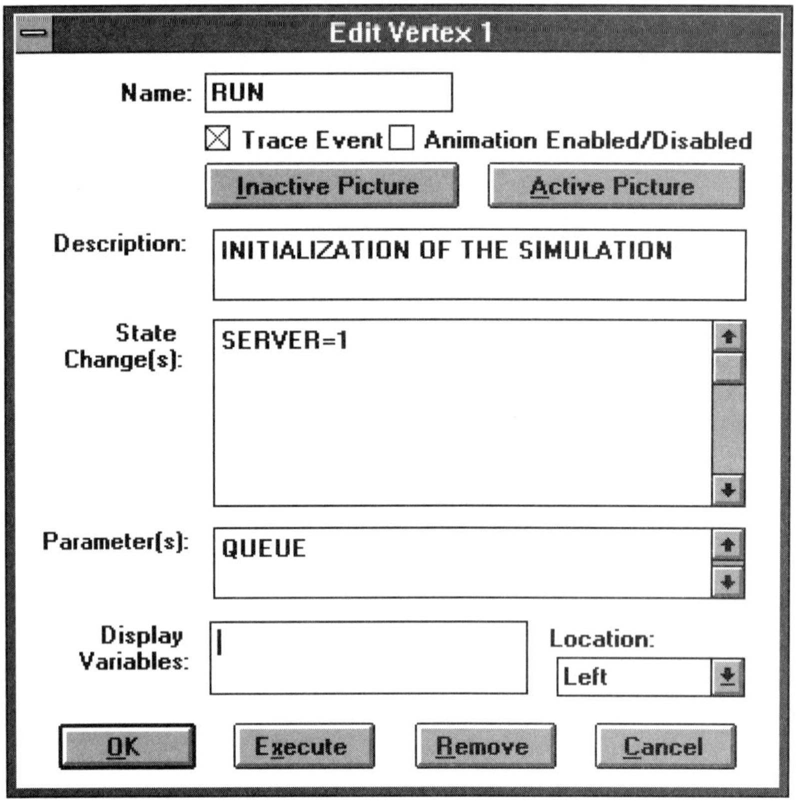

you should see a similar screen. The dialog box for state variables, like other SIGMA dialog boxes, has a line for a brief description of the object. These descriptions are important; they appear as comments in your SIGMA-generated simulation source code and make your model much easier to understand. Click on the **Cancel** command button to close the state variable dialog box and return to the simulation graph seen in Figure 3.3.

Click **Cancel** *at the lower right of the* **State Variable Editor** *dialog box.*

We will explore the model by clicking the mouse on the elements in the event graph of `CARWASH.MOD`. Make sure that the mouse pointer is in the shape of an arrow (↖) (in **Select or Edit** mode). If the mouse pointer is shaped like ⊕, SIGMA is in **Create Process** mode. If so, click on the **Select or Edit** tool or click the *right mouse button;* these actions will bring SIGMA back into **Select or Edit** mode.

As we look at the details of each vertex and edge in the event graph, read the description in each dialog box. As we will see later, the contents of

Figure 3.6: The Dialog Box for the ENTER Vertex

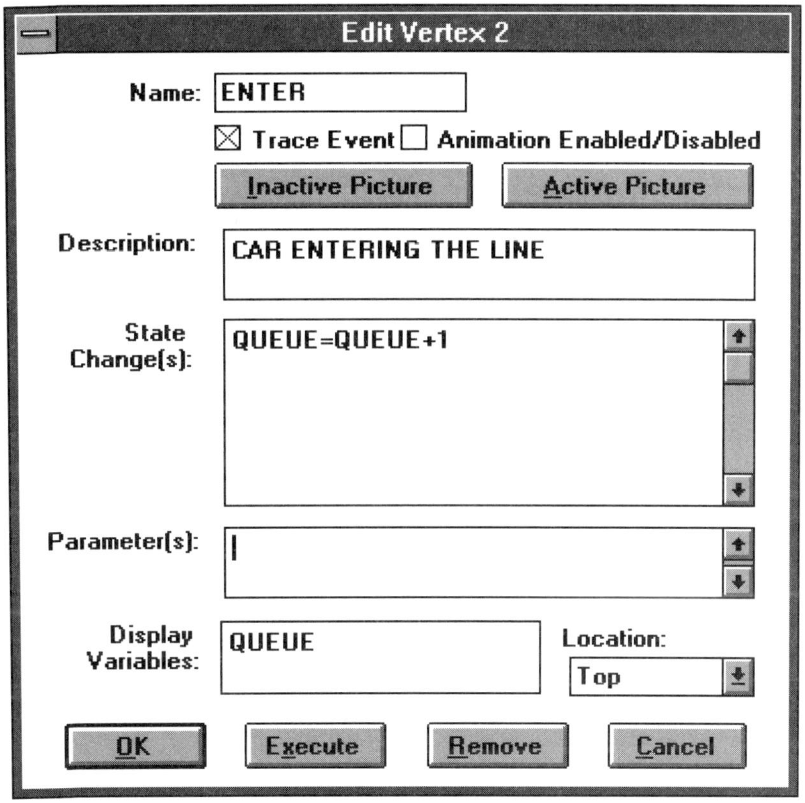

dialog boxes in SIGMA are easily changed by clicking on the line to be edited and entering the changes from the keyboard.

Double-click on the green RUN *vertex.*

The RUN vertex, shown in Figure 3.5, was the first vertex created in this model. SIGMA calls the first vertex created vertex number 1; it will always be executed first when the model is run. (This first vertex is colored green on the screen.) The RUN vertex has a parameter: the state variable, QUEUE. When CARWASH.MOD is run, you will be asked to provide an initial value for the number of customers in the QUEUE when the system opens for service. All SIGMA state variables are initialized to be equal to zero. The only state change associated with the RUN vertex is to make the SERVER available (SERVER=1). To exit, click your mouse on the **Cancel** command button.

Click the mouse on **Cancel** *in the dialog box.*

The ENTER vertex is where customers join the line. The dialog box for this vertex, invoked by double-clicking the ENTER vertex, is shown in Figure 3.6.

Figure 3.7: The Dialog Box for the `START` Vertex

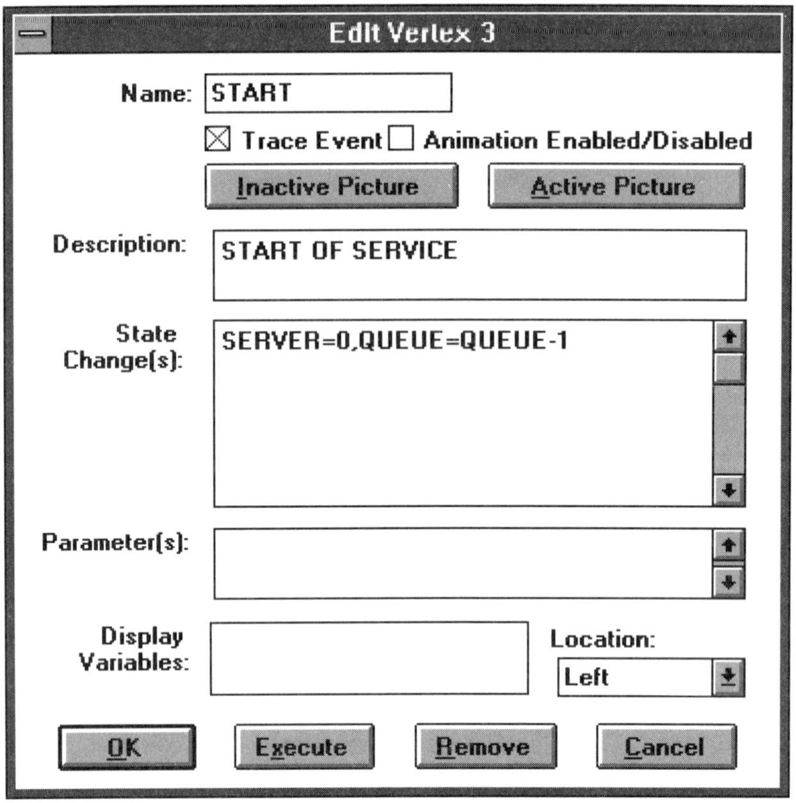

Click the mouse twice on the `ENTER` *vertex.*

The `ENTER` vertex simply increments the number of customers waiting in line (`QUEUE=QUEUE+1`). Note that `QUEUE` has been entered as a display variable, so its value will be shown while the simulation is running.

Click the **Cancel** *button on the* `ENTER` *vertex dialog box.*

Double-click the mouse on the `START` *vertex.*

The `START` service vertex is shown in Figure 3.7. Here the server is made busy (`SERVER=0`) and the number of customers waiting in line is decremented (`QUEUE=QUEUE-1`).

Open the `LEAVE` dialog box (pictured in Figure 3.8) to see the details associated with it.

Click the **Cancel** *button on the* `START` *vertex dialog box.*

Double-click on the `LEAVE` *vertex.*

Figure 3.8: The Dialog Box for the LEAVE Vertex

The LEAVE vertex makes the server available to serve other customers. Note that if the variable, QUEUE, were defined as the number of customers in the total system (in service as well as in line), QUEUE would be decremented in the LEAVE vertex rather than in the START vertex.

As we mentioned earlier, the event vertices are relatively straightforward in discrete event models. The complexity of the models comes at the edges of the event graph, where the dynamic and logical relationships between events are specified. Next, we will examine each of the edges in our model. Figure 3.9 is the edge dialog box that you should see if you double-clicked the mouse on the edge between the RUN vertex and the ENTER vertex.

Click the **Cancel** *button on the* LEAVE *vertex dialog box.*

Double-click on the edge between the RUN *vertex and the* ENTER *vertex.*

Figure 3.9: Edge Dialog Box from `RUN` Vertex to `ENTER` Vertex Schedules the First Customer Arrival

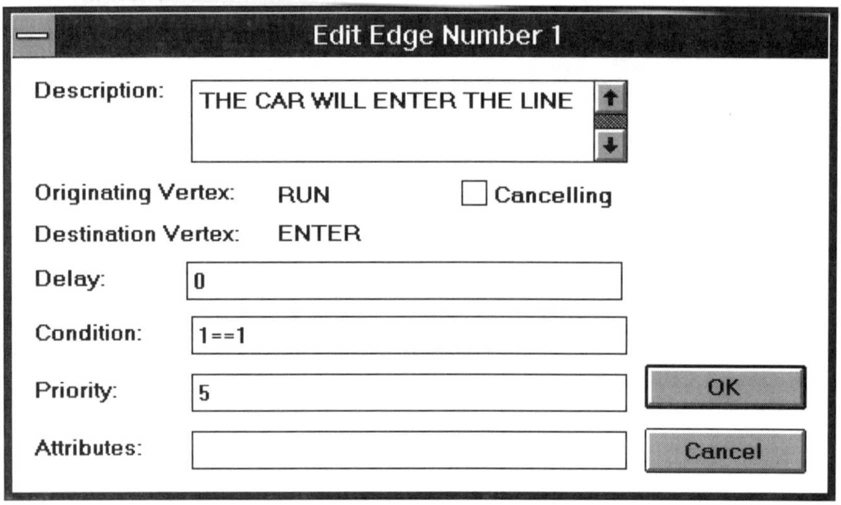

From Figure 3.9 we see that this edge has the condition (`1==1`). As in the C programming language, == is a test for equality in SIGMA. Thus, this edge unconditionally (`1==1`) schedules the first customer to `ENTER` the system. There is no time delay between starting the `RUN` and the first customer `ENTER`ing the system. Here no attribute values are passed, and the execution priority, used to break time ties between events scheduled to occur at the same clock time, is set to a neutral value of 5. (Attributes and priorities are discussed in detail in Chapters 5 and 6.)

> ➢ *Unconditional edges test the condition* (`1==1`)*, which is*

Click the **Cancel** *button on this edge dialog box.*

Double-click on the self-scheduling edge below the `ENTER` *vertex.*

If you opened the dialog box for the edge from the `ENTER` vertex to the `ENTER` vertex, your screen should look like Figure 3.10. The most notable

Figure 3.10: Edge Dialog Box from ENTER Vertex to ENTER Vertex Self-Scheduling Edge Perpetuates Customer Arrivals

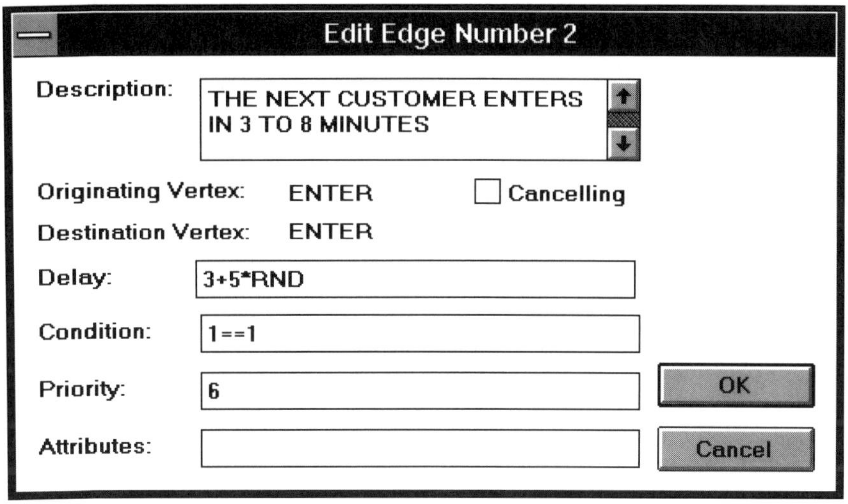

item in this dialog box is the delay time. Here, the **Delay** between successive customers ENTERing the system will be a time uniformly distributed between 3 and 8 minutes. This is done by making the delay time for this edge equal to the expression 3+5*RND. RND is a SIGMA function providing a fraction that behaves like a random number between 0 and 1. Thus, 5*RND will be a number somewhere between 0 and 5; adding 3 will shift the range of this number to between 3 and 8. Another notable item is that the **Priority** has been set to 6. This means that the execution priority for the destination vertex on this edge (ENTER) will be 6, a lower priority than the default priority (5). If the edge from ENTER to START has an execution priority of 5, the destination vertex START will be scheduled to occur before the ENTER vertex if both vertices were scheduled to occur at the same time.

Click the **Cancel** *button on this edge dialog box.*

Double-click on the edge between the ENTER *vertex and the* START *vertex.*

The dialog box for the edge from ENTER to START is in Figure 3.11. The item of interest on this edge is **Condition**: SERVER>0. This means that a customer ENTERing the system will START service without delay only if that customer finds that the server is available—i.e., if the condition SERVER>0 is true.

Figure 3.11: Edge Dialog Box from ENTER Vertex to START Vertex

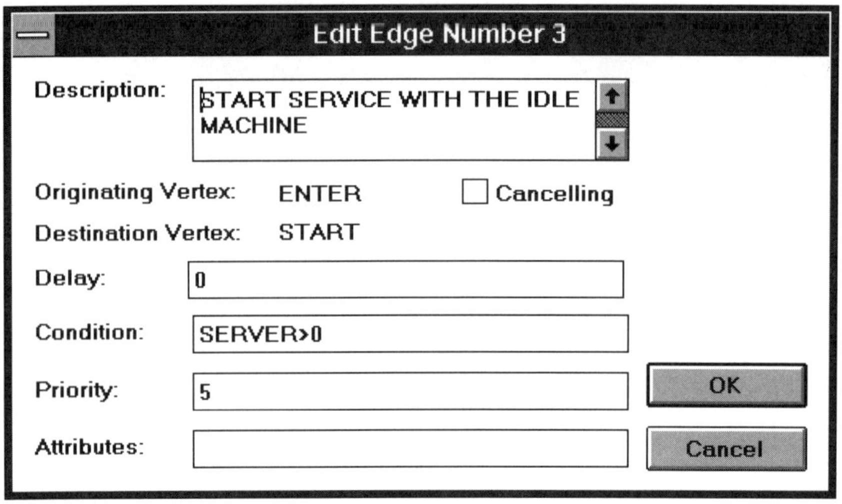

Click the **Cancel** *button on this edge dialog box.*

Double-click on the edge between the START *vertex and the* LEAVE *vertex.*

Note that the edge between the START and LEAVE vertices is a double edge. In this case, there is one edge from the START vertex to the LEAVE vertex and another edge in the reverse direction, from LEAVE to START. The dialog box for this multiple edge is shown in Figure 3.12.

Double-clicking on one of the sub-edges in the multiple edge dialog box will produce another dialog box for that particular edge. For example, if

Figure 3.12: Multiple Edge Dialog Box between START and LEAVE Vertices

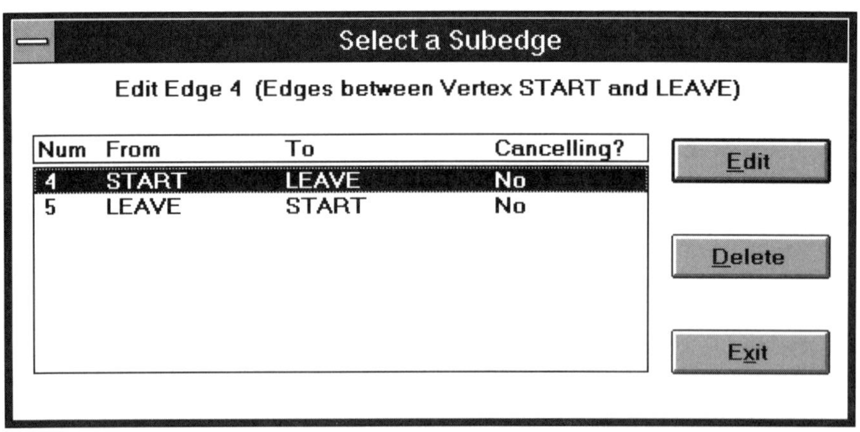

Figure 3.13: Edge Dialog Box from START Vertex to LEAVE Vertex

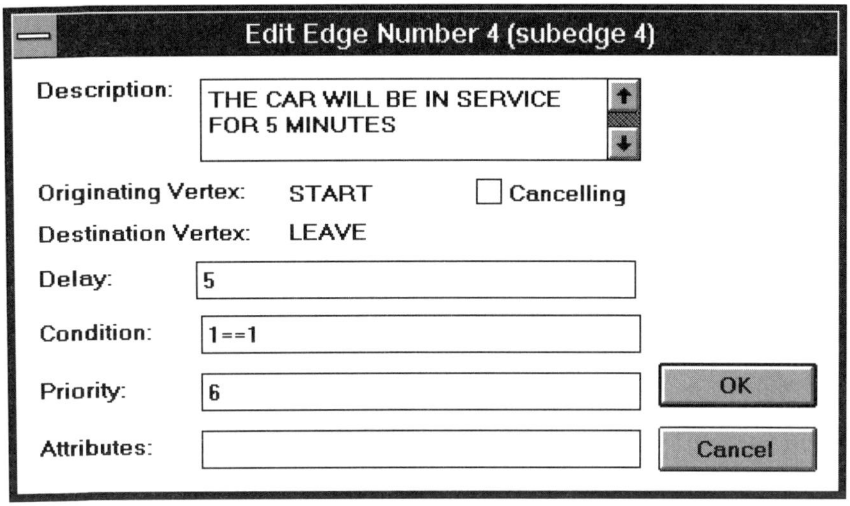

you double-click on the line for the edge from START to LEAVE, a dialog box for that edge will appear as in Figure 3.13.

Double-click on the line for the sub-edge from START *to* LEAVE.

The edge between the START vertex and the LEAVE vertex has a delay time of five minutes, indicating that it will take five minutes to wash a single car. The execution priority for the LEAVE event was also decreased to 6 to break potential time ties with customers ENTERing the system. Now cancel the dialog box for the sub-edge from START to LEAVE and look at the sub-edge from the LEAVE vertex to the START vertex.

Click the **Cancel** *button on this dialog box.*

Double-click on the sub-edge from the LEAVE *vertex to the* START *vertex.*

The dialog box for the edge from LEAVE to START is shown in Figure 3.14. This edge tells us that if there are customers waiting in line (QUEUE>0) whenever a customer LEAVEs the system, the server will START service on the next customer in line. Now exit to the event graph for CARWASH.MOD.

Click the **Cancel** *button on the dialog box.*

Click the **Exit** *command button on the multiple edge dialog box.*

To get a feel for editing graphical objects, double-click on the edges or vertices in the graph. Then click on some of the items in the dialog boxes and use the keyboard to enter changes to the model. (Pressing the **OK** button will cause your changes to be temporarily recorded in the model.)

Figure 3.14: Edge Dialog Box from `LEAVE` Vertex to `START` Vertex

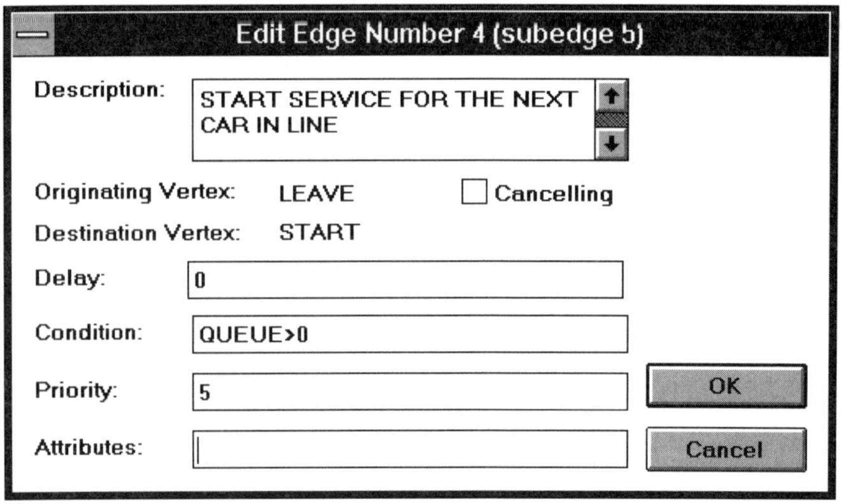

Double-click on the vertices and edges. Enter changes from the keyboard.

After you have edited a few dialog boxes, click on the **File** menu and click again on the **Open** command. Click **No** when asked if changes to `CARWASH.MOD` should be saved. (Clicking **Yes** will save the changes you just made to the model.) Next, scroll through the list of model file names until you see `CARWASH.MOD`. Double-click on `CARWASH.MOD` to reread the initial version of this model into SIGMA.

> ➢ **Important:** *Give the model you just changed a new name, say,* `JUNK.MOD`*, if you decide to save it; otherwise,* `CARWASH.MOD` *will be written over. However,* `CARWASH.BAK` *will be created as a backup of your old model.*

Open the **File** *menu in the menu bar and then click on the* **Open** *command.*

Click on the **No** *button if asked to save changes to* `CARWASH.MOD`.

Locate `CARWASH.MOD` *and double-click on it to reopen this model.*

Figure 3.15: View Text File Dialog Box Listing All Files

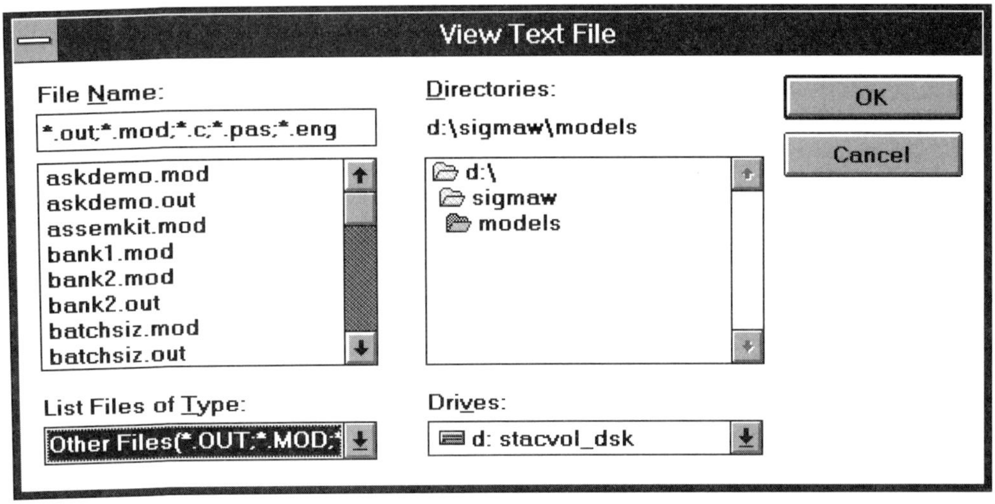

The screen in Figure 3.3 should appear again. If you saved your changes to the model, `CARWASH.MOD`, a backup copy is also in your directory as `CARWASH.BAK`. Read `CARWASH.BAK` into SIGMA and save it as `CARWASH.MOD`, if necessary.

3.6 Using Text Files

Now that we have gone over the model, `CARWASH.MOD`, in detail, you might be interested in looking at how it is stored on your computer. The model is stored in a text file by the same name, `CARWASH.MOD`. To look at this file, first open the **File** menu and click the **View Output/Text File** command. A dialog box will appear. Click on the down arrow in the drop-down list under **List Files of Type**. Click on the **Other Files** option to have all the files included in the list box of file names. The dialog box will look like the one in Figure 3.15.

Click on the **View Output/Text File** *command in the* **File** *menu.*

Click **Other Files** *under the* **List Files of Type** *box.*

Use the scroll bar to locate `CARWASH.MOD` in the list box; click once on `CARWASH.MOD` to insert this file into the **File Name** input box. Next, click the **OK** command button. When the text file appears, you will notice that SIGMA models are saved simply as copies of the dialog boxes for each of the objects in the simulation. Close the file by clicking on the **Text File Control** menu, on the left side of the menu bar, and clicking the mouse on the **Close** command.

Click on `CARWASH.MOD` *in the* **File Name** *list box.*
Press the **OK** *command button to see the text file.*
Click the **Close** *command in the* **Text File Control** *menu.*

3.7 Printing Event Graphs, Simulation Plots, and Output Files

It is very easy to print event graphs, simulation plots, and output files from models created in SIGMA. To print a graph, plot, or output file, first activate the appropriate window by clicking on it. (The title bar of the active window will change color.) Click on the **Print** command in the **File** menu. (While the different windows have different menu bars, all have the **File** menu and the **Close** command.) A dialog box will appear. Make any changes and click on the **OK** button. A copy of the desired file will be printed.

3.8 Using Spreadsheets and Word Processors

Event graphs, graphical simulation plots, and numerical output from SIGMA all can be incorporated into modern Windows spreadsheets and word processors. If you choose to copy an event graph by pressing **Select All** under the **Edit** menu and clicking on the **Copy** command and then pasting the graph into a word processing file, you may be surprised at the results. Rather than seeing an event graph, you will see the textual description of your event graph (the simulation model data). If, on the other hand, you activate the simulation graph, press [Alt-Print Screen], open a word processing file, and then click on the **Paste** command under the **Edit** menu; the event graph will appear in your word processor file.

The ease of exporting data to word processors makes it much easier to develop reports for simulation experiments. Not only can the event graph be included in the summary reports, but graphical plots, numerical output, and even an English translation of the model, discussed next, can be added to a written report. With all these features at your disposal it is much easier to inform people who are not simulation experts about your model.

Like many Windows applications, SIGMA allows you to copy, cut, or paste dialog box text within a single SIGMA modeling session, between several SIGMA modeling sessions, or between another application and a SIGMA session. This feature is particularly useful when entering lengthy, but similar, edge conditions. For example, you could write the text using Word for Windows, highlight the text and copy it using [Ctrl-c], then paste it into a SIGMA dialog box using [Ctrl-v]. To copy a SIGMA screen for insertion into a spreadsheet or word processor, click on the window you wish to copy and press [Print

Screen] while holding [Alt]. Then open your word processor file and insert the picture [Ctrl-v] (if you are using Word for Windows).

> ➢ SIGMA *allows you to copy, cut, and paste text or models between dialogs or concurrently running* SIGMA *sessions.*

3.9 Automatically Translating Models to C, Pascal, FORTRAN, or English

Once you have verified the logic of your model, you can automatically generate a simulation program in **C**, **Pascal**, or **English** by using SIGMA's **Translate** command or in FORTRAN (SIMAN or SLAM) by using SIGMA's DOS **TRANSLAT** utility. You specify the model (e.g., `CARWASH.MOD`) you wish to have translated and select a target language; the rest is automatic.

The **File** menu contains the **Translate** command, which allows you to translate your model into either **C**, **Pascal**, or **English**. The **Translate** to **C** and the **Translate** to **Pascal** commands cause your simulation model to be translated into portable standard C or Pascal source code that can be compiled and run on a variety of systems. The **English** option writes an English description of your model. Source code generation is discussed in detail in Chapter 11, where FORTRAN model translation is also presented.

3.9.1 Automatic English Translations

The automatic English translation feature exploits SIGMA's graph structure to produce an English description of your simulation. Basically the two vertices on an edge act as the subject and object of a sentence while the edge conditions and delay times form prepositional phrases; the predicate is almost always "schedule" or "cancel."

The English translation feature is very useful for checking errors (use with a printed graph), verifying a model with persons not familiar with simulation, supplementing physical animations, and checking homeworks (contrasting what you think your model is doing with what SIGMA says it is doing).

To see the English translation of the carwash model, open `CARWASH.MOD`. Activate the English translation option by clicking on the **Translate** command in the **File** menu and selecting **English** from the alternatives. A dialog box will appear with the active file highlighted in the **File Name** text box. Press the **OK** command button to see the English translation, press **Yes** to replace an existing file, and **Yes** again to view the file now.

Open CARWASH.MOD.

Click on the **Translate** *command in the* **File** menu.

Click on **English**.

With CARWASH.ENG *highlighted, press* **OK** *in the dialog box.*

Press **Yes** *when asked to replace the existing file.*

Press **Yes** *to view the English translation now.*

The following English description of our basic carwash model was obtained using the **Translate** command on the graphical model.

```
The SIGMA Model, CARWASH.MOD, is a discrete event simulation.
It models an automatic carwash.

I. STATE VARIABLE DEFINITIONS.

For this simulation, the following state variables are
defined:
   QUEUE:      number of cars in line          (integer valued)
   SERVER:     machine is idle/busy = 1/0      (integer valued)

II. EVENT DEFINITIONS.

1. The RUN(QUEUE) event models the initialization of the simu-
   lation. Initial values for, QUEUE, are needed for each run.
   This event causes the following state change(s):
      SERVER=1
   After every occurrence of the RUN event:
   Unconditionally, the car will enter the line;
      that is, schedule the ENTER() event to occur without delay.

2. The ENTER() event models the car entering the line.
   This event causes the following state change(s):
      QUEUE=QUEUE+1
   After every occurrence of the ENTER event:
   If SERVER>0, then start service with the idle machine;
      that is, schedule the START() event to occur without
      delay.
   Unconditionally, the next customer enters in 3 to 8 minutes;
      that is, schedule the ENTER() event to occur in 3+5*RND
      time units.

3. The START() event models the start of service.
   This event causes the following state change(s):
      SERVER=0
      QUEUE=QUEUE-1
   After every occurrence of the START event:
   Unconditionally, the car will be in service for 5 minutes;
      that is, schedule the LEAVE() event to occur in 5 time
      units.
```

```
4. The LEAVE() event models the end of service.
   This event causes the following state change(s):
      SERVER=1
   After every occurrence of the LEAVE event:
   If QUEUE>0, then start service for the next car in line;
      that is, schedule the START() event to occur without
      delay.
```

You can see that if you completed the sentences in the **Description** line in all of the dialog boxes for the vertices and edges in a simulation, the English translation of your model should be quite readable. Again, clicking on the **English Translation Control** menu and on the **Close** command under it will close this file.

Press the **Close** *command in the* **English Translation Control** *menu (to the left of the menu bar).*

4

Running a SIGMA Simulation

The **Run Options** dialog box controls how a simulation of a SIGMA model will run. Details associated with running a model are presented—in particular, the speed of the simulation, how the simulation terminates, and how the numerical data will be plotted.

4.1 Running the Model: A Tutorial

Before you create your own simulation, you should learn how to run SIGMA models. Here, we will continue to use the tutorial format of Chapter 3 and the carwash model to show the basic components of a simulation run. Restart SIGMA by clicking on the **SIGMA** icon in the Windows **Program Manager**. Then, read in the model, `CARWASH.MOD`. Next, open the **Run Options** dialog box.

Double-click on the **SIGMA** *icon.*

Click on the **Open** *command in the* **File** *menu.*

Locate `CARWASH.MOD` *in the* **File Name** *list box and double-click on the model.*

Click on the **Options** *command in the* **Run** *menu.*

A **Run Options** dialog box, like that in Figure 4.1, will appear. This dialog box controls how `CARWASH.MOD` executes. The **Description** of the model is: `AN AUTOMATIC CARWASH`. The **Output File** is the name of the file on your default disk drive where the numerical output from the simulation will be written; here it is `CARWASH.OUT`. The **Random Seed** is set at `12345`, and the **Run Mode** chosen for this model is **Graphics** mode, meaning that we will see a logical animation of the model during execution. The **Variables** to be traced are `QUEUE` and `SERVER`.

The **Initial Attribute** for the model is `5`. Recall from Chapter 3 that the first vertex created in `CARWASH.MOD` was the `RUN` vertex, which has the single

Figure 4.1 Run Options Dialog Box for CARWASH.MOD

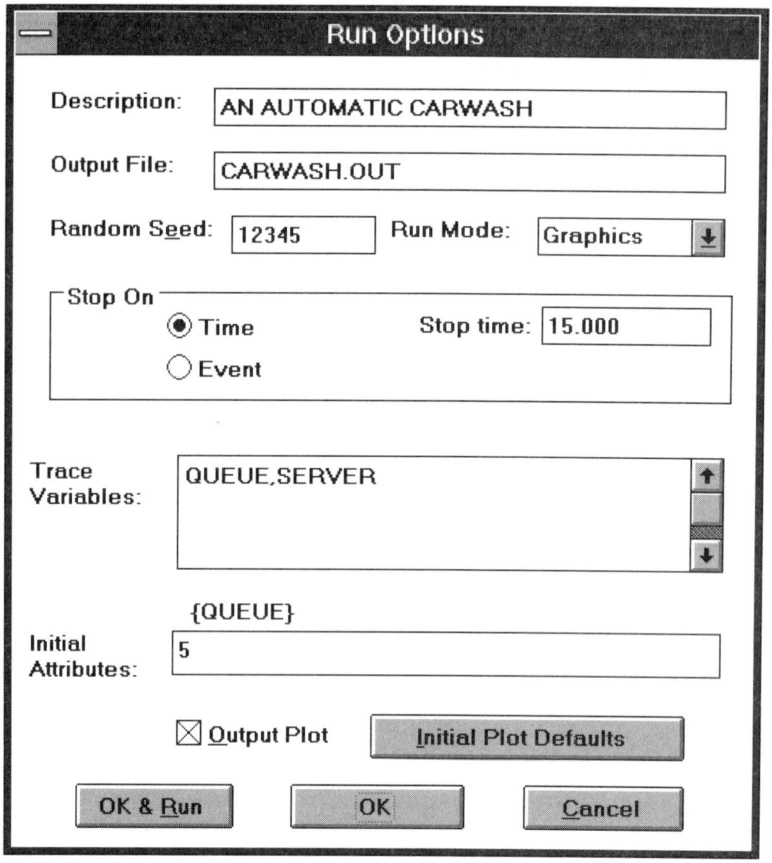

input parameter, QUEUE. In order to run this model, we will need to specify an initial value for QUEUE as prompted in this dialog box. Here the initial value for the variable QUEUE is given as 5, meaning that there will be five customers in line when the carwash opens.

In this model, the ending condition chosen is **Stop On Time**. The run will stop after the clock has advanced to a time equal to or greater than 15. This dialog box also controls output plots. Here the **Output Plot** check box is selected, so a simulation plot will appear when the model executes.

Three command buttons appear across the bottom of the dialog box. Clicking on the **OK & Run** button will incorporate any changes and cause the simulation to execute. If the output file, CARWASH.OUT, already exists, click on the **OK** command button to write over it. (If you are on a network, you need to specify a local drive (c:) for your output!)

Figure 4.2: Standard SIGMA Output File for the Model, `CARWASH.MOD`

```
                 MODEL DEFAULTS

Model Name:              CARWASH.MOD
Model Description:       AUTOMATIC CARWASH
Output File:             CARWASH.OUT
Output Plot Style:       NOAUTO_FIT
Run Mode:                GRAPHICS
Trace Vars:              QUEUE,SERVER
Random Number Seed:      12345
Initial Values:          5
Ending Condition:        STOP ON TIME
Ending Time:             15.000
Trace Events:            ALL EVENTS TRACED
Hide Edges:
```

Time	Event	Count	QUEUE	SERVER
0.000	RUN	1	5	1
0.000	ENTER	1	6	1
0.000	START	1	5	0
3.483	ENTER	2	6	0
5.000	LEAVE	1	6	1
5.000	START	2	5	0
10.000	LEAVE	2	5	1
10.000	START	3	4	0
10.653	ENTER	3	5	0
15.000	LEAVE	3	5	1

Click the mouse on the **OK & Run** *button in the* **Run Options** *dialog box.*

Click the **OK** *command button to write over the previous output.*

Watch the graph as the model runs. A simulation plot window with graphical data should appear beside the simulation graph window. When the run is finished, you can look at the numerical output by clicking the **Yes** button when asked to "View output trace now?" Enlarge the output window by pressing the **Maximize** button; scroll through the file to view the entire contents.

Click the **Yes** *button to view the output trace.*

Click the **Maximize** *button of the output window.*

The numerical output for this run is given in Figure 4.2; it is a record of the run history. There is an entry for each occurrence of every event that was monitored. (For `CARWASH.MOD`, the **Trace Event** box for every vertex was clicked on in the **Edit Vertex** dialog box, indicating that all events were to be traced.) Here we see the simulated time, the name of each event that was traced, the number of times each event took place, and the values of the **Trace Variables**, `QUEUE` and `SERVER`, at those times. Note that there is a separate column for each traced variable.

To return to SIGMA, click the **Close** command under the **Output Control** menu.

Open the **Output Control** *menu at the left of the* **Output** *menu bar.*

Click on the **Close** *command to return to* SIGMA.

4.2 The Run Options

As mentioned earlier, a **Run Options** dialog box similar to the one in Figure 4.1 will appear when the **Options** command under the **Run** menu is clicked. The following sections provide additional information concerning the various options available under the **Run Options** dialog box.

4.2.1 Description

The **Description** text box allows you to provide a brief description of your model. Please note that all of the descriptions in SIGMA are important, even though they are not executable. These descriptions will appear as in-line comments in your SIGMA-generated simulation source code and English translation.

4.2.2 Output File

The **Output File** text box allows you to name the file in which you want the numerical output recorded. The default file is the name of the current model with the file type `.MOD` replaced with `.OUT`. The name of the event, the time each event executed, the number of times each event occurred, and the current values of all state variables that were chosen to be traced are recorded in your output file. (You choose the events that are to be traced by clicking the **Trace Event** check box **On** or **Off** in the dialog box of each vertex.)

> ➢ **Warning:** *Do not write your output over your model. It is advisable to end output files with* .OUT *and model files with* .MOD.

After you have looked at the output file for a model, you can use a button on the output window to view the recent history of the output while the model is running. Press the "Refresh" button [↓] in the output window while the model is running to update the output file during the run.

The output from SIGMA models is in standard ASCII format that is compatible with most statistical analysis packages. For very large output files, the **View Text** window in SIGMA will not be able to show the entire output file. If this is the case, a message will appear on the screen. Most likely, too many vertices have been traced. Turn off some traced events in the **Edit Vertex** dialog boxes or use any ASCII editor (e.g., DOS Edit) to view the entire file. The DOS **SIGPLOT** utility, as discussed in Chapter 10, can also be used.

> ➢ **Warning:** *You will not be allowed to save your output on a write-protected or an unrecognized disk drive. If you are using a network, you must specify your complete path, including the drive letter, so you do not write on the network drive.*

4.2.3 Run Mode

The four run modes available in SIGMA can be found in the **Run Mode** drop-down list. They are:

- **Single Step**, which allows you to step slowly through the simulation;
- **Graphics**, which uses color graphics to illustrate the logic and dynamics of the simulation model;
- **High Speed**, which simply writes an output file; and
- **Time Steps**, which is used for generating spreadsheet data.

The run mode can be changed during a run. Simply open the **Run Options** dialog box during the simulation, click on the **Run Mode** drop-down list, click on the new run mode, and click the **OK** command button.

In **Single Step** mode, the simulation will halt after each vertex is executed and wait until the **Single Step** tool is pressed. This run mode permits you to monitor state variable changes and the list of scheduled events. This mode is particularly useful when verifying the logic of a simulation. When you run a model in **Single Step** mode, the **Single Step Window** will automatically open on the screen. This window will show the current clock time, the event being executed, the number of times the event has executed, the count for each state variable being traced, and the pending events list. Included in the window is the **Single Step** tool. Click the mouse on the **Single Step** tool or press

Figure 4.3: Single Step Window

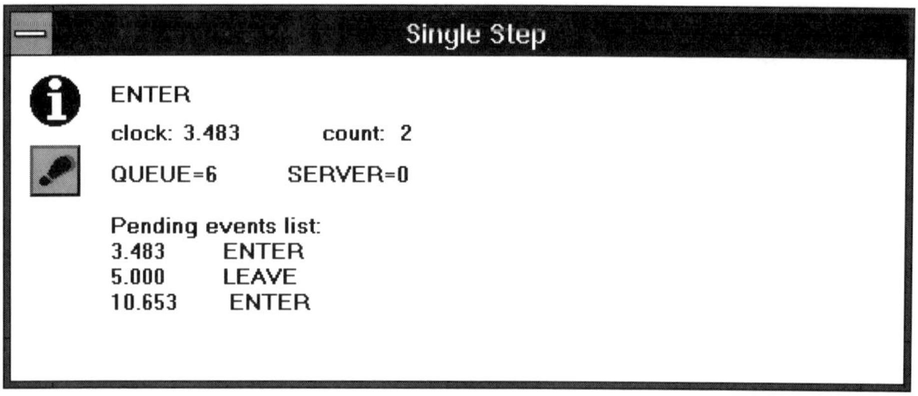

[←Enter] to advance the simulation to the next scheduled event and update the **Single Step Window.** An example of this window is given in Figure 4.3. You close this window by clicking on the **Single Step Control** menu and then clicking the **Close** command. Please note that if you close the **Single Step Window** during a run, the simulation will revert to **Graphics** mode. If you want to return to **Single Step** mode during a run, you must click on the **Run Time Information** tool to reactivate the **Single Step Window**.

In **Graphics** mode, vertices and edges change color as the simulation progresses. Edges change color when their conditions are tested as being true, and vertices flash when they are executed. You see the model being executed. Any event that does not execute during a run will remain shaded. The presence of vertices that never execute may indicate an error in your model logic. This run mode allows you to get a feel for how the model behaves. Hence, it is a good initial method for reviewing your model. If you choose to activate the **Run Time Information** tool during **Graphics** mode, a **Trace Window** (see Figure 4.4) will appear that is very similar to the **Single Step Window**. However, you do not need to do anything to advance the simulation; it progresses automatically. If the *simulation graph* window is active, pressing [F2] will slow the model execution and pressing [F3] will restore it to its original speed.

High Speed run mode bypasses the graphics in SIGMA and produces an output file. **High Speed** mode is useful particularly when running large simulations for long periods. While **High Speed** mode does produce a simulation plot as the model runs, it is wiser to turn the **Output Plot** check box **Off** so that the plot is suppressed or minimize the plot window. While the simulation does not change color during the run, the title bar indicates that the simulation is running. If execution speed is really important, compiling SIGMA-generated C source code is recommended. In fact, those with

Figure 4.4: Trace Window

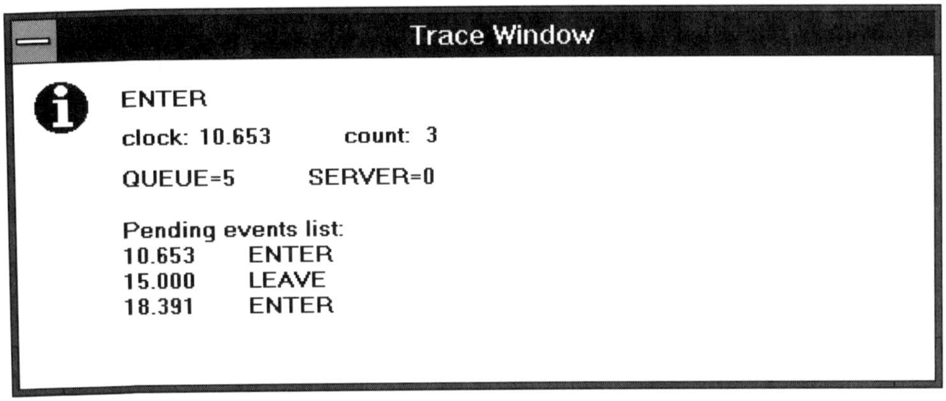

experience in SIGMA will often rough out the logic of a model graphically, immediately translate the model to C source code, and then work directly with the generated source code.

Time Steps run mode is useful for working with spreadsheets. The graphs, plots, and output files are updated only when the simulated time advances.

> ➢ *Translate your model to C for dramatically faster run times. Also, minimizing the number of open windows, including plots and graphs, will speed up the runs considerably.*

4.2.4 Ending Conditions

There are two methods available within the **Run Options** dialog box to terminate a run: **Stop On Event** and **Stop On Time**. With the first, the simulation will terminate after a particular event occurs a specified number of times. The second will end after the simulation has reached a particular clock time. To control the run duration based on a particular event, click the mouse on **Event** in the **Stop On** block of the dialog box. Two boxes will appear requesting additional information: a **Stop Event** drop-down list with all the events in the simulation and an **Iterations** input box. Suppose, for example, that our carwash simulation is to run until the tenth customer departs. Thus, the run would be controlled by the `LEAVE` vertex, and the number of executions of this vertex would be `10`. You would activate the **Stop Event** option, click `LEAVE`, and then type "10" in the **Iterations** box.

If you want to run your simulation for a specific time, click the **Time** option. You will be asked to specify how much simulated time the run is to take. (SIGMA runs until the first event after the specified time.)

To stop in the middle of a run, click the mouse on the **End Run** tool. This stops the current simulation run; however, confirmation is requested to prevent accidentally halting the run. Pressing [F5] also stops the simulation. Of course, if the future events list becomes empty during a run, the run will also terminate.

Ways to Terminate a SIGMA Run

1. Stop at a particular time (the **Stop On Time** option).
2. Stop after a particular event occurs a specified number of times (the **Stop On Event** option).
3. Stop because there are no events scheduled on the future events list.
4. Click the **End Run** tool in the lower right-hand side of the window.
5. Press [F5].
6. Open the **File** menu and click on the **Exit** command.
7. Open the **SIGMA Control** menu and click on the **Close** command.

4.2.5 Trace Variables

In the **Trace Variables** text box, you select the state variables to be recorded and displayed during the run. You list the state variable names (with subscripts in square brackets if appropriate) in a string separated by commas. It is advised to list only a few variables in each run. More than five or six traced variables can make a messy output file when viewed with text editors that wrap around after 80 columns.

4.2.6 Initial Attributes

In the **Initial Attributes** text box, you can specify the initial values for some state variables. These are the values for the parameters of the first vertex you created in this model. When you run a model, you must give initial values for all the variables you specified as parameters for the first vertex you created regardless of how you might have named them. Initial attribute values are entered as a string of numbers separated by commas.

4.2.7 Random Seed

Another starting condition for a simulation is the seed for the pseudo-random number stream; this is any valid integer between `1` and `65000`. Enter a random number seed in the **Random Seed** text box or use the default random seed—`12345`.

Figure 4.5: Initial Plot Defaults Dialog Box

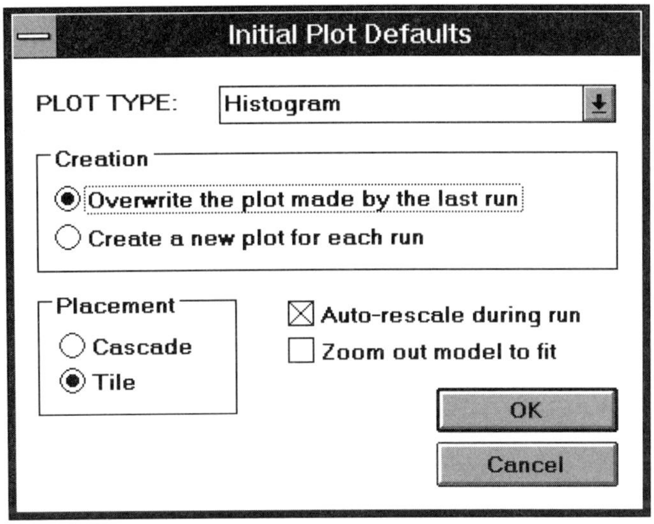

4.2.8 Output Plot

Graphical plots of the data from a simulation are available to you while the simulation is running. If you choose to observe the plots during a simulation, make sure that the **Output Plot** check box is clicked **On**. To suppress the plot, click the box **Off**. A dialog box will appear when the **Initial Plot Defaults** button is clicked. This box, shown in Figure 4.5, allows you to set up the plots as you wish.

One choice available in this dialog box is **Plot Type**. This is a drop-down list containing the following plot types: step plots and line plots (which show how variables change over time), scatter plots (which show the relationship between pairs of variables), histograms (which count the values of variables), autocorrelation plots (which show second-order dependence in the output), and standardized time series (which can be used to detect trends and initialization bias). Another choice involves plot creation: Should a new plot overwrite the plot made by the last run or should a new plot be created for each run? Activate the desired plot creation feature by clicking on your choice. Another plot option involves placement of plots created: should the windows cascade or tile on the screen? Again, click on the preferred placement choice. Two other items on this box use check boxes: **Auto rescale during run** and **Zoom out model to fit**. Click the **OK** button to save your changes and return to SIGMA, or click **Cancel** to disregard your changes and return to SIGMA.

Figure 4.6: Output Plots Dialog Box

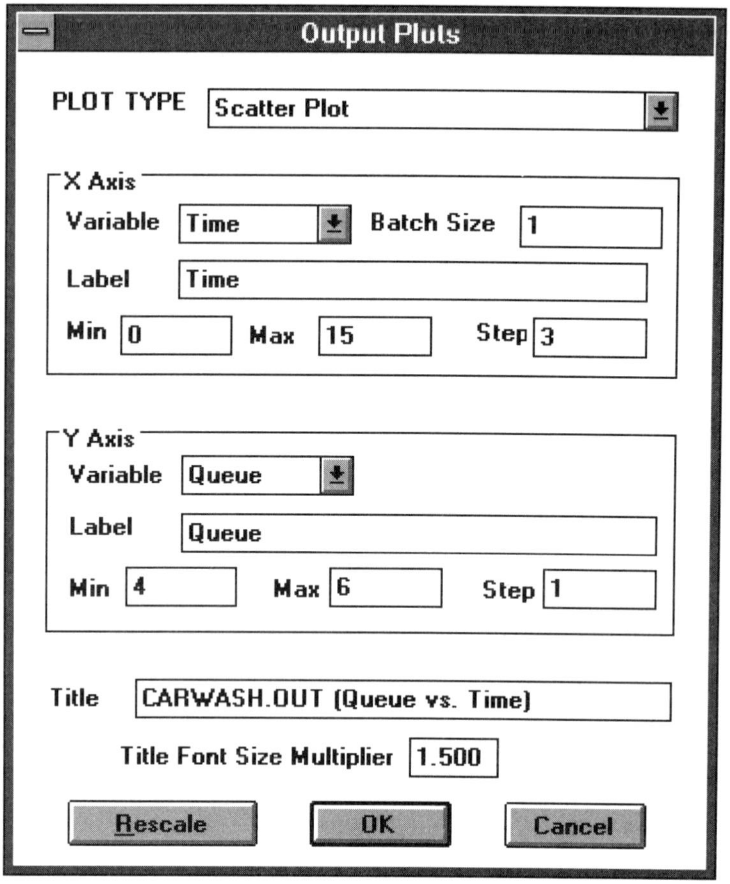

Double-clicking anywhere in the simulation plot window during a run will open the **Output Plots** dialog box, shown in Figure 4.6. In it, you can change the plot type and its characteristics. If you again activate the simulation plot window and select **New** from the **File** menu, a second plot is created, which also can be double-clicked to change its plot type.

Printing and Saving Plots: Simulation plots are printed in the usual manner: by activating the plot window and clicking on the **Print** command under the **File** menu. To save a plot, activate the simulation plot window and click on the **Save** command under the **File** menu. You can retrieve a saved simulation plot file by activating the simulation plot window, clicking on the **Open** command under the **File** menu, and then double-clicking on the file name. You can also activate the simulation graph window, click on the **View Plot** command under the **File** menu, and double-click on the file name.

Copying to Spreadsheets or Word Processors: To move output data from SIGMA into a spreadsheet: activate the *simulation plot* window in SIGMA, click on the **Edit/Copy Data** command, open the spreadsheet program, and click the **Edit/Paste** command. To export a simulation plot to a word processor: activate the *simulation plot* window, click on the **Copy Plot** command in the **Edit** menu, open a word processing file, and click on the **Paste** command in the **Edit** menu.

Labels and Axes: You can select a font type for the title and axes labels for all plots by clicking the **Select Font** command under the **Plot/Edit** menu. The **Title Font Size Multiplier** box (on the **Output Plots** dialog box) can be used to make the title of the plot larger or smaller than the axes labels. The **Step Plot**, **Line Plot**, and **Scatter Plot** all have identical **Output Plot** dialog boxes. For these plots, you can select the **X Axis** (horizontal) and **Y Axis** (vertical) and their limits. The **Histogram**, **Autocorrelation**, and **Standardized Time Series** have slightly different dialog boxes, features of which are discussed shortly.

Data Truncation and Scaling: The **Min** (lower) limit and **Max** (upper) limit for the **X Axis** can be used to eliminate data from each end of a run that might be contaminated by run initialization or termination bias. Note that truncating biased data in this way is only effective after a run has been completed since these limits will be rescaled during a run (if the automatic rescale switch is turned on as it should be). Although it is much less common, you might also want to set maximum and minimum limits for the **Y Axis** to focus on a particular range of values or to plot several different output series on the same scale for comparison purposes.

Batching: In the **X Axis** group, you are also given the option of setting a batch size for the output data. Batching simulation output data is a common smoothing technique where adjacent and exclusive groups of observations are averaged. The resulting series of "batched means" can then be plotted and analyzed. A detailed example of using batched means to estimate confidence intervals is given in Chapter 10.

Histograms: The histogram plot gives the relative counts of observations in different intervals (called cells or "slices"). The **Histogram Plot** dialog box has as its **Y Axis** the count of the number of observations in each slice. You can change the number of slices to obtain smoother or more detailed histograms.

Autocorrelation Plots: The autocorrelation plot gives the correlations between observations in the output series as a function of how close they are to each other. The **X Axis** for this plot is the "lag" between the observations (a lag of 1 is for neighboring observations and a lag of 2 is for observations that have one observation between them, etc.). Setting a fairly small maximum value for the lag is a good idea for two reasons: computing the values for this plot will be faster with a small maximum lag, and correlation estimates for observations that are far apart are not very accurate. In the detailed example in Chapter 10, the autocorrelation function is used to examine the residual correlations between batched means when estimating a confidence interval.

Trend Detection: The standardized time series (STS) plot is a powerful tool for both confidence interval estimation and detecting trends in the output data. Standardized time series are sensitive to changes in the level of a sequence of observations. This is particularly useful in detecting initialization bias in a simulation output series. If the STS plot seems to be rather jagged and spends about the same time above and below zero, then there is probably not much of a trend in the output. If the STS plot is smooth and pulled off in either a positive or negative direction, an increasing or decreasing trend is indicated. A positive trend pulls the STS series to the positive side of zero, and a negative trend pulls the STS plot to the negative side of zero. For practical purposes, you can simply look to see if the STS plot tends to be positive (negative) during a run, indicating an increasing (decreasing) trend in the data.

Examples of using STS plots to detect very weak trends in the output data are presented in Section 10.3. A detailed discussion of using STS information to estimate confidence intervals is deferred until the advanced material in Section 10.5.

4.2.9 Command Buttons

The command buttons in the **Run Options** dialog box are **OK & Run**, **OK**, and **Cancel**. The first saves changes and runs the model, the second saves changes and returns to the static simulation graph, and the third simply closes the dialog box without saving the changes.

4.3 Exercises

The models referred to in these exercises are on your SIGMA *disk.*

4.3.1 A Semi-Random Walk

Build a simulation of a semi-random walk. The location of the walker on the line is given by the variable X. Every step is in an opposite direction and has an expected step length equal to 4 feet. However, the steps to the right are uniformly distributed between 3 and 5 while steps to the left are exactly 4 feet long. Would you expect the location of the walker to change much over time?

4.3.2 Stopping a Run Based on Event Counts

Run the model of a single server queue, `CARWASH.MOD`, until 10 customers `LEAVE` the system.

4.3.3 Time Scaling

Without changing the run stopping criterion in the **Run Options** dialog box, double the effective run duration of `CARWASH.MOD`. (Hint: Rescale the unit for measuring time from minutes to half-minutes.)

4.3.4 Event List Dynamics

Twenty jobs were run through a computer system with one CPU. They all had one of three priorities (lowest number has higher priority and is executed first). A historical data file of these jobs is as follows:

Job number	Time job was submitted	Job priority	CPU time used by the job
1	.00	1	.02
2	.00	2	.01
3	.01	3	.02
4	.02	2	.04
5	.04	3	.02
6	.05	2	.01
7	.07	1	.01
8	.12	1	.01
9	.14	2	.02
10	.15	1	.01
11	.15	2	.01
12	.17	1	.02
13	.18	3	.04
14	.21	1	.03
15	.22	2	.05
16	.23	1	.02
17	.23	1	.01
18	.26	1	.03
19	.33	2	.02
20	.34	1	.03

(a) By hand, schedule the job submission and job completion events as they would occur if all jobs had the same priority; assume that nothing else changes except the priorities. Schedule only the next job submission and next job completion event, not all future job submissions (that is, at most two events will be scheduled at any given time). At time 0.25, what is the state of the system, i.e., the number of jobs in the queue, the status of the CPU (busy/idle), and the events that are scheduled to occur in the future (and when they are scheduled)?

(b) Do part (a) with the execution priorities enforced.

(c) Assume that a second identical CPU has been installed and that the two processors operate in parallel on the same single queue of jobs. A single CPU will finish a complete job before taking the next job in the queue. With job priorities enforced, plot the queue size and number of idle CPUs every .01 time units.

4.3.5 A Theater with Limited Seating Capacity

Suppose that customers arrive at a movie theater at a uniform rate of one every 10 to 25 seconds and each is served in constant time of 20 seconds. There is limited seating in the theater, so the ticket window closes after it has sold 100 tickets. Model this queue.

4.3.6 A Restaurant

A popular restaurant, which does not accept reservations, serves parties in the order that they arrive. For dinner, parties arrive with a rate uniformly distributed between 5 and 15 minutes. Parties range in size from 2 to 6 people, each with the same probability of arrival. Service time for each party, regardless of size, is 2 hours. Assume the restaurant has a capacity for 12 parties. Model this system.

5

Event Graph Modeling

This chapter presents numerous ways to enrich and modify the basic queueing model introduced in Chapter 2 to develop sophisticated simulation models. Among the models discussed are those used to simulate multiple servers with identical capabilities, multiple servers working in parallel with different capabilities, batching operations, assembly operations, service failures, and systems with closing times. Three nonqueueing event graph applications can be found in this chapter: financial risk analysis in coupon bond pricing for an investment bank, continuous time modeling of an aquatic ecosystem, and critical path evaluation of a construction project. The process modeling viewpoint is also illustrated. Several features of event graphs are expanded upon including edge attributes, event parameters, and event cancelling as well as methods for modeling multiple resources and transient entities. This chapter includes a discussion of the modeling technique of using Boolean variables, which allow alternatives to be expressed more easily, as in "if-then-else" statements, "do-while" loops, and nested loops.

5.1 Enrichments of Our Basic Model

In this section we will look at some of the ways that our basic queueing model can be enriched. The models that follow can all be found on your SIGMA distribution disk. You will find that the following discussions are much easier to understand if you read while looking at the models on a computer. Remember to focus only on the edge or vertex being discussed in each model. One of the major advantages of event graphs is that you do not have to look at the whole graph to understand what is happening; you only need to consider one vertex at a time and its exiting edges.

Figure 5.1: Multiple Server Queue

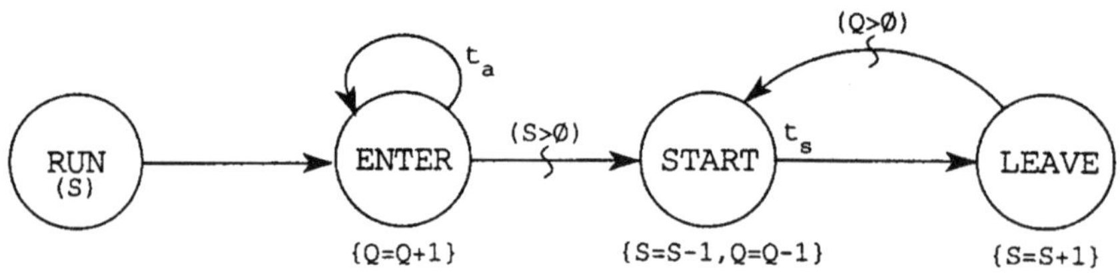

5.1.1 Multiple Identical Parallel Servers

We will simulate a system with several identical servers operating in parallel on a single waiting line of customers (e.g., tellers at a bank). The model BANK1.MOD on the SIGMA distribution disk is an enrichment of CARWASH.MOD, discussed in the previous chapters. Using the 1 = available and 0 = unavailable convention for a single server allows us to easily change the number of servers available in our model. We simply let SERVERS denote the number of idle tellers in a simulated bank. No matter how many tellers we have in our model, the condition, SERVERS>0, will always mean that at least one is available. The only modification necessary of our basic model to change it from a single server system to a multiple server system is to set SERVERS equal to the total number of tellers in the system in the RUN vertex. All edge conditions remain the same, but we now make the service times random.

The SIGMA graph of this system appears in Figure 5.1. The state variables we use to describe this system are:

QUEUE	The number of customers currently waiting in line, initially equal to 0 by default.
SERVERS	The number of idle tellers, specified as an input parameter to the initial RUN vertex.

(To make the model easier to read, QUEUE and SERVERS are represented by Q and S on the event graph.) We initialize the number of servers as an input parameter so we can change the number of servers easily each time we run the model.

As before, we will "read" this model by sequentially considering the state changes and the edges exiting from each vertex. The edges entering each vertex will take care of themselves. First, we look at the state changes for each vertex.

In the RUN vertex, the number of SERVERS is input and the run started.

In the ENTER vertex, the arrival of the next customer is modeled with the state change, QUEUE=QUEUE+1.

In the START service vertex, the queue and the number of free servers are both decremented with state changes, QUEUE=QUEUE-1 and SERVERS=SERVERS-1.

When the service is finished, the customer can LEAVE. In the LEAVE vertex, the number of idle servers is incremented with the state change, SERVERS=SERVERS+1.

Next, we read the edges that exit from each vertex.

When the RUN is started, the first customer is unconditionally scheduled to ENTER right away.

Subsequent customers ENTER at intervals that are uniformly distributed between 3 and 8 minutes.

When a customer ENTERs, if there is an idle server (SERVERS>0), service will START without delay.

Once service STARTs, the customer will be scheduled to LEAVE after a time delay equal to the service time of between 2 and 6 minutes.

When a customer LEAVEs the bank, if there are still customers waiting (QUEUE>0), the server will immediately START service on the next customer.

Notice that the vertices for this example are identical to those in the carwash model. The only difference is that rather than setting the SERVER to busy or idle (0/1) when service starts and finishes, we increment and decrement the total number of idle servers. In fact, the single server carwash model is a special case of this model if the variable SERVERS is initialized to equal one in the RUN vertex.

We may wish to study the behavior of this system under different service speeds and demand rates. For the time being, we are only interested in resident entities—i.e., the servers and queues. We will observe both the utilization of the servers and the size of the queue. There is no reason here to model individual customers, as they are assumed to be identical; however, modeling customers is important in later examples. Modeling only resident entities simplifies a model considerably, as we shall see when we enrich this model to explicitly include each customer. With a little practice, either type of model is very easy to build.

5.1.2 Batched Service

Batched service occurs when more than one item is processed at the same time. Examples include a furnace that processes multiple parts, an oven in a

Figure 5.2: Event Graph for a Queue with Batched Service

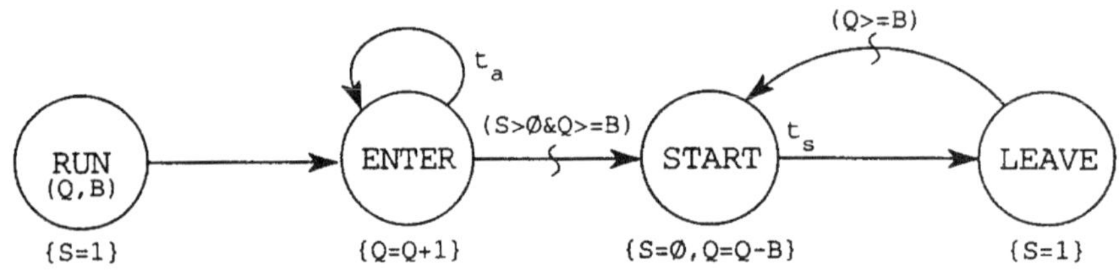

bakery, or a shuttle bus for airline passengers. Figure 5.2 is a model of such a system (BATCHSIZ.MOD on your SIGMA disk).

For this enrichment, we will denote the batch size in the graph with the variable B. If a full batch is required for processing, this would be indicated on the conditional edge between the ENTER and START vertices. Using our carwash model, we would simply change the edge condition for the edge between ENTER and START to S>0&Q>=B. (Note that & is the symbol for a Boolean "and" operator that indicates that both conditions must be true.) We also would change the edge condition between LEAVE and START to Q>=B. The state change vector for the START event is now

S=0,Q=Q−B

so that a full batch is removed from the waiting queue every time a START event takes place. If we were simulating a system where it is possible to process a partial batch, the edge conditions for our original carwash model would not change. The state change for the START vertex would decrement Q by the minimum of the Q and B, Q=Q−MIN{Q;B}.

5.1.3 Rework

In some cases, it may be necessary to rework a part that has just been processed. This situation is most common when layers of material are applied to a part, as in a painting operation. The only change needed in the carwash model to create this new model is to add a feedback loop, an edge from LEAVE to REWORK and back to START as shown in Figure 5.3 (REWORK1.MOD on your SIGMA disk). Here the probability of rework, P, is an input variable to the model. A random number, RND, that falls (strictly) between 0 and 1 is drawn; if this number is less than P, rework is required. The probability that the condition RND<P is true equals P.

Notice that if we model REWORK in this manner, LEAVE, REWORK, and ENTER might all schedule a START vertex at the same time. To break time

Figure 5.3: Event Graph with Rework

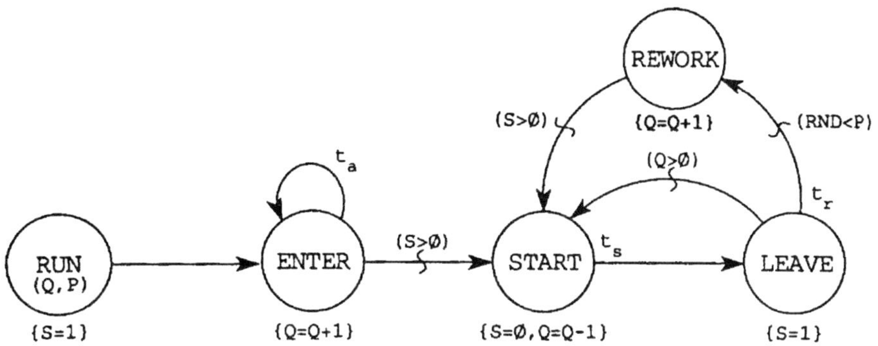

ties correctly, the execution priority for the START vertex (assigned by the edges scheduling this event) should be higher than the execution priority for all other vertices. If not, an ENTER or REWORK vertex might schedule a START event (if the server already was made free by the LEAVE event) at the same time that the LEAVE event scheduled a START event. These START events would each, in turn, schedule LEAVE events, creating "phantom" extra servers in our model. If the START event is executed before any other events, there is no problem since this makes the appropriate edge conditions (S>0) false.

This model illustrates problems that occur when two events are scheduled at the same time. Several popular professional simulation languages have no mechanism for breaking ties in the times that simultaneous events are scheduled. This is a bigger problem than one might think at first glance, since in a "balanced" system, time ties are intentionally designed into the system. The so-called Just In Time production systems invented in Japan are examples.

> ➢ **Warning:** *Watch out for unwanted side effects that come when events are scheduled simultaneously!*

Sometimes rework requires an additional preparation time, called rework setup time. To model this additional rework preparation time (e.g., to remove paint), we simply place a delay on the edge from LEAVE to REWORK equal to the rework setup time, here t_r.

Figure 5.4: Event Graph with Limited Waiting Space

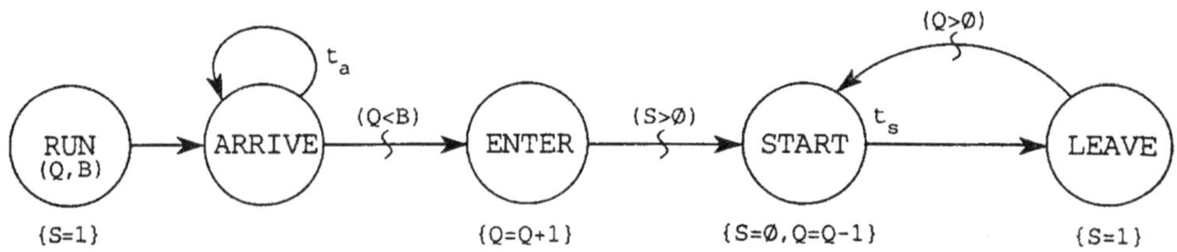

5.1.4 Limited Waiting Space

In our next model, we will simulate a system with limited waiting space in the queue. The amount of waiting space is called the buffer size. We define variable B as the buffer size and specify this as a parameter for the RUN vertex, to be initialized when the model is run. To create this model, we modified our basic carwash model by adding an ARRIVE vertex between the RUN vertex and the ENTER vertex. The self-scheduling edge used to create customer arrivals is moved from the ENTER vertex to the ARRIVE vertex. We also conditioned the edge from ARRIVE to ENTER to require that there be an empty space for the arriving customer to wait. The event graph for this new model is shown in Figure 5.4 and implemented as BUFFERQ.MOD on your SIGMA disk.

It is also possible to model this system using a Boolean variable. When using Boolean variables, a condition takes on the value of 1 if it is true and 0 if it is false. Using the carwash model, we can incorporate limited waiting space by altering the expression for the state change in the ENTER edge from Q=Q+1, which models an arriving customer unconditionally joining the queue, to the expression,

Q=Q+(Q<B).

Figure 5.5: Event Graph with Boolean Variables to Model Limited Waiting Space

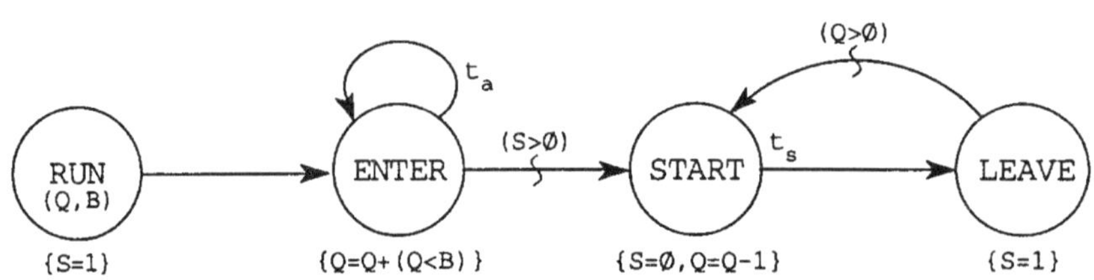

Figure 5.6: Event Graph for an Assembly Operation

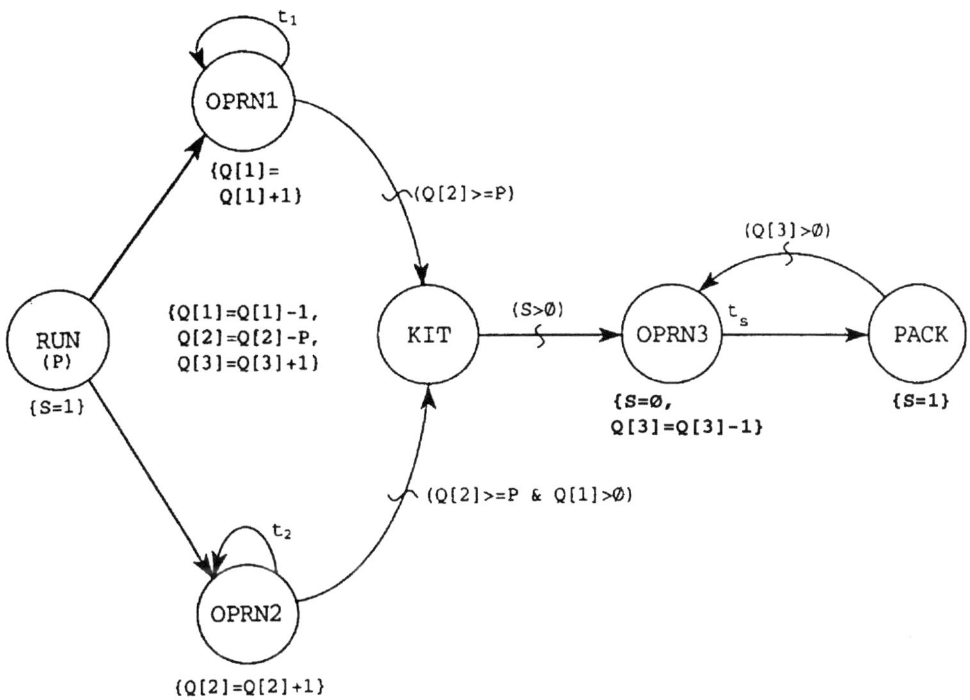

If the condition (`Q<B`) is true, there is waiting space for an arriving customer and the Boolean variable in parentheses will be equal to `1`. Then `Q` will be increased by `1`. If the `Q` equals or exceeds the buffer size, there is no waiting space. Consequently, the condition will evaluate to `0`, and `Q` will not be incremented (`0` is added to `Q`). See Figure 5.5 for the event graph for this model.

5.1.5 Assembly Operations

In an assembly operation, several different types of parts are put together into a single unit. The collected parts for a finished assembly are sometimes called a "kit." A kitting and assembly operation, where one part from Operation `1` is joined with `P` parts from Operation `2` to form a kit for assembly Operation `3`, is modeled in Figure 5.6 and is `ASSEMKIT.MOD` on your SIGMA disk.

Figure 5.7: Event Graph with Two Dissimilar Servers Working in Parallel

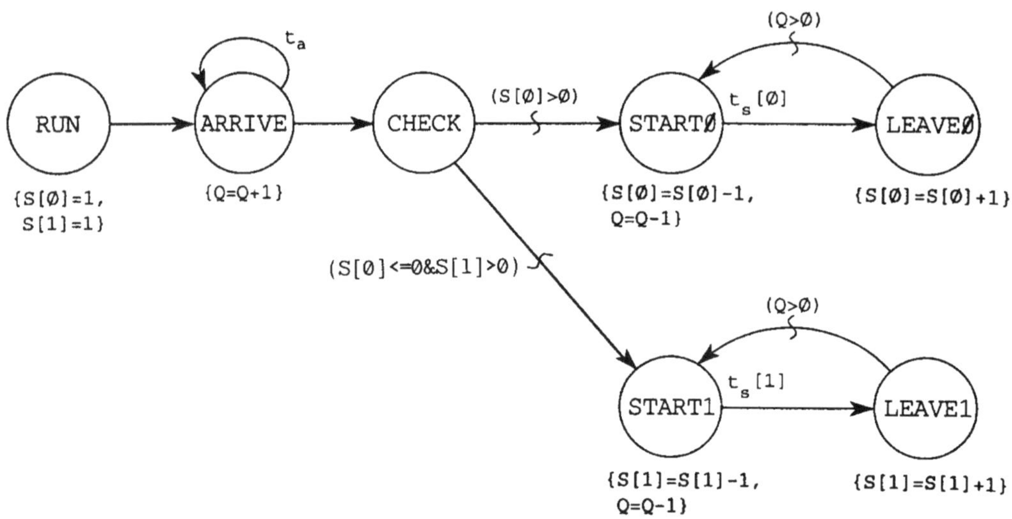

5.1.6 Multiple, Nonidentical Servers Working in Parallel

Suppose that we have two servers with different characteristics operating in parallel (e.g., machines with different average processing speeds). In this example, there is a new, faster machine working with last year's slower model.

We will designate each type of machine with an index, A, that indicates the age of the machine. For the new machine, A=0; for the older machine, A=1. The status of each machine is given by the values of state variables S[0] and S[1]. The status of a machine will be equal to 0 if the machine is busy and equal to 1 if the machine is idle. We will denote the average processing times for the two machines by t_s[0] and t_s[1]. We assume that when both machines are idle the faster machine, (A=0), is preferred.

The most direct way to model these two types of machines operating in parallel is to add a second pair of START and LEAVE vertices for the second server. This was done in Figure 5.7 and is the model SLOFAST0.MOD on your SIGMA disk. From the viewpoints of the servers, this model with a single waiting queue and two servers is the same as a model with separate waiting lines for each server with line "jockeying" (customers in a queue will change lines if they see the other server is idle).

Parts arrive at the ARRIVE vertex in the usual manner with a (perhaps random) interarrival time of t_a. We will increment the count, Q, of the number of parts in the queue at the ARRIVE event. At the CHECK vertex, we check to see if there is an idle machine. If the faster machine is available, work

Figure 5.8: Event Graph of Many Servers of Two Types

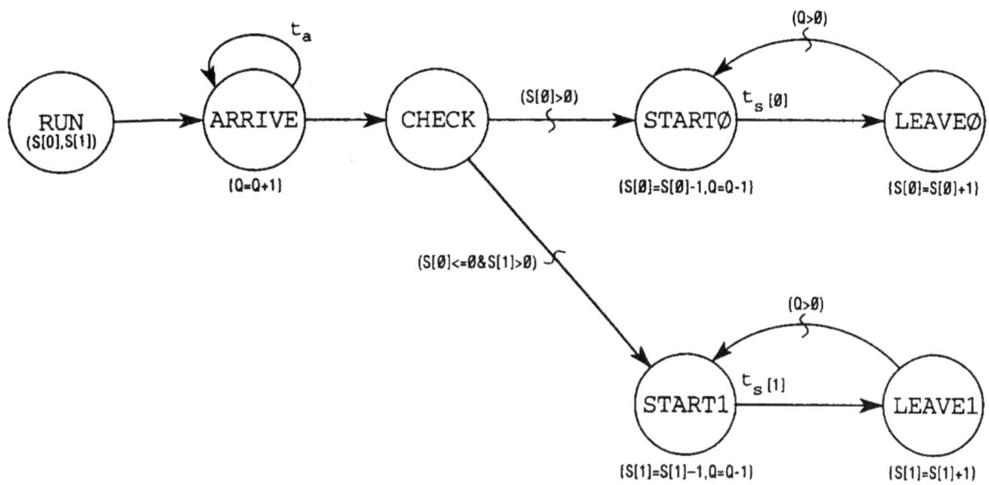

will start with that machine. In the `START0` vertex, the state change, `S[0]=S[0]-1`, makes machine `0` busy; `S[0]` goes from a value of `1` to a value of `0`.

If the fast machine is busy and the slower machine is idle, work will start with machine `1` at the `START1` vertex. The test for this is the condition, `S[0]<=0&S[1]>0`, on the edge from `CHECK` to `START1`. When the conditions on both edges exiting the `CHECK` event are false, both servers are busy and nothing further will happen until the next event occurs (which will be an `ARRIVE`, `LEAVE0`, or `LEAVE1` event).

Just as we enriched our model of the single server queue to include multiple identical servers working in parallel, we can easily enrich this model to include many servers of two types. We simply redefine `S[A]` to be the number of idle servers of type `A` and initialize our model (at the `RUN` vertex) with the total numbers of each type of server. This model is shown in Figure 5.8 and is implemented as `SLOFAST1.MOD` on your SIGMA disk.

5.2 Event Cancellation

In some cases, the occurrence of an event will cause some previously scheduled event to be cancelled. For example, if a machine in a factory simulation happens to break, the completion of the current job will have to be cancelled. In event graphs, cancelling edges are shown as dashed arrows. Conditions under which the originating vertex will cancel the destination vertex are shown

Figure 5.9: Event Graph with Closing Time

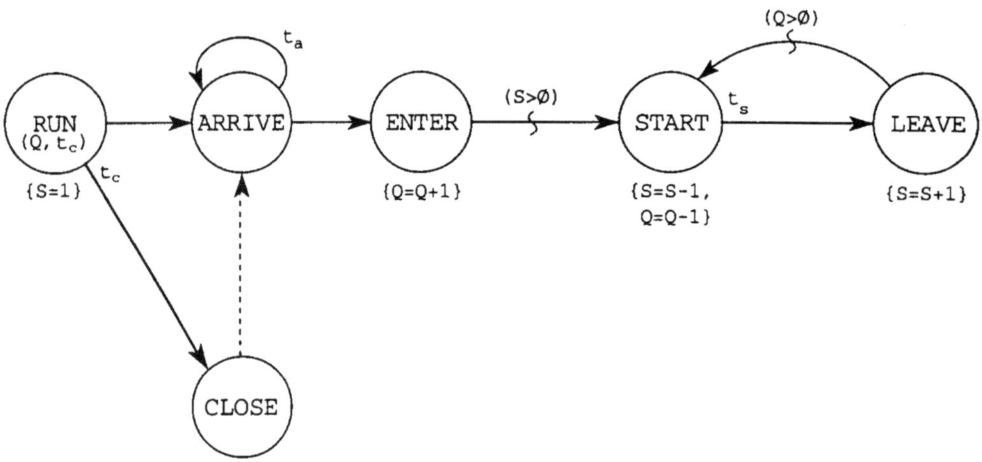

in the same manner as scheduling edges. If the edge condition for a cancelling edge is true, cancellation of the destination vertex is assumed to occur immediately; all the delay times for cancelling edges are equal to zero.

5.2.1 Closing Time

Here we expand the carwash model to include a daily closing time. When the simulated time, CLK, reaches the value of the input variable, CLOSING_TIME, we will no longer admit customers to the system. Of course, customers already waiting in line when we close will be served. There are several ways to model this. A straightforward way might be to add an ARRIVE vertex like we did in section 5.1.4 and place a condition on the edge from ARRIVE to ENTER that the current time be less than the value of CLOSING_TIME. The problem here is that we will not know in advance how many customers are waiting in line when we close; therefore, we will not know when we should stop the simulation run. We could set the run time to a large number so that the customers in the system have ample time to leave the system before the simulation ends.

Since customer arrivals are generated by having each ARRIVE event schedule the next ARRIVE event, a more efficient model for closing the queueing system would be to cut off the stream of customer arrivals at CLOSING_TIME. However, placing the condition, CLK<CLOSING_TIME, on the self-scheduling edge that generates arrivals would not be correct. Before closing time, an ARRIVE event might be scheduled to occur after CLOSING_TIME.

Figure 5.10: Event Graph with Service Failures

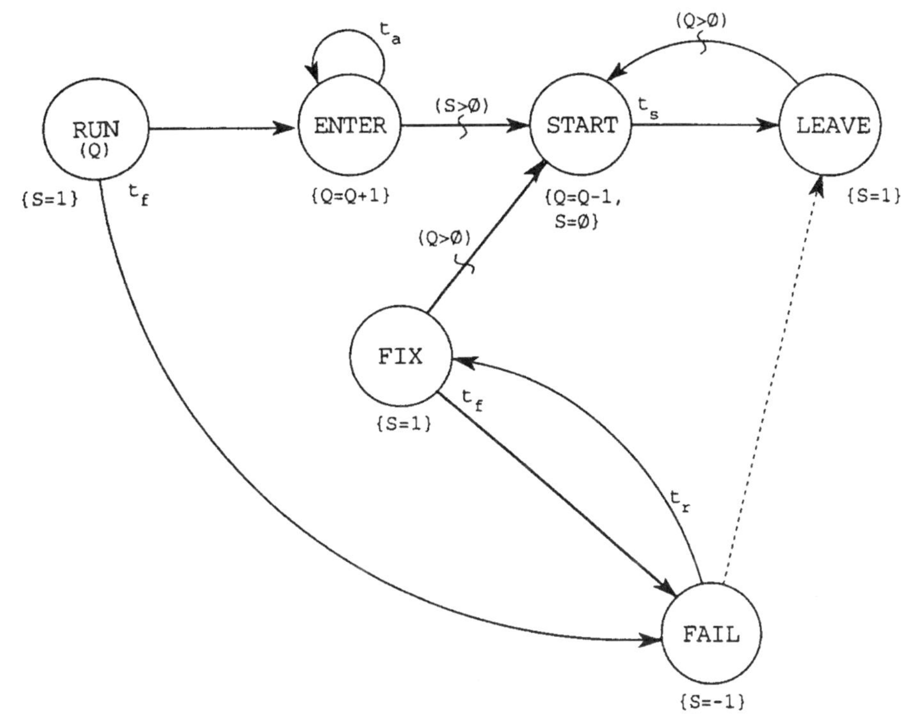

A correct way to stop the arrival of customers at closing time is to cancel the next scheduled ARRIVE event (and thus all subsequent customer arrivals) at CLOSING_TIME. Any waiting customers will be serviced until there are no more events on the future events list; by default, the run will stop with an empty events list. (An empty future events list is a default run termination condition for almost all discrete event simulation systems, including SIGMA.) This model for closing a system is illustrated in Figure 5.9 and is given as CLOSEIT.MOD on your SIGMA disk (closing time is denoted as t_C in the event graph in Figure 5.9).

5.2.2 Single Server with Intermittent Service Failures

The model BRKDN.MOD on your SIGMA disk is an enrichment of our basic carwash model that allows us to model periodic breakdowns of service. The event graph for this model is pictured in Figure 5.10. We added two vertices and expanded the definition of the status of the server to include "broken."

Now server status is represented by 1 (available), 0 (busy), and -1 (broken). The breakdown process is modeled with the following vertices:

> FAIL is the vertex where a service failure occurs. Any job that may be in progress and scheduled to LEAVE the system is cancelled. The part being worked on when the machine broke down is destroyed. The server's status is changed to "broken" with the state change, SERVER=-1.
>
> FIX is the vertex where the server is repaired. The state change, SERVER=1, makes the server once again available.

Additional edges added to the carwash model to simulate server breakdowns include the following:

> An unconditional edge from RUN to FAIL is used to schedule the first service breakdown when the run starts (t_f).
>
> An unconditional edge from FIX to FAIL is used to make the server break down after a randomly distributed time interval (t_f). This is regardless of whether or not the machine actually did any work during this interval.
>
> A cancelling edge from FAIL to LEAVE is used to cancel the LEAVE event without delay if the server is busy. Note that if the server is idle when a failure occurs, we will attempt to cancel a nonexistent LEAVE event (which does nothing if the server is not busy).
>
> An edge from FIX to START, conditioned by (QUEUE>0), is used to immediately start the server working after being repaired if there are parts waiting in the queue.
>
> An unconditional edge from FAIL to FIX, with a delay time of t_r, is used to schedule the server to be fixed after the repair time.

If we assume that a part in service is not affected by a machine failure, we would add a variable to keep track of the amount of service time remaining on a part when failure occurs. Also, it might be more realistic to model machine failures as being dependent on how much work was done since the last failure rather than on the elapsed time. This situation could be modeled by defining a new state variable to accumulate the working time until the next failure.

5.3 Event Parameters and Edge Attributes

An important enrichment of our basic model is the parameterization of event vertices: similar events can be represented by a single vertex with different parameter values. For example, say that there are several machines working in a factory. A "start processing" event might be parameterized to indicate which machine is involved. We might call this event START(M). START(3) would indicate that machine number 3 is starting. Similarly, a "finish processing" event might be parameterized to indicate which machine has just become

Figure 5.11: Conditional Edge with Delay Time and Parameter Passing

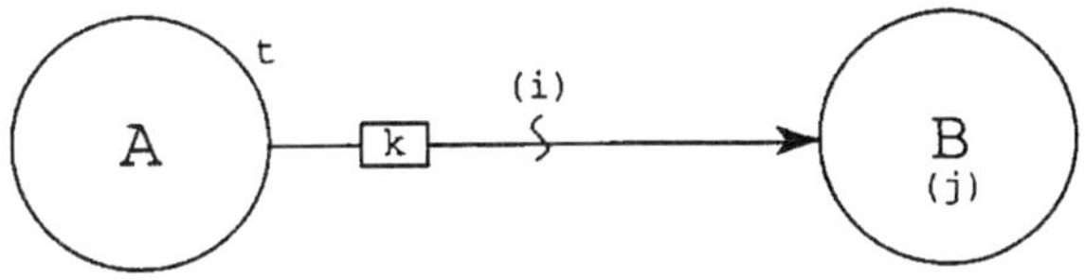

idle. We might call this event FINISH(M); FINISH(3) would indicate the end of service on machine 3.

We parameterize event graphs using the notation in Figure 5.11. The edge on a simulation event graph is now "read" as follows:

> *if condition* (i) *is true at the instant* A *occurs, then event* B(j) *will be scheduled to occur* t *minutes later with the parameter,* j, *equal to* k.

In general, the attribute value, k, can be a string of expressions and j can be a vector of state variables.

Consider a network of waiting lines, such as those at an airport terminal. The number of customers in each queue in the system might be represented by a variable called NUM_IN[QUEUE]. Here [QUEUE] identifies a particular line and NUM_IN is an array of integers (an integer state variable with a size greater than one). Whenever a new customer joins a waiting line, the number of customers in that queue is increased by one. The vertex in the graph representing this event will contain the state change, NUM_IN[QUEUE]=NUM_IN[QUEUE]+1. A copy of the dialog box for this vertex is shown in Figure 5.12. This vertex will require a value for the parameter, QUEUE, telling which line in the system the customer joins. A value for the parameter, QUEUE, is passed as an attribute of the edge that scheduled this vertex.

With cancelling edges, like scheduling edges, it is sometimes necessary to designate which of several scheduled instances of an edge destination vertex is to be cancelled. If several machines are working and one breaks, an edge attribute can be used to identify which machine has broken so that its job completion vertex can be cancelled. If no edge attributes are specified, only the first scheduled occurrence (if any) of the edge destination vertex is cancelled. If attributes are given on a cancelling edge, the future events list is searched for an exact match by vertex type and attribute values; only the first scheduled event with an exact match of edge attribute values is cancelled. If you want to cancel all scheduled events of a particular type, an asterisk (*) is placed as the edge attribute. Setting an edge attribute to an * might be useful,

Figure 5.12: `EVENT` Vertex Dialog Box

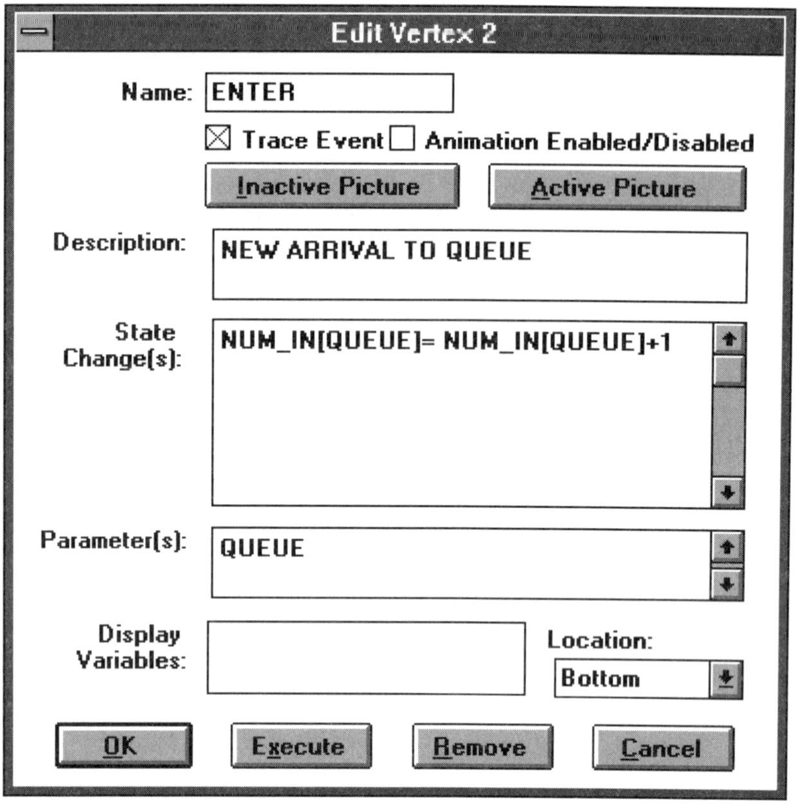

say, if you wish to temporarily shut down a portion of the simulation (e.g., a fire drill in a factory would cancel all job completion events).

> ➢ **Note:** *Pass array elements explicitly; e.g., if* `Q=3`*, pass* `WAIT[3]` *and* `Q`*, not* `WAIT[Q]`.

Passing edge attribute values to parameters is illustrated in the following examples.

5.3.1 Many Servers of Many Types

A generalization of the model with two types of servers (seen in Figure 5.7) is a model of many types of servers with many servers of each type. Our

Figure 5.13: Using Event Parameters to Simulate Many Servers of Different Types

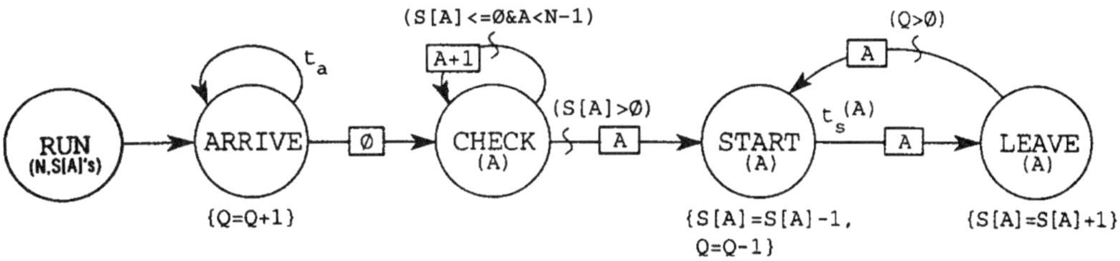

example will be a production department with N different machines of different models and ages.

As before, we will designate the type of machine by its age, A, and let S[A] denote the number of idle machines of type A. If we merely added more event vertices for each type of machine, the model would become cumbersome when we simulate a system with many types of machines.

This problem is easily solved using vertex parameters. For example, a START vertex with parameter A will denote the start of work with a machine of age A. A LEAVE vertex with parameter A will mean that a job has been finished by a machine of age A. When necessary, we will place vertex parameters in parentheses following the vertex name—e.g., START(A) and LEAVE(A). See Figure 5.13 for this model, which is SLOFAST2.MOD on your SIGMA disk. We have parameterized everything (state variables, edges, and vertices) that pertains to the type of server with the parameter A.

This graph may look complicated when viewed as a whole. Perhaps the most confusing part of this model is the CHECK vertex; this vertex checks each type of server in turn until either an idle server is found (S[A]>0) or all servers are checked (A>=N-1). These two conditions are the same as the compound condition (S[A]<=0&A<N-1) being false.

Notice that the graph structure for this model (vertices and edges) is similar to that of our original single server queue. We can think of these models as being in the same "family" of models. Using event parameters allows us to use simple graphs to model very large systems; we exploit the similarities of subgraphs by parameterizing them. We could use this model for very large systems with perhaps hundreds of servers of hundreds of different types and still be able to run the corresponding simulation program on a small personal computer.

5.3.2 Multiple Servers—Single Line with Waiting Times

In the model BANK2.MOD on your disk, we keep statistics on the waiting times of individual customers in a multiple server queue (e.g., bank tellers). This

Figure 5.14: Multiple Server Queue with Customer Waiting Times

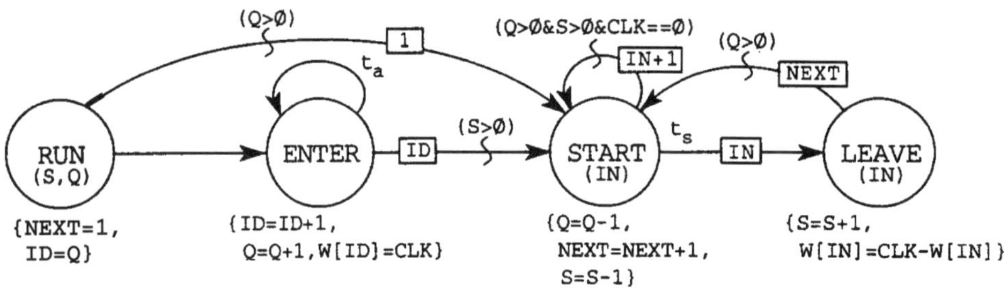

model is an enrichment of `BANK1.MOD` discussed in Section 5.1.1 The event graph for `BANK2.MOD` is shown in Figure 5.14.

The state variables for this model include:

`QUEUE`	The number of customers currently waiting in line (denoted by `Q` on the graph).
`SERVERS`	The number of idle servers, initialized each time the model is run (denoted by `S`).

Additional variables that allow us to model the flow of transient entities are:

`W[I]`	An array of `W`aiting times for the `I`th customer.
`ID`	The customer `ID`entification number.
`IN`	The identification number of a customer currently `IN` service.
`NEXT`	The customer `NEXT` at the front of the line.

Recall that `CLK` is the current simulated time, initially set at `0` and automatically updated at each event.

Our graph now represents the flow of customers passing through the system. This model has the flavor of a process flow model. The process being modeled is that of customers moving through a bank.

This model has the same four vertices as the simpler resident entity model, `BANK1.MOD`, and their graph structures are very similar. The vertices, along with their state changes, are given below:

The `RUN` vertex (the first vertex to be executed) is where we initialize the run parameters and start the run. The state change is as follows:

`NEXT=1`	customer `1` is initially first in line.

The event parameters, `S` and `Q`, are input as initial conditions.

The `ENTER` vertex models the arrival of new customers. The state changes are as follows:

`ID=ID+1`	increment the customer `ID` counter.
`Q=Q+1`	increment the number in line.
`W[ID]=CLK`	mark customer arrival time.

The `START` vertex is the start of service for the customer with identification number = `IN`. The state changes are as follows:

`Q=Q-1`	decrement the waiting line.
`NEXT=NEXT+1`	update `ID` of the customer next in line.
`S=S-1`	reduce the number of idle servers.

The event parameter, `IN`, is the customer going into service.

The `LEAVE` vertex models the end of service for the customer `IN` service. The state changes are as follows:

`S=S+1`	free one server.
`W[IN]=CLK-W[IN]`	compute customer waiting time.

The event parameter, `IN`, is the customer who was in service and is now finishing.

Here the situation is considerably more complex than in previous models. However, it is still easy to read since our graph allows us to concentrate on one edge at a time. As before, you should try to identify each sentence in this system description with an edge in Figure 5.14.

The `RUN` begins with the first customer `ENTER`ing the system. Any customers initially in line may `START` service.

When a customer `ENTER`s the system, if there are any idle servers available `(S>0)`, this customer will start service. (That is, we immediately schedule a `START(IN)` event with the customer identification number for the customer to go `IN` service being customer, `ID`, who just arrived.)

Successive customers will `ENTER` the system after a time delay of t_a minutes.

The `START` vertex will make all initially idle servers busy if there is an initial queue.

The customer who `START`s `IN` service can `LEAVE` t_s minutes later after receiving service. (The parameter, `IN`, is passed from the `START(IN)` event to the `LEAVE(IN)` event since the same customer is involved. Note that we do not know the actual waiting times for customers who were initially in the queue when we opened the system for services, so their waiting times should be ignored.)

Whenever a customer `IN` service finally `LEAVE`s, if there are still customers waiting `(Q>0)`, the `NEXT` customer in line can immed-

Figure 5.15: Numerical Example of BANK2.MOD

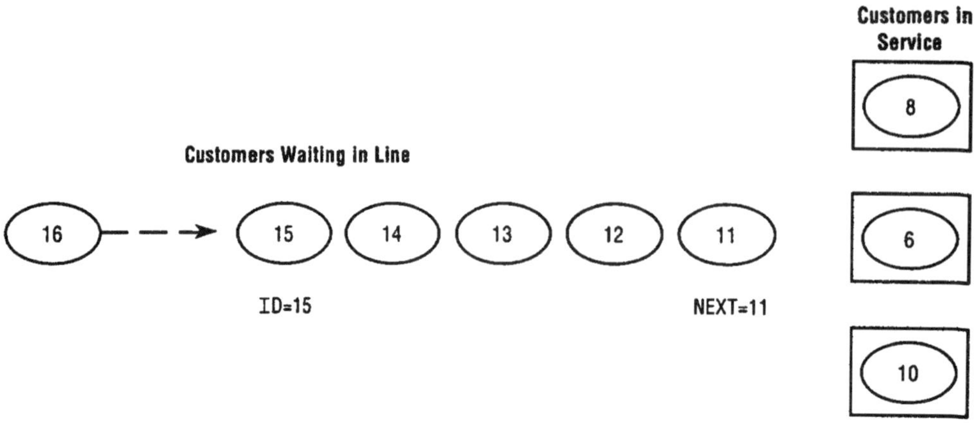

iately START IN service. (The NEXT customer in line will be able to go IN service since the value of the edge attribute, NEXT, is passed to the parameter, IN, of the START vertex.)

To learn how to read event graphs, reread the above edge descriptions without looking at Figure 5.14 and *ignoring all the parenthetical remarks.* You might want to lightly cross out all these remarks with a pencil. You will see that the edge descriptions give a simple, concise, and accurate description of the system dynamics.

To clarify these ideas, it is helpful to walk through an example with three servers. Consider this model at time 2.50 (CLK=2.50). Suppose that an ENTER event has just occurred. The entering customer found five customers waiting in line (Q=5) and no available servers (S=0). The customer at the front of the line is customer 11 (i.e., NEXT=11) and the last customer in the line is customer 15 (ID=15). The three servers are now serving customers 8, 6, and 10. The customer who just arrived would be customer 16 (ID+1) and Q would be increased to Q=6. Suppose the random time generated until the next arrival was 1.71. The next ENTER event would occur at time = 4.21 (2.5 + 1.71). The situation is illustrated in Figure 5.15. The future events list for this example is given in Table 5.1. It shows when the three customers currently in service will LEAVE the system and when the next customer will ENTER. At CLK=3.243 the LEAVE event occurs where customer 8 is the customer IN service (IN=8). At this LEAVE vertex, the total time in the system for customer 8 can be computed as the difference between the current value of the clock, CLK, and the time customer 8 arrived, W[IN]=W[8]. Since there

Table 5.1: Future Events List with Customers 6, 8, and 10

Time	Event		Priority	Attributes
3.243	LEAVE	(customer 8)	6	8
4.210	ENTER	(next arrival)	6	
5.593	LEAVE	(customer 6)	6	6
6.478	LEAVE	(customer 10)	6	10

are customers waiting in the queue (Q=6>0), a START event will be scheduled to occur without delay at time 3.243. The value of the vertex parameter IN, which indicates which customer is starting "IN" service, will be the current value of NEXT (11) and will be passed by the edge from LEAVE to START. The START event will occur with parameter IN=11 and schedule a LEAVE event with customer 11 (say at time 8.243). The current value of IN is the attribute value for the parameter IN of the LEAVE event that has just been scheduled. Also, in the START event vertex, NEXT will be increased to 12 since customer 12 is now at the head of the line. The system and future events list now looks like Table 5.2. When the ENTER event occurs at CLK=4.210, the identification number of the customer who is last in line is increased to ID=17.

We see that only the values of edge attributes are placed on the list of scheduled future events. All connection with the value of an attribute and the particular state variable or expression that was evaluated to get that attribute value is lost once the event vertex is scheduled.

Until you get some practice in reading simulation event graphs, the graph in Figure 5.14 might appear very complicated. Indeed, this is a fairly complicated simulation. You can take some comfort in knowing that in Chapter 7 we will introduce two SIGMA functions (called PUT and GET) that file entities in ranked lists and make this model very simple by eliminating the need for event parameters or edge attributes. Using these functions is a more straightforward way to model queues of transient entities.

Table 5.2: Future Events List After Customer 8 Leaves and 11 Starts Service

Time	Event		Priority	Attributes
4.210	ENTER	(next arrival)	6	
5.593	LEAVE	(customer 6)	6	6
6.478	LEAVE	(customer 10)	6	10
8.243	LEAVE	(customer 11)	6	11

> ➣ *Only the* ***values*** *of edge attribute expressions are placed on the events list. These values are assigned to the list of vertex parameter* **State Variables** *when the event is later executed. Do not use array elements as edge attributes.*

Two models on your SIGMA disk, BANK1.MOD and BANK2.MOD, illustrate how the same system can be modeled differently. The first example focuses only on the behavior of resident entities, those physical system components that remain a part of the system for long periods (e.g., servers in a queueing system). The second model enriches the first to include details on the flow of transient entities, those entities that occasionally enter and leave a system (e.g., customers in a queue). Each type of model has advantages: modeling resident entity cycles tends to be easy and efficient, while modeling the details of transient entity flow gives more information.

5.3.3 Limited Rework

Reworking does not always involve the removal of a coating that has just been applied; it sometimes involves the removal of original material. In a limited rework model, a particular part is not reworked more than a specified number of times before it is discarded. In this model, we will assume that a part can be processed no more than the number of times specified by the limit, LM. Starting with the rework model of Section 5.1.3, we can set up a counter, called RW, which is incremented each time rework is necessary on a part and reset to zero whenever a new part is started. This is easily done by making the RW counter an attribute of the START vertex. In the REWORK event, this counter is incremented from its current value by passing the edge attribute value of RW+1 into the vertex parameter RW for the REWORK vertex. When a new part is started, a value of 1 is passed into the rework counter. This model is implemented in Figure 5.16 and as REWORK2.MOD on your SIGMA disk. In this model it is vital that the REWORK vertex have a low execution priority so that rework will not start at the same time that a new job is starting.

5.3.4 Generalized Assembly Operations

Using vertex parameters, we also can generalize the assembly operation found in Figure 5.6. We let N represent the number of different types of parts that go into the final assembly (see Figure 5.17). The number of parts needed from operation I will be given by the input variable P[I]. The graph for this model simply identifies the operation being finished in the OPRN event with

Figure 5.16: Event Graph with Limited Rework

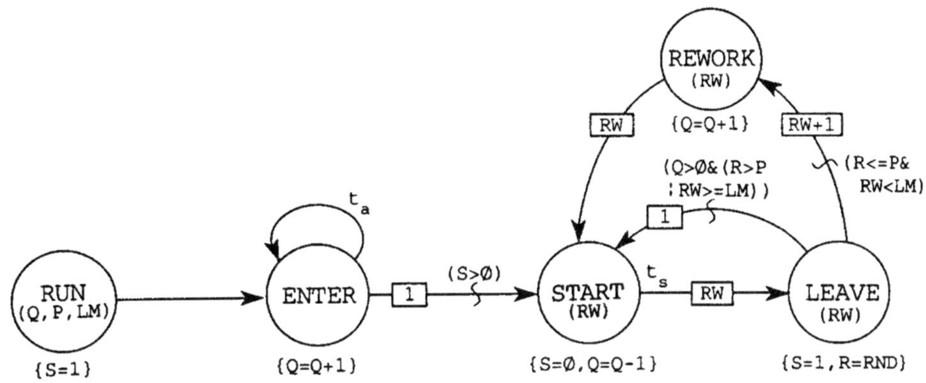

the parameter I, denoting the type of part being produced. In this model, we use the mathematical notation ∀ to mean "for every"; thus the condition (Q[I]>P[I]∀I<N) is mathematical shorthand for "the number of finished parts in queue I is greater than the number of that type of part needed in the kit for every type of part."

Figure 5.17: Using Event Parameters in an Assembly Operation

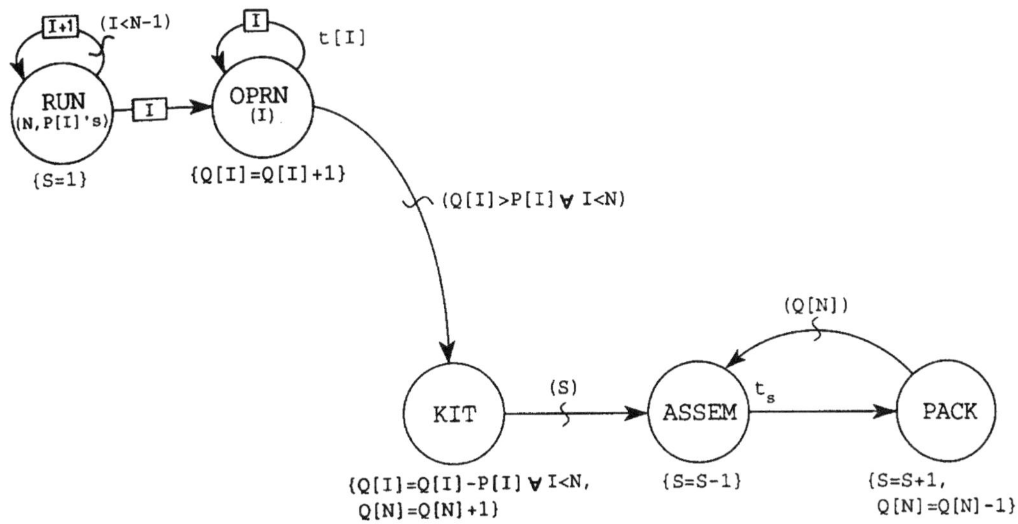

5.3.5 Sequential Service with Blocking

A queueing network where customers proceed through successive service operations along a single path is called a tandem queue; basically the queues are lined up one after another. An example of this might be a serial production line with several different machining steps. Typically, the service time for one of the steps is a bit slower than the others; this is called the bottleneck. Work will tend to pile up at the bottleneck created by the slower server, and successive servers will become starved for work. If there is limited waiting space between the servers (called a capacitated queueing system), blocking might also occur. A server becomes blocked when there is no space to unload a finished job. Both blocking and starving will degrade the performance of a tandem queue. Attempts to avoid both situations are major tasks to be faced when designing queueing networks with limited waiting space.

We will start with the simplest example of a capacitated tandem queueing network. In this example there are two servers with a waiting space (buffer) for only `B[1]` customers in front of the first (upstream) server and waiting space for `B[2]` customers in front of the second (downstream) server. This is model `TWOQUES1.MOD` on your SIGMA disk.

The values of `B[1]` and `B[2]` will be input as parameters of the initial `RUN` vertex. Since we have only one server for each queue, we can use a single state variable, `S[I]`, to denote the status of the server, `I`, as `BUSY=0`, `IDLE=1`, and `BLOCKED=-1`. The status of each server can be passed as the value of an edge attribute into the vertex parameter `S[1]` or `S[2]` depending on which server is involved.

The event graph for two queues in tandem, shown in Figure 5.18, looks like two of our basic queueing models wired end-to-end. Customer arrivals are generated in the usual manner at the `ARRIVE` vertex. If customers find space in the first queue, they will enter the first queue at the `ENTER1` vertex. We assume, as we did for our single capacitated queueing model, that customers who arrive when the first queue is full will simply leave.

Customers that enter the system will eventually start and then finish service with the upstream server (`START1` and `LEAVE1`). If there is room in the second queue, the customer will then enter the second line for the server at the `ENTER2` vertex. When the upstream server finishes and there are already `B[2]` customers waiting for the downstream server, the first server will become blocked. It must wait for the downstream server to finish with its current customer to make space to unload. It is possible to model blocking with a separate vertex; however, since we have only a single server for each operation, we can avoid using a separate blocking vertex. Instead we will use edge attributes to change the status of each server. When the first server finishes at the `LEAVE1` vertex and finds the second queue full (`Q[2]>=B[2]`),

Figure 5.18: Event Graph for Sequential Service with Blocking

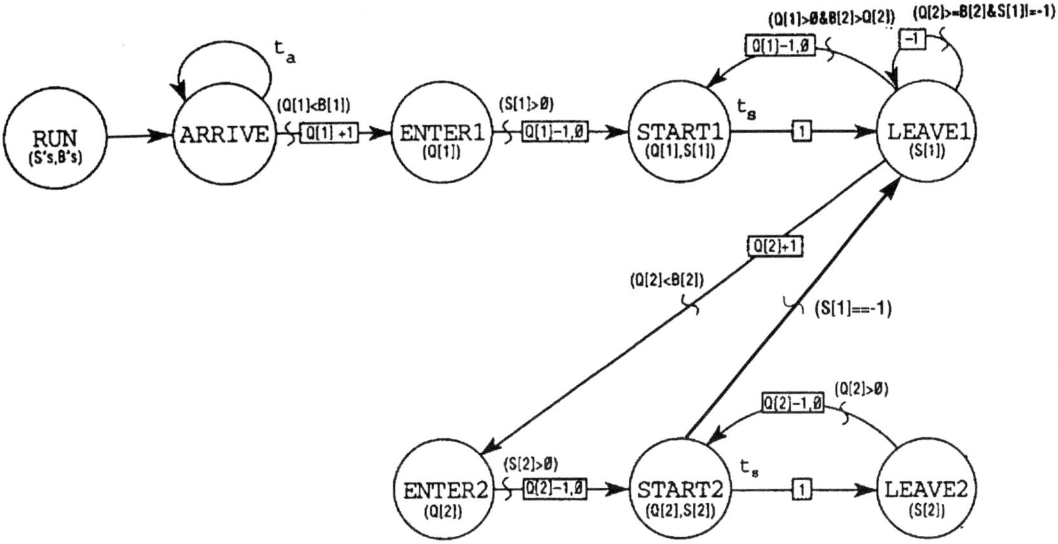

a self-scheduling edge will pass the value `-1` back into the `LEAVE1` vertex parameter, `S[1]`, unless `S[1]=-1` already. Setting `S[1]` equal to `-1` indicates that the first server is blocked.

As soon as the second server finishes its current service epoch, the first server can become unblocked. Thus, when the second server finishes service at the `LEAVE2` vertex and finds that the first server is blocked (`S[1]==-1`), the edge from `LEAVE2` to `LEAVE1` will pass `1` (idle) into the status of the first server, `S[1]`, which is a parameter of the `LEAVE1` vertex.

We will resolve time ties between the two finish event vertices, `LEAVE1` and `LEAVE2`, by unblocking a blocked server before trying to start service. We will also block server 1 before trying to start with the next customer in the `START1` vertex. You should look at the execution priorities on the edges for this model on your SIGMA disk to see how this is done; it is important!

An easy and common technique for modeling networks of queues with limited waiting space is to not permit a job to `LEAVE` a queue before it can `ENTER` the next queue. This overlapping of capacitated queues is illustrated in `TWOQUES2.MOD` on your SIGMA disk.

We can generalize the tandem queue model to include any number of queues in series by having an additional vertex parameter that indicates which queue is involved in each event. For example, the `ENTER1` and `ENTER2` vertices can become a common `ENTER` vertex with the parameter,

I, indicating which queue is being entered. This general tandem queue is modeled as TANDQ.MOD on your SIGMA disk.

5.4 Multiple Resources

Sometimes several resources must be available for an event to happen. For example, in a factory it may be necessary that both a worker and a machine be idle before a part can be processed. Assigning 0 to the "not-available state" makes multiple resource constraints very simple to model. If several types of resources are needed to schedule an event, simply list the names of these resources on the scheduling edge in your SIGMA graph. If WORKERS is the number of idle workers, PARTS the number of parts available, and MACHINES the number of idle machines, then the edge condition, WORKERS & PARTS & MACHINES, is sufficient to check if all three resources are simultaneously available (assuming, of course, that there are no codes for states of the workers and machines that are negative numbers).

The reason this works is that in SIGMA (like C and not like Pascal) zero indicates a condition is false and *any* non-zero value indicates it is true. Note that if you are going to generate Pascal code for your model, you still need to explicitly write conditions (e.g., WORKERS>0 & PARTS>0 & MACHINES>0).

Our next model enrichment is a conceptual prototype for models where several resources are required to do a task. Here the machines are semi-automatic—they only need to be loaded and unloaded by workers. Once loaded, processing is automatic. Since one of the prime motivations for automation is to reduce labor requirements, we will assume that there are fewer workers than machines. We will add the event vertices, STRTL (start loading) and ENDL (end loading), to model the worker loading a job onto a machine and the vertices, STRTU (start unloading) and ENDU (end unloading), to model the worker unloading a machine. It is necessary that there be both an idle machine and an idle worker to start loading a job onto a machine. The event graph for this model is given in Figure 5.19.

5.5 A Problem in Finance

So far we have focused on models of queueing systems that are applicable to such areas as manufacturing, health care, and communications. The applications of SIGMA are by no means limited to these systems. Here we will use SIGMA to analyze a problem in finance: determining fair pricing for coupon bonds in the presence of randomly fluctuating interest rates. The simple model we will develop can serve as a basis for more complicated cash stream

Figure 5.19: Event Graph for System Requiring Multiple Resources

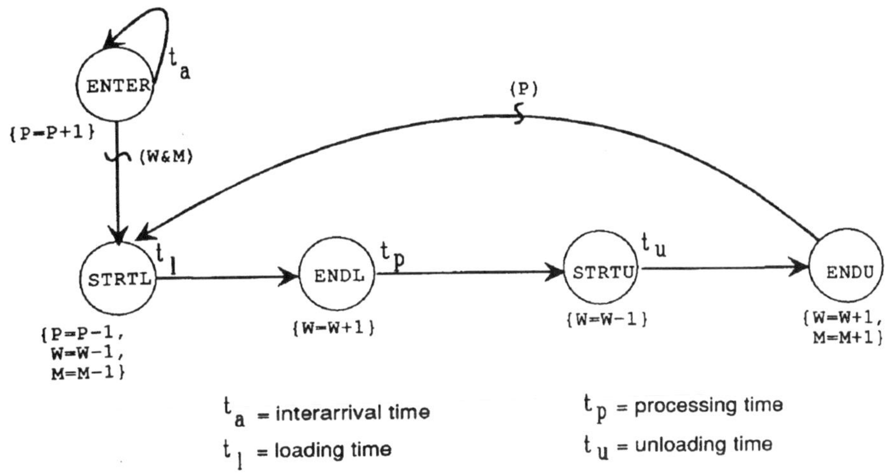

analysis; indeed, this model can be enriched to study financial risk in general cash flow scenarios.

In determining a fair price for a coupon bond (or any other investment), it is important to consider alternatives. For our example, we consider the decision faced by an investor who is offered shares in a variable rate mutual fund with a guaranteed minimum interest of 8%. Interest returns on this kind of investment are expected to remain about 15% over the next 5 years, but are highly variable. A more conservative option is being offered by an investment banker: a 5-year coupon bond that pays $10,000 at the end of each year with a $100,000 value upon maturity. How much should our investor be willing to pay for the coupon bond?

Discount factors are used to account for interest. With an interest rate of `I` for a particular year, cash is worth `(1+I)` as much at the end of the year as at the first of the year. Equivalently, cash at the end of the year is worth `1/(1+I)` as much at the beginning of the year; the factor, `R=1/(1+I)`, is called the discount factor for that year. Therefore, multiplying a cash payment at the end of the year by `R` gives its present value.

In addressing this problem, we will assume that yearly interest rates for the mutual fund can be modeled using a normal probability distribution with a mean of 15% and standard deviation of ±5%. Our simulation can be used to simulate thousands of replications of the next five years. For each replication we can determine the fair price for the bond. If the bond is offered at less than this price, the investor would have been better off buying it. In a few seconds, the investor can use our simulation to gain 5000 years of experience before making a decision. The simulation for this SIGMA model appears on your distribution disk as `BONDRATE.MOD`.

Our model has the following input variables.

`LIFE`	Life of the bond until maturity
`INT`	Average annual interest rate over the life of the bond
`STD`	Standard deviation of the interest rate
`MINR`	Minimum interest from alternative investment
`PAYMENT`	The coupon bond yearly cash payment
`VALUE`	Face value of bond at maturity

The following intermediate variables are used in our calculations.

`N`	Index for year during planning horizon
`I`	The normally distributed random future annual interest rate
`R`	Cumulative discount rate
`NREP`	Number of replications you wish to run
`REP`	Index for which replication currently is being run
`CFLAG`	Flag indicating if you want a cash flow diagram (1/0=yes/no)

The model computes the following for each year of the investment life.

`CASH`	End of year cash flow (only used for cash flow diagrams)
`PRICE`	Fair price of bond on maturity
`NPV`	Net present value of cash flow (before taxes)

The dynamics of this model are simple; all of the action takes place in a single vertex loop where each year's interest rate is generated. Then the net cash flow for the year is discounted back to the present and added to the net present value of the investment. Initially, the cumulative discount factor is

Figure 5.20: Line Plot of Five Year Discount Rate Fluctuations

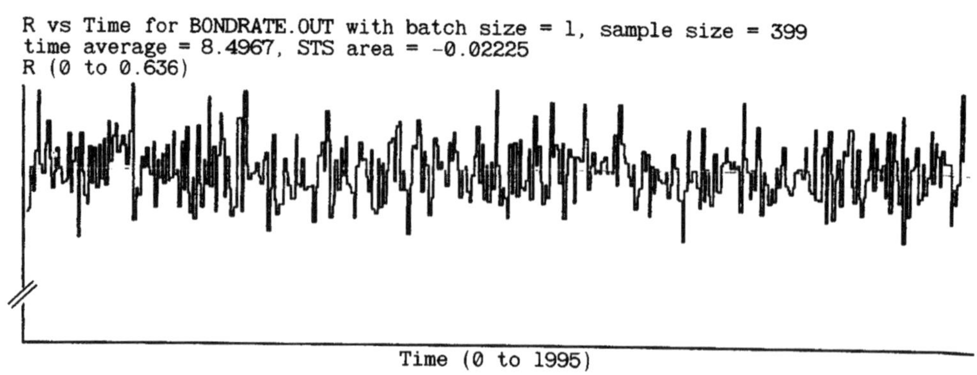

Figure 5.21: Scatter Plot of Observed NPV for the Investment

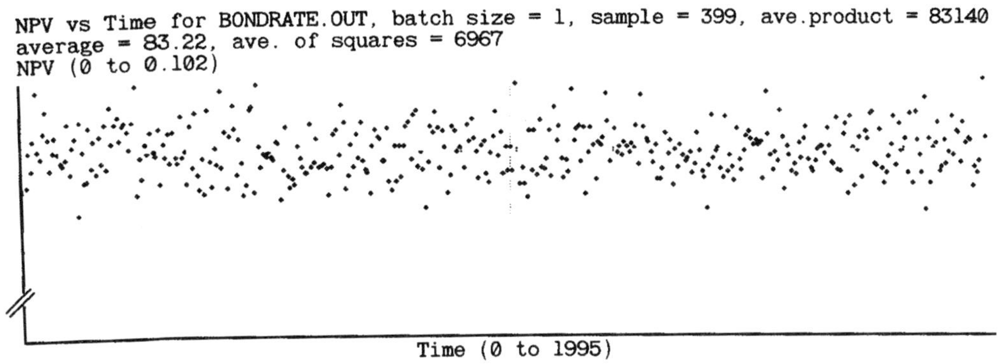

set to R=1. Next, a loop with year, N, going from 1 to LIFE is executed. For every year, the computations are the following.

`I=NOR{INT;STD}`	Generate the year's variable interest rate
`I=MAX{I;MINR}`	Guarantee the minimum interest rate
`R=R*(1/(1+I))`	Compute cumulative discount factor for the year
`CASH=PAYMT`	Place payment in the cash flow stream
`NPV=NPV+CASH*R`	Roll cash back to the present

In the last year when the bond matures, the face VALUE for the bond is collected. This VALUE is rolled back to the present and added to the net present value of the investment in exactly the same manner as for each annual cash payment.

`NPV=NPV+VALUE*R`	Roll cash back to the present

The result is the fair price of the bond, which is the net present value of the same amount of cash invested in the variable rate mutual fund for the simulated five year period.

If the number of replications is less than the number desired, the investment is again simulated. Experimental results from our risk analysis model are the line plot of discount rates shown in Figure 5.20, the scatter plot of the net present value of the investment shown in Figure 5.21, and the distribution of prices for the bond shown in Figure 5.22. (These plots use the **SIGPLOT** charts discussed in Chapter 10.)

We can see from Figure 5.20 that the minimum interest rate (reflected in the observed upper limit for the discount rate) was important even though it was only about half of the prevailing rate. This is due to the high variability of the interest rates we used in our "what-if" experiment. We see from Figure 5.22 that if the bond is offered for a price less than most of the simu-

Figure 5.22: Fair Bond Price Histogram

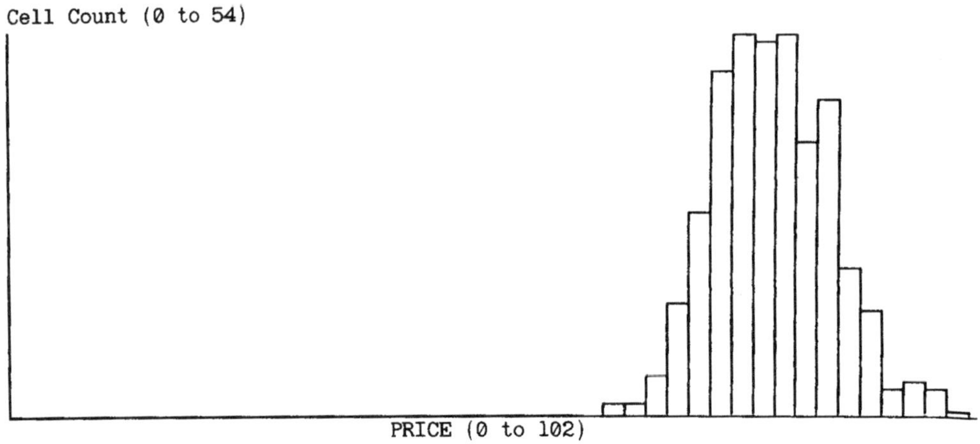

lated fair prices, it would probably be a good investment. Of course, many more scenarios should be explored before funds are committed. These experiments should consider alternative models for the future interest rates. The model structure would remain essentially unchanged. Such experimentation only takes a few seconds.

Starting with this model, it is possible to build a very sophisticated, *customized,* financial risk model. In fact, a New York investment bank uses a SIGMA model to explore the pricing of "cocktail" bonds, which can be cashed in one of several foreign currencies (Berg, 1992).

5.6 Project Management (PERT/CPM)

In a large project, such as the construction of a new building or the development of a major software package, there are typically several activities that may proceed in parallel as well as some precedence constraints among the different activities. When erecting a building, it might be possible to have the windows installed at the same time as the plumbing and electrical wiring; if so, these three activities can proceed in parallel. On the other hand, there might also be precedence requirements among activities: the scaffold must be finished and secured before starting the outside facing, the frame must be finished before starting work on the roof, etc. When planning or bidding for a large project it is important to know as much as you can about how long it might take to finish before resources are committed.

A popular technique for managing large projects is to study activity precedence networks, which use graphs showing the activities that must be

Figure 5.23: Activity Precedence Network for a Project

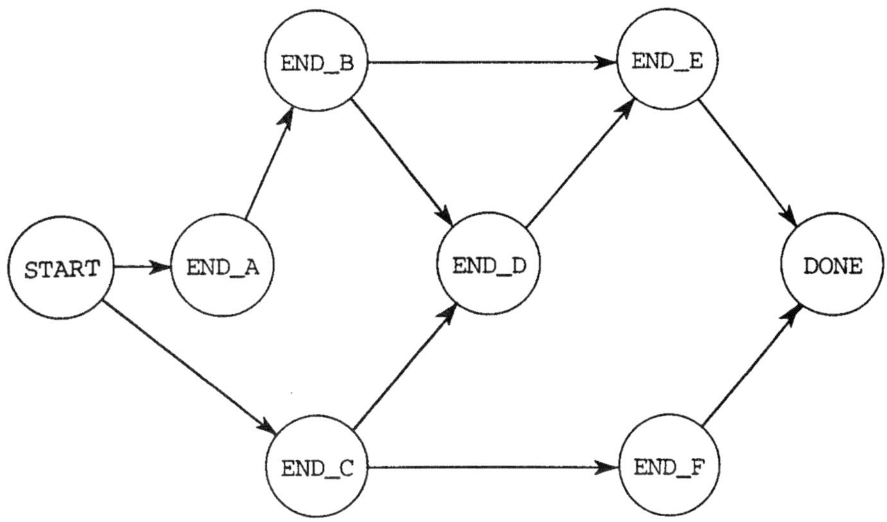

completed before others can start (see Figure 5.23). The end of each activity is represented by a node and the duration of the activities by the edges. In Figure 5.23, activity B must be finished before activities D and E can be started; therefore, the node, END_B, also represents the simultaneous starting of activities E and D.

The most common approaches to the static analysis of these networks are called PERT (Program Evaluation and Review Technique) and CPM (Critical Path Method). These two similar techniques are discussed in most textbooks on management or industrial engineering. Traditional CPM and PERT assume that the activity durations are either known or, if random, independent of each other. Clearly, in a real project the activity times are random as well as dependent (e.g., bad weather, labor disputes, or competition for resources generally will delay more than one activity). Using simulation, we can "dry-run" a project hundreds or thousands of times to learn what might happen before we submit a bid or commit to a contract.

We will illustrate this with a simple example. Suppose we are planning a project that has the activity precedences given in Table 5.3 and graphed in Figure 5.23. The event graph on your SIGMA screen for this project will look exactly like the activity precedence network in Figure 5.23. Associated with each vertex, I, is a counter of *unfinished precedent activities,* initialized to equal the number of incoming edges for the vertex. We will call this activity counter COUNTER[I]. The counter for the project START vertex

Table 5.3: Activity Precedences for a Project

Activity	Must Follow Activities	COUNTER[I]
A	None	0
B	A	1
C	None	0
D	B and C	2
E	B and D	2
F	C	1

is always `0`, and the counter for the `DONE` vertex in this example is `2`. The state change for each vertex is simply to decrement its counter by one, `COUNTER[I]=COUNTER[I]-1`. All edges have the condition that the counter for the originating vertex has been reduced to zero (`COUNTER[I]==0`) indicating that there are no more unfinished precedent activities. The delay times are simply the activity times associated with activities that end at the destination vertices; they can have any distributions you want (e.g., they might be dependent on a weather pattern you generate).

5.7 Modeling Transient Entities

Most of our models so far have dealt primarily with resident entities: the servers and the waiting lines. Suppose that we want to know the average waiting time in line for each customer. If we modeled each customer, their average waiting times would be easy to compute (as we did in Section 5.3.2). However, modeling transient entities in a queueing simulation may require more computer memory and significantly greater processing time. Furthermore, as the simulation becomes more congested, it will become less efficient. It is not uncommon for transient-entity-oriented network simulation languages to become so congested that they abort a run. When the run aborts, there is often no useful information given about that run, possibly just the message that the run has terminated with an error! Thus, the most interesting runs of the simulation (when the system was the busiest) and the most expensive (when the most customers were simulated) are exactly those runs that are aborted. Not observing the simulated system when it is congested can lead to an overly optimistic evaluation of system performance. Pure resident entity models are considerably more efficient; furthermore, this efficiency does not degrade as the system becomes congested.

A situation where we do not need transient entities is when we are only interested in aggregate information about the transient entities, such as the average customer waiting time. Suppose that we want to know the average time spent by our customers waiting for service during a simulation run. We will denote this average waiting time as W. To observe customer waiting times, we might enrich (and complicate) our simulation by including each customer in our model. Alternatively, we could leave our model like it is and use the idea behind "Little's Law" from queueing theory to indirectly estimate W without adding transient entities to our model. We will illustrate this with a straightforward dimensional analysis.

Say we have N customers in a resident entity simulation run that is T simulated hours long. Denote the observed average queue length as L customers. The average number of customers waiting in line during the run multiplied by the amount of simulated time gives us the total customer-hours spent waiting by all of the customers during the run. If C is the total simulated customer-hours, then

$$C = L*T \qquad \text{(in customer-hours).}$$

If we divide this total customer-hours by the total number of customers simulated, N, we get an estimate of the average time each customer spent waiting;

$$W = C/N = (L*T)/N.$$

Therefore, by keeping track of the average queue length in a pure resident entity simulation, we can estimate the average waiting time of the transient entities.

Although this is a popular way to estimate average waiting times in queues and it is used by some commercial simulation languages, it is not quite as accurate as directly collecting the waiting times of each customer. This is because some customers might be in line when the run ends, causing different numbers of customers to contribute to the numerator and denominator of the ratio C/N used to estimate W. Each customer waiting in line contributes to the total customer-hours waiting, C, continuously as they wait; however, the total cumulative customer count, N, is only incremented at discrete times. If we count customers when they leave, we might overestimate W since customers who have made partial contributions to the total customer-hour waiting time have not yet been counted. If we count customers when they enter the system, we would tend to underestimate W since customers who remain in line when the run ends will not make their full contribution to the total customer-hours until they leave. We might adjust for this problem by generating the unfinished backlog of customer-hours of work for the server at the end of the run and add it to C or, equivalently, by cutting off the arrivals and letting the system empty as in the example in Section 5.2.1.

5.8 Programming with Event Graphs

An event graph can be used as a general flow chart for designing computer programs that have nothing to do with simulation models. If all the edge delay times are zero, each vertex would be a block of assignment statements; edge conditions would show the logic flow. All branching is represented by edges in the graph, including `goto`'s, `if-then-else`, and function calls. The values of edge attributes passed to the vertex parameter variables act like values passed to functions, as in a C program. The main difference, and it is an important difference, between event graphs and traditional flow charts is branching. In SIGMA more than one branch might be taken, or perhaps none of a set of possible branches might be followed.

> ➢ *Recall that when edge conditions are tested they are considered false only if they are equal to zero. Expressions for edge conditions that are non-zero are always considered true.*

5.8.1 Boolean Variables

Although condition testing is done on the edges of an event graph, it is possible to evaluate conditional expressions within a vertex by using Boolean variables. Boolean variables take the numerical "value" of a conditional expression such as `(X>Y)`. The rule is simple: If the condition is true, the value of the Boolean variable is 1; if the condition is false, the value of the Boolean variable is 0. Embedding a logic condition in a state change means that the number 1 is substituted for the condition if the condition is true and a 0 is substituted for the condition if it is false.

For example, you might want to increment the length of a waiting `QUEUE` if and only if there are no idle `SERVERS` available. This can be done with the single statement

```
QUEUE=QUEUE+(SERVERS==0)
```

which is the same as setting `QUEUE=QUEUE+1` if `(SERVERS==0)` and leaving `QUEUE` otherwise unchanged. This statement would model the queue increasing only if there are no servers available to a newly arrived customer. As another example, examine the expressions

```
R=RND,
Q=54+(R>.5)*3+(R>.7).
```

Note that here only one random number, `RND`, is generated. In SIGMA (and in C), this will have the following effect:

`Q` = 54 with a probability of 0.5 `(R<=.5)`

Figure 5.24: `If-Then-Else` Graph Structure

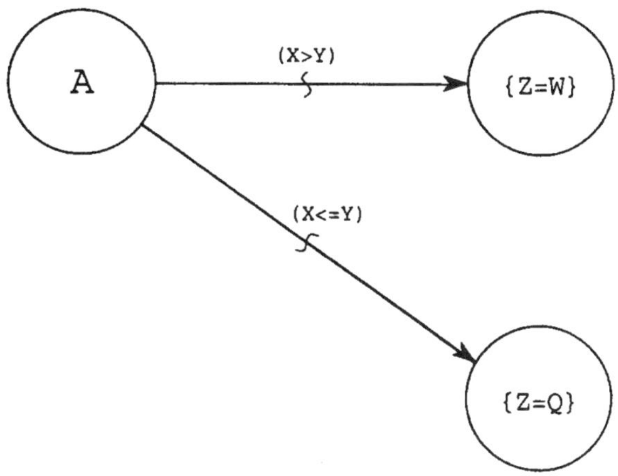

Q = 57 with a probability of 0.2 (.5<R<=.7)
Q = 58 with a probability of 0.3 (R>.7).

Another example would be to use three successively generated random numbers, X=(RND<.5)+2*(RND<.5)+4*(RND<.5), to generate a value of X uniformly over the integers 0 to 7. These are efficient ways to generate samples from a simple discrete probability distribution.

A common use of Boolean variables in event graph modeling is in expressing alternatives, as in the "if-then-else" logic structure explained next.

5.8.2 Conditional Expressions (If-Then-Else)

There are several ways to write conditional expressions. Consider the following "if-then-else" sequence in C,

```
if (X>Y)  Z=W;
else Z=Q;
```

In SIGMA, one would either define an edge conditioned on X>Y as in Figure 5.24 or use the expression with embedded Boolean variables,

```
Z=W*(X>Y)+Q*(X<=Y)
```

in a vertex. If X>Y, the above expression will be equivalent to

```
Z=W*(1)+Q*(0)=W,
```

and if X<=Y, it would become

Figure 5.25: Do-While Loops

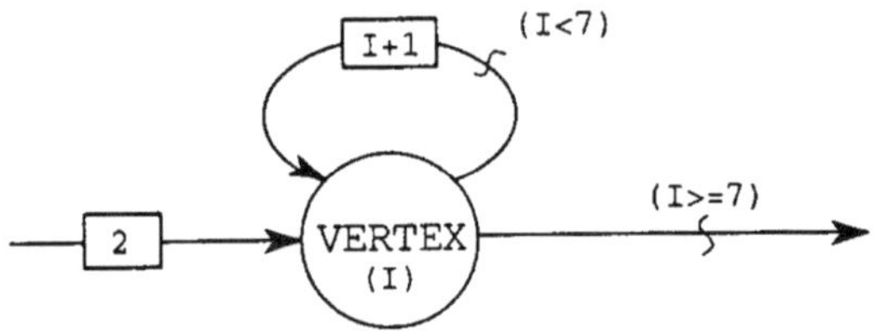

Z=W*(0)+Q*(1)=Q

as desired. Using embedded Boolean variables here is more efficient.

5.8.3 Do, While, and Nested Loops

"Do" and "while" loops are easy to implement in event graphs. In fact, loops of code are naturally pictured in the graphs as loops. Figure 5.25 shows how the expressions in a block of code called VERTEX can be executed with a parameter, I, that goes from a value of I=2 to a value of I=7.

It is worth going through the logic in Figure 5.25 in detail. We want the state changes in VERTEX to be executed for the last time when I=7. This will happen here because edge attribute expressions are evaluated only after edge conditions are tested as being true. When I=6, the condition on the loop, (I<7), is true; therefore, the value of the attribute expression, 7=I+1, is then passed to VERTEX parameter, I. This is done by scheduling VERTEX on the list of future events with an attribute of 7. When VERTEX occurs the next time, the first thing that happens is its parameter, I, is set to 7. Unless the state changes in VERTEX reduce the value of I (which would probably be a programming error), the condition (I<7) is now false and the loop is not scheduled. Nested loops are only slightly more complicated. In Figure 5.26 there are two loops, an outer loop indexed with the variable, I, and an inner loop indexed with J. The values of I range from the constants 2 to 7 as before; however, the values of J will range from 0 up to the current value of I.

5.9 Model Complexity and Model Size

Although some of the models discussed here may appear complicated at first, keep in mind that a large model is not necessarily a complex model. When building simulations, it is important to distinguish between a model that is inherently complicated and a model that is large but otherwise simple. Complexity occurs when a model is composed of many different *types* of

Figure 5.26: Nested Loops

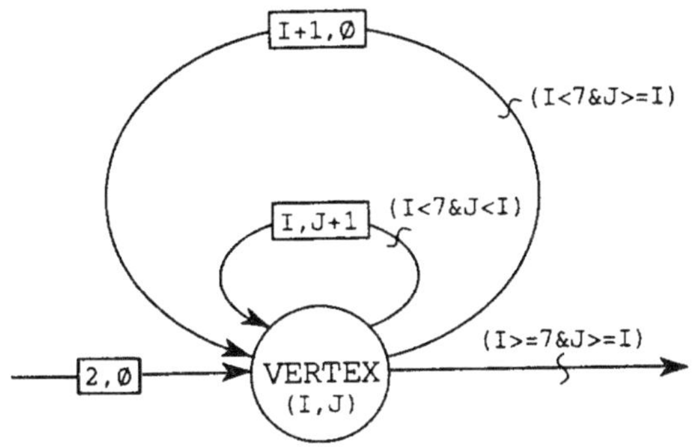

events; a large simulation might be made up of many events but only a few different types of events.

A large simple model might be built from many copies of a few, essentially identical, subgraphs. It is the commonalities of these subgraphs that keep the model simple. Indeed, special purpose simulators are developed by focusing on the commonalities of the elementary components of a particular type of system. For instance, a typical commercial factory simulation package will have a generic subgraph to represent a machine as its basic building block. A crude model of a factory is built by putting together many machine subgraphs, each of which is distinguished only by different parameter values. The parameters for each machine (processing time, distribution of the time between failures, repair time distributions, etc.) can be selected from simple menus. The fundamental differences between simple simulators like that just described and block-oriented, general-purpose simulation languages are the number and the richness of the building blocks available with the language; however, both are limited to a finite set of preprogrammed modules. If you want to simulate a situation not already anticipated by the software vendor, you are out of luck.

Using event graphs, we can construct a simulator of a large scale queueing network by first developing an event graph of the basic building block for the network, a single service center. Using this approach, in Chapter 13 we will develop a simulation of an arbitrarily large queueing network of service operations with several different types of customers. Each customer will follow a different path through the service network and will have different sets of service times. Starting with a simple queueing system model like those presented in this chapter, we will quickly build a simulator of an entire queueing network.

Once we are satisfied with the richness of the event graph of a basic building block, we can then use edge attributes and vertex parameters to make as many distinct copies of this subgraph as we want (the *picture* of our graph will not change). The complexity of our model will be determined by the detail we put into the basic building block; the size of our model is determined only by the number of parameterized copies of this basic event graph that our model generates during a run. It is useful to visualize the basic subgraph of a simulation model as a simulation "molecule" from which a larger model can be developed, much like a "crystal" made up of many molecules.

5.10 Continuous Time Simulations

This book is concerned mainly with simulating discrete event systems. However, there is another class of systems where the values of state variables are modeled as changing continuously. Simulations of such systems are referred to as continuous time simulations. Continuous time systems can also be simulated using event graphs and the SIGMA software; an example is presented in this section.

While discrete event models typically are used to study systems that are on a "human scale," continuous time simulations are popular for very large scale and very small scale systems. On a small scale, continuous time simulations are used in the sciences and engineering to study such things as the stress on a robot arm or the dynamics of a collection of molecules. On a large scale, this type of simulation is used to study interactions in social, astronomical, or economic systems.

Discrete event simulations have the reputation of being considerably more complicated and *ad-hoc* than continuous simulations. This is largely due to the fact that continuous time systems have an explicit mathematical representation in the form of systems of differential and partial differential equations. Differential equations model the instantaneous rates of change for the state variables. These rates can depend both on time as well as the values of the state variables. In the simplest case, we might have a system with only one variable. The value of this variable at time, t, is denoted $X(t)$. The instantaneous rate of change in this variable—i.e., its time derivative, $dX(t)/dt$—might be given as a (perhaps random) function, $f(.)$, of state and time,

$$dX(t)/dt = f(X(t),t).$$

Knowing the state value at time zero, $X(0)$, we can simulate future values of $X(t)$. On the computer, this is done recursively using a difference equation to approximate the change in state over a small time step. For a step size of Δt time units, our system can be modeled as

$$X(t+\Delta t) = X(t) + f(X(t),t)*\Delta t.$$

Typically a continuous time simulation model will involve several state variables, and these will be coupled. We need to know the values of the state variables before we can compute the changes, and we need to know the changes before we can compute the values. Therefore, the system of equations must be solved simultaneously. Approximate methods can be used to perform the integration to simulate the state variable trajectory. Consideration of such things as error accumulation require carefully designed algorithms. There is a clear trade-off; a simulation with a smaller time-step will have smaller errors but will also take longer to run. Discussions of integration algorithms can be found in any number of texts on continuous time simulation.

A realistic but simple example of a continuous time simulation is a model of a large fish breeding aquarium by Jean-Didier Opsomer. This model is included on your SIGMA distribution disk as `FISHTANK.MOD`. The population dynamics of a tropical fish called a *discus* is modeled. The simplified food chain in this ecosystem model consists of phytoplankton (algae), zooplankton, daphnia, and small fish. Several fish may be purchased and introduced into the system at once; they are typically sold one at a time. Each population in the food chain is modeled with a linear feeding and piece-wise linear growth rate that depends on the relative sizes of each population. In addition to feeding rates, a rate-limiting nutrient, phosphate, is used. Termination events for this system are eutrophication (explosive algae growth) and extinction.

Using this model, the effects of fish introduction, feeding rate, and phosphate introduction are studied with the objective of determining appropriate target populations for the plankton and daphnia. Figure 5.27 shows how the fish population changes over time in this model. Like most ecosystem models, the population has a clear periodicity; the management goal is to keep the fluctuations in the different populations under control (and the fish population large) so that one of the termination events does not occur.

5.11 Process Modeling

Many popular simulation packages are based on what is known as a *process worldview.* (The process approach is also sometimes called network modeling.) With this modeling philosophy, the focus is typically on transient entities, such as customers in a service system or parts flowing through a factory. Steps followed by these transient entities as they move through a system are identified. A simulation model is developed by placing preprogrammed blocks of code in a sequence that approximates the actual processing sequence

Figure 5.27: A Continuous Time Simulation of a Fish Aquarium, `FISHTANK.MOD`

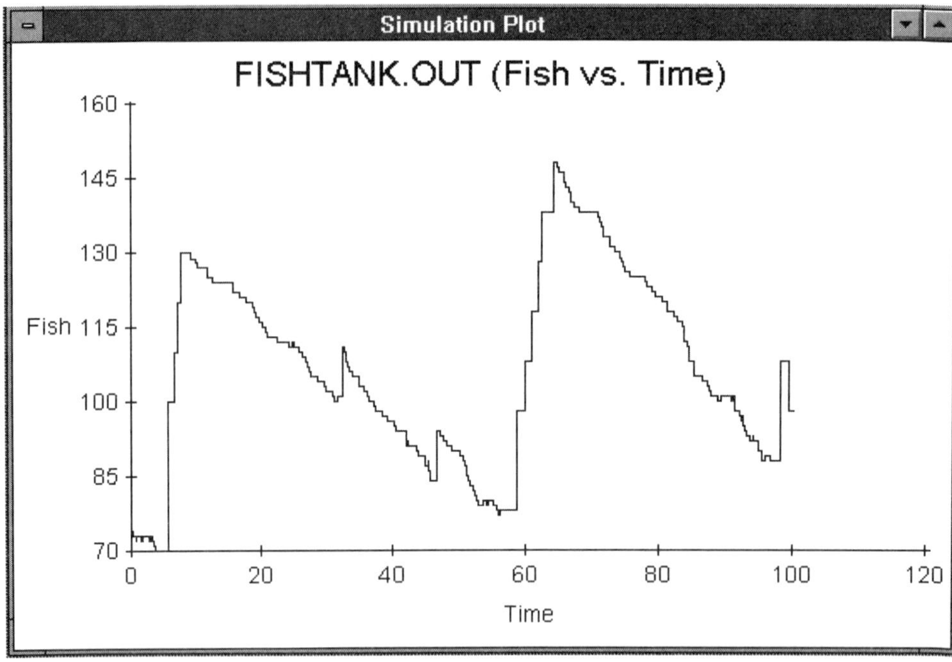

being modeled. The processing of a transient entity is conceptually viewed as the entity flowing from block to block. The process modeling viewpoint is possibly the purest form of transient entity modeling.

Process-oriented simulation languages provide a series of preprogrammed blocks that represent some of the typical processing stages in a queueing system. Examples of such blocks include a block to represent the entity waiting (i.e., a `QUEUE` block) and another to represent the start of service (i.e., a `SEIZE` block). Popular software packages that include a process-oriented feature include GPSS, SIMAN, and SLAM. A schematic diagram of the blocks in a GPSS model that represents a single server queue is shown in Figure 5.28.

The single server queue being modeled in Figure 5.28 has the customer entering the system in the `GENERATE` block and joining `QUEUE` number `1`. If server (number `1`) is idle, it is `SEIZE`d and the customer `DEPART`s from the line. After the clock `ADVANCE`s for the service time, the server is `RELEASE`d and the customer exits the system at the `TERMINATE` block.

Although each of the popular process modeling software packages is similar in function, each has its own terminology. For example, GPSS provides a `GENERATE` block, which introduces a transient entity into the system; SIMAN calls this a `CREATE` block. Time delay is modeled using an `ADVANCE` block in GPSS and a `DELAY` block in SIMAN. GPSS and SIMAN both have `QUEUE`

Figure 5.28: Block Diagram for a GPSS Model of a Single Server Queue

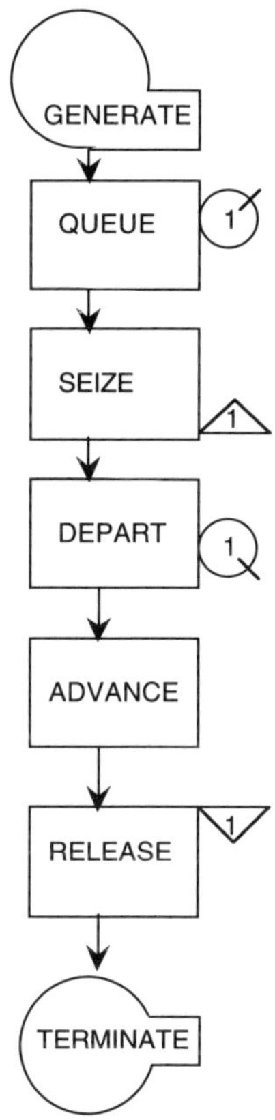

blocks to collect waiting time statistics, and both represent the entity waiting for service using `SEIZE` and `RELEASE` blocks. (Separate `ENTER` and `LEAVE` blocks are used in GPSS to model several identical parallel servers, which they call a "storage facility.") Time delays are modeled on the network arrows in SLAM, similar to the edge delay times used in event graphs.

Event graphs, while much simpler than most process languages to learn and use, are more general. In fact, you can build versions of these process languages using SIGMA. As an example, the model `GPSS.MOD` on your SIGMA disk is shown in Figure 5.29. This is a simulation of the GPSS single server queue pictured in Figure 5.28. This model uses the SIGMA `PUT` and `GET` functions, described in Chapter 7, for queue management.

`GPSSLANG.MOD` on your SIGMA disk is an actual subset of the GPSS simulation language written in SIGMA. `GPSSLANG.MOD` includes the current and future events *chains* used by this language. Here, rather than having a sepa-

FIGURE 5.29: SIGMA Simulation of the GPSS Single Server Queue

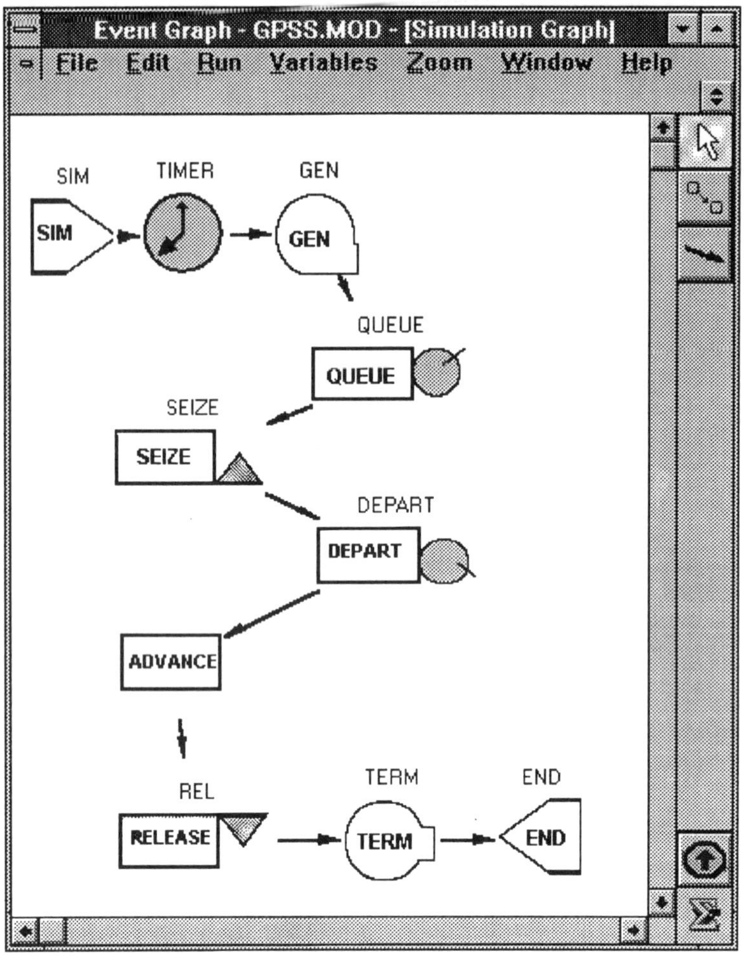

rate ENTER and LEAVE block for multiple server queues as in GPSS, you can simply initialize the number of idle servers to the desired number when you start the run. Studying GPSSLANG.MOD should offer a good introduction to GPSS. Simulated SIMAN models are on the disks as SIMAN*.mod. Versions of languages like SLAM can also be built easily using SIGMA.

Proponents of the process approach argue that it is natural to focus on the movement of transient entities since their motion "catches the eye." Once the definition of each of the preprogrammed blocks in the software package is understood, it is a simple matter to string them together into a simulated process. This is certainly one of the more easy to use modeling approaches for the beginner and largely explains its commercial success.

A disadvantage of the process modeling approach is that modeling certain situations may be difficult or impossible to simulate depending on the software you are using. You can only include in your model those features that the software vendor has anticipated and provided for with a specific block. Another drawback is that process modeling can be very inefficient. For example, a process model of a queue with hundreds of transactions can run much slower (or not at all) than the same model with only a few customers. This is because each customer that enters the system "generates" or "creates" a separate record in memory. The remarks in Chapter 2 concerning the trade-offs between resident and transient entity models apply here.

5.12 Exercises

The models referred to in these exercises are on your SIGMA *disk.*

5.12.1 Batch Arrivals to a Queue

Assume that cars arrive at a drive-up fast food restaurant with equal probability of having 1, 2, 3, or 4 customers in the car. Assume that service takes between 25 and 35 seconds per customer and cars arrive every 1 to 3 minutes (both service and interarrival distributions are uniform). Modify the carwash event graph in Figure 2.6 to model this system.

5.12.2 Parameter Passing

In the following event graph, plot the values of `X` at times `0` to `6.5`.

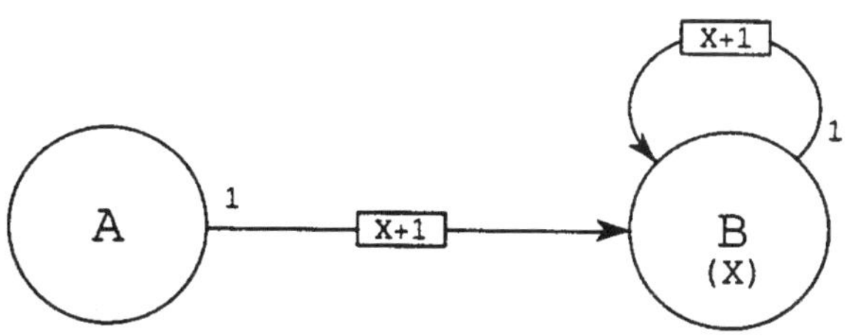

5.12.3 Future Events List

In a simulated queue with one line and five parallel servers (like `BANK1.MOD`):

(a) What is the minimum number of events on the events list while the simulation is running?

(b) What type of event(s) does this minimum list contain?

(c) What is the maximum number of events on the list during a run?

(d) What type of event(s) does this maximum length list contain?

5.12.4 Limited Waiting Space

Assume that the waiting line in BANK1.MOD has space for only five customers; there are three tellers. The maximum number of customers in the system is eight: three in service and five in line. Customers who arrive to find a full system are turned away. Change BANK1.MOD to reflect this constraint and rerun the first 30 customer service completions. Print your graph and output file. Record the number of arrivals that were turned away because the queue was full when they arrived. Again calculate the average waiting time for the first 10, 20, and 30 customers. Compute averages by hand or use a special statistics gathering vertex.

5.12.5 A Two Server Queue

Consider a queueing system with a single line and two identical parallel servers. The resident entity model, BANK1.MOD, and the transient entity model, BANK2.MOD, on your SIGMA disk are simulations of such a system.

Modify BANK2.MOD to have a finite capacity in this system of a total of at most 10 customers (a maximum of two customers in service and eight waiting in line). Arrivals that occur when the system is full are turned away. Customer arrivals occur according to a Poisson process with a constant rate of 1.5 customers per minute. (This is the same as exponentially distributed interarrival times with a mean of 1/1.5 = 0.667, given by .667*ERL{1}.) Each server has an exponentially distributed service time with mean of 1 minute. The arrival and service processes are all mutually independent. The objective for studying this system is to estimate the distributions for the customer waiting times and distributions for the server utilizations.

(a) Give the entities in this system (tell which are resident and which are transient). Give the attributes of each entity. Also list the sets of entities with their owners and members.

(b) List the events for this system. Give the state transformations for each event. Also give the conditions and delay times for scheduling each of the events. Show the relationships between events with an event graph.

(c) What event(s) should be scheduled initially to begin running this simulation for 100 simulated hours?

(d) What event(s) should be scheduled initially to run this simulation for 100 simulated customer service completions?

(e) What will happen if a customer tries to ENTER a full queue at the exact same time that another customer LEAVEs the server? Which of these two simultaneous events should be executed first?

5.12.6 Sensitivity Analysis

Customers arrive at an ice cream parlor at a rate uniformly distributed between 2 and 6 minutes and are served at a rate uniformly distributed between 3 and 8 minutes. Model this queue. After 4 hours, what is the average length of the queue? If another scooper is hired, what is the average length of the queue? How many scoopers must be hired to keep the average length of the queue below 2 customers?

5.12.7 Fast Food

Customers waiting for fast food are very impatient. If they see 4 or more people waiting in line already, they will not enter. At peak hours, customers arrive at a rate uniformly distributed between 0.5 and 3 minutes. With current processes, each customer can be served in 2 minutes. Can the processes be speeded up enough to make sure the store never loses customers? (no). Can we speed up service so that we have a very low probability of losing customers? (yes). What is the necessary processing time for a specified probability for losing a customer that you think is reasonable? Build a model that can be used to answer this question.

5.12.8 Parameter Passing

Give the number and types of events that will be on the list of scheduled events at time 21.5 in the following event graph.

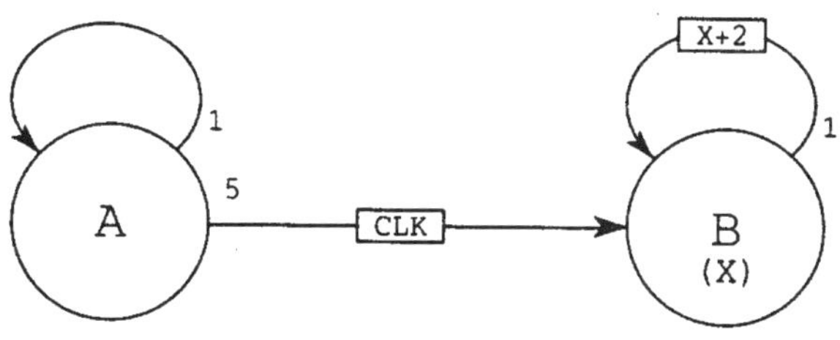

5.12.9 A Bank

(a) Suppose that cars arrive at a bank's drive-through facility at a rate uniformly distributed between 2 and 10 minutes and each transaction requires 3 minutes. Model this queue.

(b) Now suppose that the bank added two more identical tellers and customers arrive at each one at a uniform rate between 5 and 15 minutes. Model this situation by modifying your answer for (a).

5.12.10 The Post Office

(a) Suppose customers arrive at a post office at a rate uniformly distributed between 2 and 3 minutes. A postal official can serve each customer at a rate uniformly distributed between 1 and 10 minutes. Model the service at the post office.

(b) Modify this model for a post office with 3 postal officials. Upon entry, all customers line up in one queue. The first person in the queue is served by the next available official.

(c) Modify this model again for a post office where one lazy clerk takes a 5 minute break (will not serve) after he serves 3 customers.

5.12.11 An Assembly Station

A factory mass produces widgets. Each widget has 3 component parts: `A`, `B`, and `C`. Each of these 3 types of parts is produced in its own area of the factory and then transported via assembly line to the assembly area. Parts `A`, `B`, and `C` arrive at the assembly area every 4, 5, and 10 minutes, respectively. A worker takes a time uniformly distributed between 5 and 10 minutes to assemble the widget. Model this production process.

5.12.12 Communications Network Repair

A local area network has 100 identical links between work stations. Links fail at random intervals. The time until a working link fails has an exponential distribution with a mean of 5 days. Once a link fails, it must wait for a repairman to fix it. The time to repair a link has a uniform distribution between 1 and 2 hours. A single repairman is on duty at all times. Build a simulation of this maintenance system. Use your model to develop a trade-off curve between performance of the system (how should this be measured?) and the number of repairmen on duty. Hint: Use the model, `CARWASH.MOD`, as a starting place where links (instead of cars) queue up for the single repairman (instead of a carwash machine). Also note that the rate that links fail depends on the number of working links at a given time. (This failure process is called a state-dependent Poisson process.)

5.12.13 A Water Reservoir System

Three water reservoirs (at `A`, `B`, and `C`) serve a city through the pipeline system shown below.

Three identical (type 1) pumps at stations *a, b,* and *c* pump water from each reservoir to pumping station *d.* A large (type 2) pump at *d* pumps water to another type 2 pump at booster station *e,* which pumps water to the city. The time until failure of a type i pump ($i = 1$ or 2) is uniformly distribute between

$12i$ and $4(i + 1)^2$ months. Pump failures are independent, and pumps are not repaired until the water flow to the city actually stops. Model this system to predict when the city will run out of water due to pump failures.

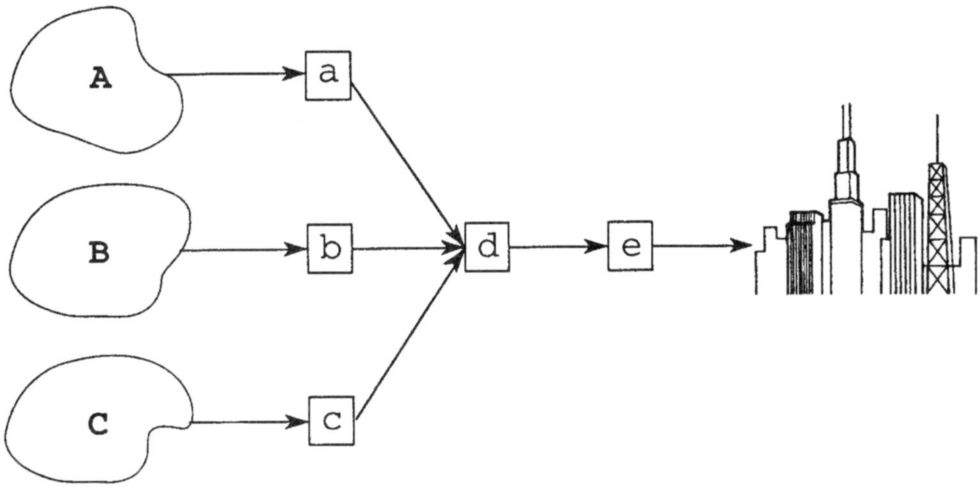

5.12.14 Preventive Maintenance Policy Optimization

A conveyor system has 40 identical rollers, each with a failure distribution uniformly distributed between 20 and 45 days. When a roller fails, it must be repaired at a cost of \$500. When preventive maintenance is performed on the conveyor, the cost is `$300+$50*N`, where `N` is the number of rollers replaced. A partial group replacement policy of performing preventive maintenance every `M` months and replacing all rollers over `A` months old is being considered. Model this system to try to suggest reasonable values for `M` and `A`.

5.12.15 Elimination of the Future Events List

Create an event graph that is logically equivalent to the carwash model but does not schedule *any* events on the future events list. (Hint: Use a generic minimum function, `min(a,b)`, to determine the next event time.)

(a) What is the main advantage of your modified model? (Consider speed.)

(b) What is the main disadvantage of your model?

5.12.16 Queues with Blocking

There are three identical and independent servers for each of two tandem queues. There is room for only 3 customers in queue 2; when queue 2 is full, no one can exit from any of the first set of three servers until a service completion for the second set of servers occurs.

(a) Identify the resident and transient entities along with their attributes. Present your entity-attribute hierarchy in outline form. Give the set of possible values for each attribute.

(b) Identify sets of entities and tell which entities (if any) "own" each set and which entities may be members of each set.

(c) Describe the discrete events in the cycles of activities for each resident entity. Also describe the events in the path of each temporary entity as they flow through the system. For each event tell what state changes occur and the conditions for these changes along with what further events will be scheduled or cancelled in a computer routine for the event.

5.12.17 Simultaneous Events

In a queueing simulation, `BRKDN.MOD` (Figure 5.10), if an idle server is scheduled to start a break (`STARTBREAK` event) at the same time a customer arrival occurs (`ARRIVAL` event), which event should be executed first? No other events are on the events list and all other events have the same execution priority.

5.12.18 Nested Loops

(a) Create a nested loop with three index variables: `I` going from `1` to `4`, `J` going from `1` to `I`, and `K` going from `0` to `I*J`.

(b) Create an event graph that finds the sum of all the elements of a 3 by 5 array.

(c) Give the event graph for a nested loop where the inner loop moves twice as fast as the outer loop.

(d) Draw an event graph for a program that produces the entries in a table that translates from 1 to 20 degrees Celsius to Fahrenheit.

6

Using SIGMA to Build and Verify Simulations

In order for a SIGMA simulation to run, three objects must be defined: vertices, edges connecting the vertices, and state variables. In this chapter, you will learn how to create and define these objects and how to make changes to them. Moreover, you will learn how to edit and build models *while they are running*. SIGMA's ability to let you interact with a simulation as it is progressing is a valuable logic checking and model enrichment feature.

6.1 The Simulation Graph Window

When you click on the **SIGMA** icon in the Windows **Program Manager**, a screen like that in Figure 3.1 will appear. There are three regions in the simulation graph window: the model creation area, the menu bar, and the toolbar. The region in the center of the window is devoted to model creation. The menu bar, located at the top of the simulation graph window, is where the various menus are arranged. Clicking on a particular menu will show a list of commands related to that menu. Some commands will open dialog boxes where additional information can be entered. The toolbar, located on the right side of the simulation graph window, contains various push buttons that change the capabilities of the mouse, provide additional information, or stop and start a simulation.

When SIGMA for Windows is started, the mouse is normally in **Create Process** mode (⊕).The graphical components of a simulation model are created in this mode. When the mouse pointer looks like an arrow (↖), it is in **Select or Edit** mode. Clicking the right mouse button will cause the mouse to alternate between the **Create Process** mode and **Select or Edit** mode. The information concerning specific vertices and edges can only be added or changed in **Select or Edit** mode. To edit a vertex or edge, double-click on it. An **Edit Edge** or **Edit Vertex** dialog box will appear. Add information or make changes by clicking on the appropriate box and entering the data from the keyboard.

6.2 Creating and Editing an Event Graph

6.2.1 Create Process

SIGMA enables you to create a connected chain of events simply by moving the mouse and clicking. Such a sequence of events is called a process. If the mouse pointer is in **Select or Edit** mode (↖), click the right mouse button to change to **Create Process** mode. (Clicking on the **Create Process** tool in the toolbar will also change the mode to **Create Process**.) Clicking with the left mouse button on the graph-creation region will cause a vertex to be created. If you move the mouse to another location and click the left mouse button again, another vertex will be created as well as an edge between the vertices. Clicking on a vertex will connect it to the last vertex clicked; no new vertex is created. As you continue clicking, SIGMA will create a chain of event vertices and connecting edges.

If you are starting a new graph, your first mouse click will create the initial vertex, which is green. It is good practice to name the first vertex you create something like `RUN`. The variables in the parameter list for this first vertex are the initial run conditions that must be entered in the **Run Options** dialog box.

> ➢ **Important:** *The first vertex created in a* SIGMA *model will always be the first vertex executed when you run your model.*

To make *self-scheduling* edges (edges that have the same originating and destination vertex), simply click twice at the same location. The first click will create the vertex, and the second click will create the self-scheduling edge. This is useful, for example, when creating an input stream of arrivals to a simulated queue, like the loop on the `ENTER` vertex in Figure 3.10.

6.2.2 Create Single Edge

The **Create Single Edge** tool allows you to create a single edge between two vertices. This tool is useful for adding edges and/or vertices to different parts of your graph or connecting graphs copied from one SIGMA session to another.

This tool is actually very similar to **Create Process** discussed previously; however, with **Create Single Edge**, only one vertex at a time is remembered. You are first asked to select an originating vertex for the edge. If no vertex exists at the location where you click the mouse, one will be created. You will then be asked to select a destination vertex. After doing so, you will be prompted to select another originating vertex. Unlike the **Create Process** tool, your next selection will not create an edge.

There may be several edges connecting a pair of vertices, and these may go in either direction; however, only one edge appears on the screen. A multiple edge is called a graphics edge with sub-edges. You can move an edge by holding the mouse key on the end of an edge and dragging it to a different vertex; press [↑Shift] and drag the mouse to copy an edge. You need to deactivate the **Create Single Edge** tool (click the right mouse button or click on the **Select or Edit** tool) before you attempt to enter or alter information about any edge or vertex.

6.2.3 State Variables

The **Variables** menu is used to define and edit the state variables in your simulation. We call these *state* variables to emphasize that they can be used in any expression, anywhere in your SIGMA model. All state variables in a SIGMA simulation must be defined before a SIGMA model will run.

When you click on the **Create/Edit Variables** command under the **Variables** menu, the **State Variable Editor** dialog box will appear. It is here where state variables are entered or edited. The insertion point will be in the **Name** text box. Enter the name of each new state variable here. Use the mouse or [Tab] to activate the **Size**, **Type**, and **Description** text boxes and enter the appropriate information. Clicking **Add** or pressing [←Enter] will cause the state variable information to be entered in the list box. The insertion point will automatically revert back to the **Name** text box. When you have created more than eight state variables, a scroll bar will appear to allow you to view all the state variables. You can use the mouse, [PgDn] and [PgUp], or [↑] and [↓] to scroll through the list of state variables. The number of state variables may be limited by the available memory on your machine or the version of SIGMA you are using.

To edit an existing state variable, click on that state variable in the list box. This will cause the state variable information to appear in the text boxes above. (Refer to Figure 3.4.) Use the mouse to activate any boxes where changes are needed, then enter the new information from the keyboard. To change just the name of a state variable, use the **Rename** button. To change other information regarding a state variable, click **Change**. To eliminate a state variable, use the **Delete** button. Be sure to click on the **OK** button to save the changes you have made. Clicking on the **Cancel** button will close the dialog box without making any changes to your model.

> **Note:** *Be sure to click on the* **OK** *button after clicking* **Rename**, **Add**, **Delete**, *or* **Change** *to save any information you may have entered. Clicking on the* **Cancel** *button will close the box without saving any changes.*

The **Name** you give to a state variable can be used in vertex state change expressions and in expressions for edge conditions, delay times, priorities, and attribute strings. State variable names have a maximum length of 8 characters. Names should begin with a letter but may be composed of letters and numbers. SIGMA will not let you enter names that do not follow this format. If you intend to automatically translate your model to C, you should use C naming conventions. Similar advice applies to SIGMA models that will be automatically translated into Pascal or FORTRAN (SIMAN or SLAM). Also, the two functions reserved for SIGMA (`CLK` and `RND`) cannot be used as state variable names. In SIGMA, variable names and expressions are in upper-case. This is because reserved words in ANSI standard C are in lower-case, and we do not want to confuse C when we translate our models to source code. Compilers typically have some non-standard functions added to their libraries, so you must avoid using these function names. This is discussed further in Appendix B.

You can select a **Size** for a variable. (If `Size>1`, it is an array.) The maximum array size allowed may be limited by the free memory you have on your computer or the version of SIGMA you are using. Following the convention in C, in SIGMA we start indexing arrays with zero (not 1 as in FORTRAN); you will see that this makes all of our work with arrays much easier. Array elements in a model can be recycled using the modulus function included in SIGMA. This is discussed in Chapter 7. In SIGMA, variables can be up to four dimensions. Two-dimensional variables are used for modeling tables of data. To define a variable that is a two-dimensional table, specify the maximum size of each dimension separated by a comma (e.g., `5,6`). The default size is a scalar of size `1`. (Modeling arrays of any dimension is discussed in Section 12.4.) You select the size of each array, within default limits. Array index values can be scalars or arrays of real or integer numbers. Real valued numbers are rounded down when used as indices for an array. If `X` is a one-dimensional array with `Size=5`, we reference the elements of `X` in SIGMA expressions as `X[0]` through `X[4]`. If `Y` is a two-dimensional table with `Size=5,6`, we can reference the entries as `Y[0;0]` through `Y[4;5]`. (Note that indices for elements of a table are separated by a semicolon.)

At the **Type** drop-down box, you can choose one of three types of variables currently supported in SIGMA. In addition to the usual integer and real (floating point) variables or arrays, you may create a general type of variable called a USER variable. A USER variable is actually an executable function on your default disk drive. This can be a program compiled in FORTRAN, Pascal, ASSEMBLY, C, etc. USER defined functions are discussed in Section 12.5.

The **Description** of each state variable is very important. It is strongly encouraged (but not required) that at least brief descriptions be given whenever a SIGMA object is created; descriptions become valuable comments in SIGMA-generated source code. Text descriptions of each state variable are always available at the click of a mouse and should be used.

6.2.4 Editing Vertices

Changes in the values of state variables occur only when a vertex is executed. Formulas for the state changes associated with a particular vertex are entered using an **Edit Vertex** dialog box, which is displayed when the mouse is double-clicked on a particular vertex. An **Edit Vertex** dialog box contains the following input boxes:

Name and Description: Vertex names must be six characters or less. Vertex descriptions provide valuable comments in SIGMA-generated simulation source code.

Trace Event: When the **Trace Event** check box is **On**, the vertex will be traced in the output file. The SIGMA default is to have **Trace Event** automatically **On** when a vertex is created. Thus, if no action is taken, all events will be traced in the output file. The **Trace Event** mechanism for a vertex can be deactivated by opening the dialog box for that vertex and clicking the **Trace Event** check box **Off**. The **Trace Event** feature can be turned **On** (or **Off**) in several selected vertices by holding down [↑Shift], clicking on the vertices, and then clicking **Trace Off** (**Trace On**) in the **Edit** menu. Once the correctness of a model's logic has been verified, only a few event vertices should be traced.

Animation Enabled/Disabled: When the **Animation** check box is **On**, the active and inactive bitmap pictures for the vertex have been defined. Clicking this check box **Off** will clear the pictures.

Inactive Picture/Active Picture: This feature is used for animations. See Chapter 8 for more details.

State Change(s): There are typically one or more state variable changes associated with each vertex. The operators available for use are +, -, /, *, and ^ for add, subtract, divide, multiply, and exponentiation, respectively.

For example, the value of the expression X^2 is the square of X. Multiple state variable changes are separated by commas.

Parameter(s): Parameters are the values of state variables passed to a vertex as attributes of the scheduling edge. The parameter list is a string of state variables separated by a comma. The main value of vertex parameters is in defining the particular system entities to which a vertex pertains. For example, suppose that there were two identical machines in a simulated factory. The same START vertex may be used for both machines if the vertex has a parameter telling which machine is to start.

To solidify our understanding of vertex parameters, consider a vertex in a queueing simulation that occurs when a customer starts to be served. The state changes are given as the string

```
QUEUE[S]=QUEUE[S]-1,  STATUS[S]=0.
```

When this vertex executes, the number of customers waiting in the QUEUE for station S is decreased by one, and the STATUS of the server at station S is set equal to 0 (BUSY). A value for the parameter S (denoting which of several possible service stations is involved) is passed to the vertex as an attribute of the edge that originally scheduled this vertex.

Display Variables: A state variable and its value at a particular time can be displayed during a run. The current value of the display variable is updated every time any event is executed. To display more than one variable, separate each with a comma. Display variables are useful for animation and debugging.

Location: This drop-down list shows where a display variable will be located relative to a vertex: to the left, right, top, or bottom.

6.2.5 Editing Edges

Edges connect pairs of vertices in a simulation graph and define how one event may cause (or prevent) the occurrence of another event. There can be multiple edges between any pair of vertices in the model. Multiple edges are useful, say, if different conditions or parameters imply that different probability distributions should be used for the times events are to be scheduled.

Information concerning an edge can be found in its dialog box. If you double-clicked on an edge and the dialog box in Figure 6.1 appeared, it would tell us the following:

> Every time the vertex DRILL is executed, if the variable QUEUE is greater than 2 and the variable BUFFER is less than or equal to 8, then the vertex MILL will be scheduled to occur. The time until the scheduled occurrence of vertex MILL is read sequentially from a disk data file named TIME.DAT. A value for the

Figure 6.1: Edit Edge Dialog Box—`DRILL` to `MILL`

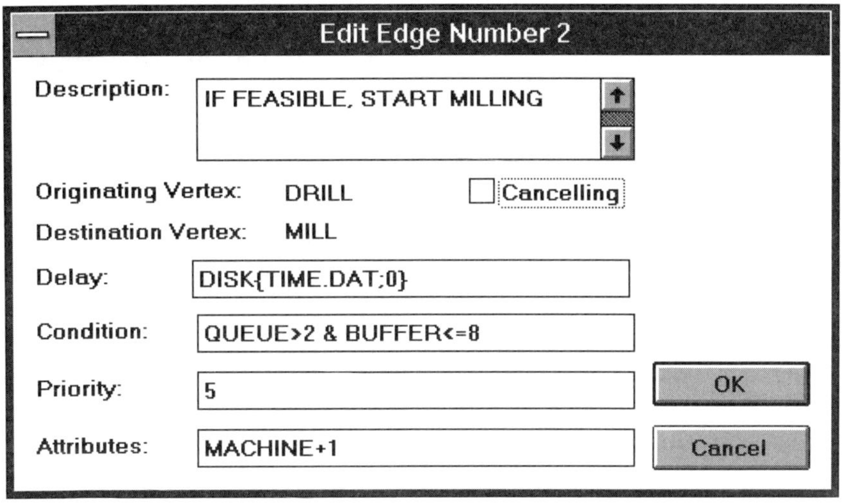

attribute expression `MACHINE+1` (maybe the next machine) is computed and specified as the parameter value for the occurrence of the `MILL` vertex being scheduled. The vertex `MILL`, if scheduled, will have an execution priority of `5` to break time ties with simultaneously scheduled vertices.

To change characteristics of this edge, you would click the mouse on the text box of interest and enter the change from the keyboard. An **Edit Edge** dialog box contains the following input boxes:

Originating and Destination Vertices: The originating and destination vertices for an edge are entered automatically from the event graph. You can change the originating and destination vertices by copying or moving edges on a graph (drag edge end points with the mouse).

Cancelling or Scheduling Edges: The cancelling option is a check box. If checked on, it is a cancelling edge and can cancel the destination vertex. If checked off, it is a scheduling edge and can schedule the destination vertex. The SIGMA default is the scheduling edge. (Cancelling edges are represented by dashed lines on the graphical model; scheduling edges by solid lines.) When a vertex cancelling edge is executed, it cancels only previously scheduled vertices of the same type as the destination vertex of the edge. If the edge has any attribute expressions, only scheduled vertices with parameter values that are an exact match with the values of these edge attribute expressions are cancelled. If the attribute on a cancelling edge is entered as an asterisk (*), all scheduled occurrences of the destination vertex will be cancelled regardless of their parameter values. If a cancelling edge has no attributes, only the next scheduled vertex of the same type as the edge destination vertex (if any) is cancelled.

Edge Delay Time: This is the expression for the delay time between the occurrence of the originating vertex and the occurrence of the destination vertex. An example of an edge delay time is `-3*LN{RND}`, which is an exponentially distributed random variable with a mean of `3` (as demonstrated in Section 9.10.1). Cancelling edges have zero delay times; cancelling is immediate, regardless of a delay expression or execution priority.

If the expression for the condition on a scheduling edge in SIGMA is true and the delay time expression is simply an asterisk (`*`), SIGMA will execute the vertex state change immediately. This is called *pre-emptive vertex execution;* the vertex is executed without being placed on the future events list. The effect is that the two vertices on this edge are condensed into a single vertex. Bypassing the future events list generally speeds up model execution without making the state changes for each vertex more complicated. While far from universal, the customary notion of a "simulation event" includes all vertices that are connected with edges that have an asterisk (`*`) for their delay times. For an example of how this might be used to eliminate the scheduling of events during a simulation run, see Section 12.3 on vertex reduction.

Caution should be used with pre-emptive vertex execution. Pre-emptive vertex execution makes execution priorities moot; potential problems in simultaneous vertex execution have to be considered. You should try to avoid having a cycle in your graph where all the edges have pre-emptive execution, such as a self-scheduling loop. The resulting loop is likely to run until there is a stack overflow due to recursive function calls. Finally, recall that there must be at least one event on the future events list or your SIGMA run will terminate; a generic `STOP RUN` event (scheduled when the run starts) is appropriate if all edges in a model have pre-emptive execution.

> ➢ *If four or five pre-emptive vertex execution edges are placed in sequence, a stack overflow may occur. (While this is not a serious limitation, you may be able to avoid this by increasing your Windows stack size.)*

Edge Conditions: The cancelling (or scheduling) of the destination vertex can be made conditional on the state of the system at the time the originating vertex executes. Edge conditions are entered as expressions. The operators you may use in edge conditions are +, -, /, *, ^, defined earlier in this chapter, along with:

`==` (equal to)
`!=` (not equal to)
`<` (strictly less than)
`>` (strictly greater than)
`<=` (less than or equal to)
`>=` (greater than or equal to)

You may combine conditions by using the Boolean operators `&` (and) and `|` (or). For example, the edge condition `QUEUE>1&STATUS==0` means that the destination vertex will be scheduled to occur (after the edge delay time) only if `QUEUE` is currently greater than one *and* `STATUS` is equal to zero. Readers familiar with C should note that the exclamation mark (`!`) is not used by itself in SIGMA to negate a general condition and a single `&` and `|` are used for Boolean operators rather than the double `&&` and `||` used in C.

Execution Priority: This is an expression for a scheduling edge that computes an execution priority for the destination vertex being scheduled. Edge priorities are used to break time ties in scheduled vertices. When two or more vertices are scheduled to occur at the same time, the event with the higher priority (the lower numerical value) will be executed first. Remaining ties are broken by giving precedence to the vertex that was scheduled first.

In SIGMA, the default execution priority is `5`. The execution priority of events that are to be executed earlier should be changed to a higher priority (e.g., `1`, `2.4`, `3.6`, or `4`). The execution priority of events that are to be executed later should be changed to a lower priority. When a delay time greater than zero is entered in the **Delay** input box, a SIGMA message will appear to remind you to change the execution priority to a number greater than `5`. You can choose to suppress this message for the duration of the SIGMA session.

Event time ties occur with surprising frequency in some discrete event models. In fact, the occurrence of simultaneous events happens regularly in simulations of mechanized or automated systems such as paced assembly lines found in modern factories. Since a machining line is intentionally balanced, event time ties may be designed into the system.

If simultaneous events are executed in the wrong order, the logic of the simulation may be incorrect. Consider the example where a customer arrives at a capacitated queue that is full and a service completion coincides with that arrival. If the customer arrival event is executed first, the customer will see a full line and depart. If the service completion event is executed first, a space will be made in line for the arriving customer and the customer will not depart. In simulations of serial systems (factories, communication networks, etc.), executing simultaneous events in the wrong order can cause the model to behave in a very strange manner. Recall the discussion of the "phantom" server in Section 5.1.3.

No good rule of thumb for assigning execution priorities has been devised to replace thinking through the chain of consequences of simultaneous events. However, you should be alert to the possibility of simultaneous vertex problems whenever

the state changes in one vertex and the conditions tested in the exiting edges for another vertex involve the same variables.

Any two such vertices should have appropriate execution priorities passed to them. The order in which the different expressions are computed can be found in the Event Execution Sequence in Appendix A.

Edge Attributes: (Values passed to vertex parameters) Each edge has an attribute list, and each vertex has a parameter list. These are simple but powerful modeling tools. The edge attribute list is a string of expressions separated by commas. When the originating vertex for an edge is executed, the expressions in the edge attribute list are evaluated. These will be the values assigned to the state variables in the destination vertex parameter list when that vertex is subsequently executed.

For example, consider an edge with attribute list

`X+1,5,QUEUE*N.`

Say that the destination vertex for this edge has the parameter list

`Z,N,QUEUE.`

Suppose when the originating vertex for this edge is executed, the state variables have values `X=5`, `N=10`, and `QUEUE=2`. When the destination vertex is subsequently executed, the values for the state variables `Z`, `N`, and `QUEUE` will be set equal to `6`, `5`, and `20`. This parameter list assignment is made before any vertex state changes and regardless of the values for `X` and `QUEUE` when the scheduled vertex executed. The expression `QUEUE*N` was evaluated when the vertex was scheduled; the values of `N` and `QUEUE` at that time were `10` and `2`, respectively, so `QUEUE*N` was equal to `20`. The number `20` is literally placed on the future events list as a parameter of the scheduled event.

> ➢ **Important:** *Remember that any state variable in* SIGMA *may be changed indirectly, by passing values to vertex parameters, as well as directly, by the state changes in vertices.*

Figure 6.2: A Simple Event Graph and Events List

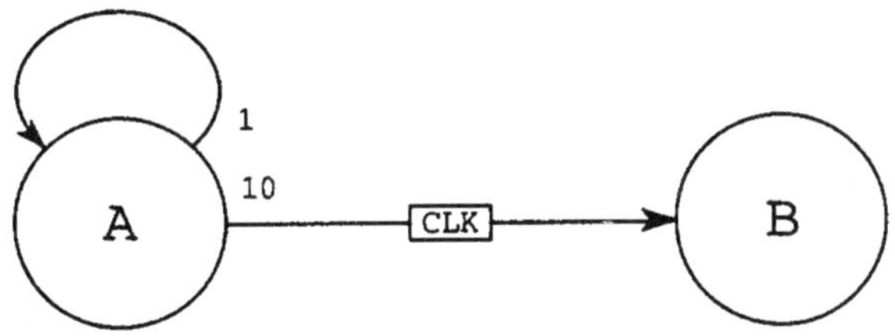

Time	Event	Priority	Attributes	
13	A	5		(A has just executed)
14	B	5	4.00	
14	A	5		(Next A event, after B)
15	B	5	5.00	
16	B	5	6.00	
17	B	5	7.00	
18	B	5	8.00	
19	B	5	9.00	
20	B	5	10.00	
21	B	5	11.00	
22	B	5	12.00	
23	B	5	13.00	(Just scheduled by A)

If an edge has more attribute expressions than its destination vertex has parameters, the extra edge attribute values are ignored. If an edge has fewer attribute expressions than needed, an error message occurs. As another example, consider the situation in Figure 6.2, which shows the events list at time `13`, just after vertex `A` executes. (Execution priorities are all equal, so time ties are broken on a "first-in-first-out" basis.)

Reminder: Initial attribute values for the parameters required by the first vertex must be specified in the **Run Options** dialog box.

> ➢ *Array elements must be specified explicitly—e.g.,* `A[3]`*, not* `A[Q]`.

6.2.6 Deleting Parts of an Event Graph

To delete a particular vertex, click on the vertex once (the vertex will change color) and click the **Delete** command under the **Edit** menu or press [Delete] on the keyboard. A dialog box will appear asking for confirmation to delete the highlighted vertex and all associated edges. Click **Yes** to delete the item. If you would like to delete several vertices and edges, hold down [↑Shift] and click on each vertex and edge to be deleted. Again, after pressing [Delete], a dialog box will appear requesting confirmation to delete. If you press the **Yes** button, you will be asked to confirm the deletion of each vertex and its associated edge. If you wish to delete all quickly, press the **Yes To All** button.

If you wish to delete a particular edge, click on the edge and then press [Delete]. This time, the edge will be deleted without a request for confirmation. Deleting multiple edges works in a similar manner. Use [↑Shift] with the mouse to highlight multiple edges to be deleted. Multiple edges between a pair of vertices are deleted one at a time. You can also select multiple edges or vertices by dragging the mouse around these objects, a process called "lassoing."

6.3 Moving a Simulation Graph

All or part of a simulation graph can be moved around the graphical window relatively easily. First click on the object to be moved with the mouse, hold down the left mouse button until the pointer changes shape, and drag the object to the desired location. Multiple edges and vertices can be highlighted using [↑Shift] and the mouse and moved by clicking the mouse on *one* vertex in the group and dragging that vertex to the new location. Edges outside the group that are connected to the vertices that are to be moved will shrink or stretch to accommodate the move. You can also lasso a group of vertices by dragging the mouse around the group.

You can move an edge by pressing and *holding* the mouse on the edge until the mouse pointer changes to a cross-shape. Then drag the end of the edge to a new *vertex*. There must be a vertex to serve as a destination for that edge, or the move will not be successful. You cannot move an edge from a vertex to the middle of another edge; you must move it to a vertex. Notice that other edges that occupy the same bounding rectangle on the screen as the selected edge may be moved unless the associated vertices are moved off to the side before attempting to move an edge.

If you wish to move the entire graph, you can open the **Edit** menu and choose the **Select All** command. This command will highlight the entire graph and allow you to move it across the screen. Just make sure that you position the mouse pointer on a vertex, or the move will not be successful. If a vertex is dragged out of the screen, it can be retrieved by choosing the **Select All** command under the **Edit** menu and dragging any of the highlighted vertices until the lost vertex reappears.

Vertices in event graph models can also be moved one pixel at a time by highlighting the vertex and using the arrow keys. This method can be used to straighten crooked edges and tidy up graphs. (The scroll bars at the right side and at the bottom of the simulation graph window also allow you to manipulate the location of the graph on the screen.)

6.4 Viewing a Simulation Graph

6.4.1 Zoom

The **Zoom** menu contains commands that allow you to alter the size of the simulation graph on the screen. The **Normal Size** command resets the graph to its original size. With **Zoom Out**, the graph appears smaller with each mouse click. Use this command to avoid crowding your simulation model or to view different sections of a large model. With **Zoom In**, the graph appears larger on the screen. The **Fit to Screen** feature resizes the graph so that most of the vertices appear in the window. A running model will execute more slowly when it is not its normal size.

6.4.2 Window

The **Window** menu is useful to control the arrangement of windows and icons in SIGMA. The **Cascade** command will arrange the open windows in an overlapping manner, with all title bars exposed but only the top window readable. The **Tile** command will arrange the open windows so all can be seen. The **Arrange Icons** command will arrange whatever icons are active at the bottom of the screen. The **Refresh Graph** command will clean up any scraps that may have been created by moving edges and bitmaps during a run.

> ➢ *Under the* **Window** *menu is a* **Refresh Graph** *command that will clear up any scraps that may have been left on the screen. You also should become familiar with the* **Tile** *command to display multiple windows.*

6.5 Saving, Retrieving, and Copying Your Work

6.5.1 Save and Save As

Before you invest the effort in building a simulation model, you should know how to save it. This is done with the **Save** and **Save As** commands in the **File** menu. If a model has not been saved previously, clicking on the **Save** or the **Save As** command will produce the dialog box shown in Figure 6.3. You will be asked to provide a name for the file where the model is to be saved. The convention for naming files containing SIGMA graphs is to use the .MOD file type (e.g., CARWASH.MOD). File names must be 8 or fewer characters and begin with a letter or number.

If a model has been saved previously, the **Save** command will save it under its current name. The **Save As** command will allow you to save the model under a different name and under a different directory. A backup copy of the last model saved is retained with the extension .BAK.

> ➢ *It is strongly suggested that all* SIGMA *models be saved with the file type ".MOD." This is useful for debugging and documentation.*

6.5.2 Open

The **Open** command under the **File** menu lets you open a previously saved model. After clicking on the **Open** command, a dialog box will appear showing a list box of all the models in your default directory (those files whose file type is .MOD). Click twice on the name of the file to open the model. Alternatively, click once on the name of the file and then click the **OK** command button.

6.5.3 Recall

Using the **Recall** command under the **File** menu is an easy way to retrieve models that were used recently. After clicking on **Recall**, a box will appear listing the last ten models used. Clicking once on the appropriate file name will cause that model to appear in the simulation graph window.

6.5.4 Copy and Paste

SIGMA allows you to copy and paste information within a single SIGMA modeling session, between several SIGMA modeling sessions, and between another application and a SIGMA session.

Figure 6.3: Save Model As Dialog Box

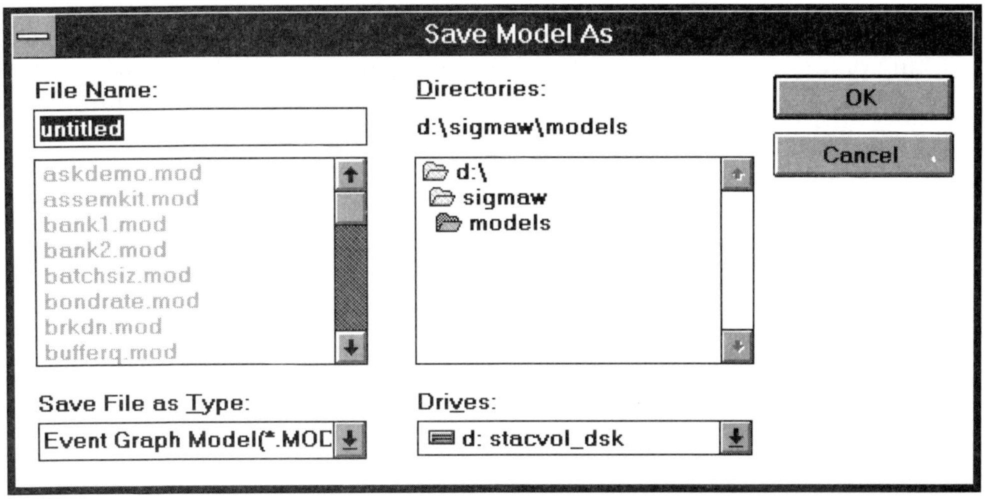

Vertices and connecting edges in an event graph can be copied and pasted in the same event graph to build a model quickly. Select the items to be copied by using the mouse and [↑Shift] (or the **Select All** command under the **Edit** menu), click on the **Edit/Copy** command, and then click on the **Edit/Paste** command. Copies of the vertices and edges will appear on the screen. Make sure the copied items are still highlighted so that you can drag them to a new location, if necessary. (Place the mouse on *one* vertex to drag a subgraph.) Connect the copied subgraph to the original graph using the **Create Single Edge** tool.

Edges are copied in the same way they are moved (press and hold down the mouse pointer on the desired edge until the mouse pointer changes shape) except [↑Shift] is also pressed during the operation. Recall that unless other edges that occupy the same bounding rectangle are moved out of the way they may also be copied.

Copied state variables are added to the current set of state variables; duplicate names are deleted. Copied vertices with duplicate names are renamed. The Copy-Paste feature is particularly useful when developing a model containing similar but complex vertices or edges.

Event graph models (or parts of models) also can be selected, copied, and pasted between different SIGMA sessions. First, open the SIGMA session with the model to be copied. Highlight the components to be copied, then click on the **Edit/Copy** command. Open a second SIGMA session from the icon in the Windows **Program Manager**. Use the **Edit/Paste** command to paste the first model into the new SIGMA session. Move the newly pasted subgraph to the desired location. It is suggested that you save intermediate graphs under different names.

The model BRKDN.MOD in Chapter 5 was actually created by copying BRKDN.APN from one SIGMA session to another session while running the model QUEUE.MOD. The Copy-Paste feature is also useful when several persons are working on different parts of the same simulation model. This allows a team of modelers to create separate parts of a simulation model in different SIGMA windows and later connect them together into a larger simulation.

> ➢ *For text in dialog boxes,* [Ctrl-c] *will copy information,* [Ctrl-x] *will cut it, and* [Ctrl-v] *will paste it into another dialog box (or to and from another Windows application, such as Word for Windows).*

6.6 Dynamic Run-Time Model Building and Analysis

SIGMA has the unique ability to allow a modeler to interact with a model during the run. You can alter your model in virtually any way you wish *while it is running!* For example, with a running model, you can change an edge condition or delay time expression by double-clicking on the edge and making the necessary changes in the dialog box. If you double-click on a vertex, you can modify the state changes or displayed variables. You can change the run mode by making changes in the **Run Options** dialog box during a run. You can even add and delete edges or vertices during a run. You should work along with the example below and try things as they are discussed.

> ➢ *Changing a simulation during execution is simple: just make the changes as if the model were not running!*

6.6.1 Changing the Value of State Variables During a Run

To illustrate the usefulness of changing variable values during a run, we will examine a model of a multiple server single-line queue such as that found in an airport check-in line—AIRPORT.MOD. If you open AIRPORT.MOD, your screen should look like the one in Figure 6.4. (This model is very similar to BANK1.MOD but an INPUT vertex has been added.)

Start this simulation by pressing [F5]. Watch the queue increase for a few seconds in the simulation plot window. Next, double-click on the INPUT vertex; it will not have executed since it is not connected to the graph. The **Edit Vertex** dialog box for the INPUT event should look like the one in Figure 6.5.

Figure 6.4: A Multi-Server Queueing Model—`AIRPORT.MOD`

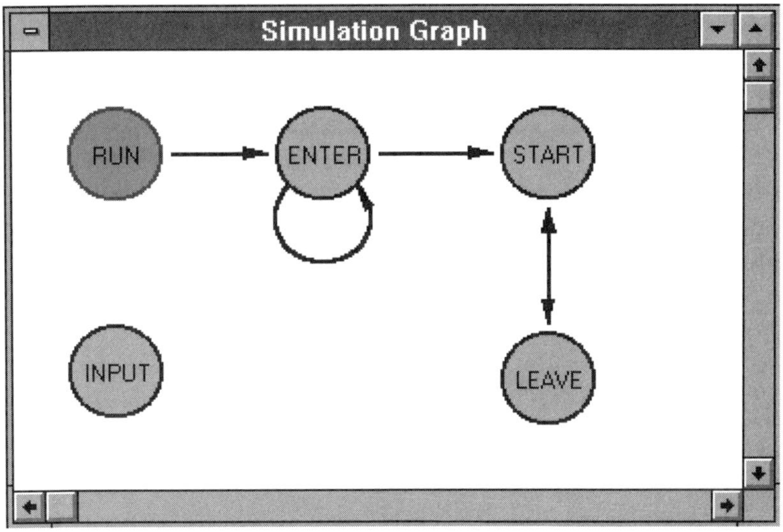

Figure 6.5: The Dialog Box for the `INPUT` Vertex

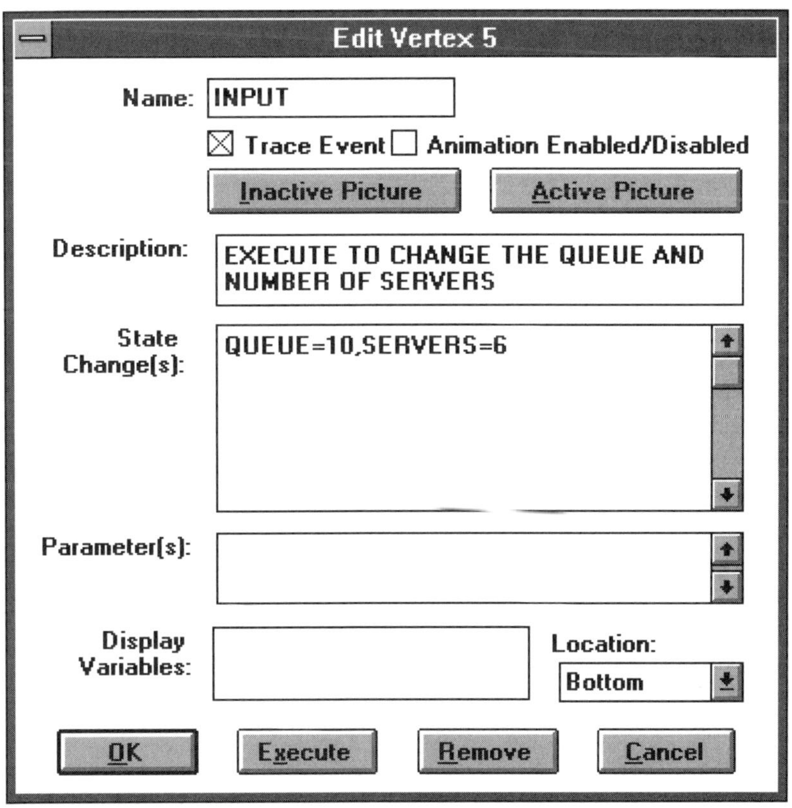

When you click on the **Execute** button in an **Edit Vertex** dialog box during a run, that vertex will be the next event executed. State changes for this vertex will then occur. Try this by pressing **Execute**. You will see the `QUEUE` jump to `10` in the simulation plot, and the number of idle servers will be reset to `6`. Continue to increase the number of idle servers in the running model until the system appears to stabilize. Do this by repeatedly editing and executing the state changes for the `INPUT` event. Note that in this model the variable, `SERVERS`, is defined as the number of *idle* servers. Thus, servers that are busy will stay in the system; only the `QUEUE` and number of idle servers are changed.

To delete servers, double-click on the `LEAVE` vertex and close the resulting dialog box with the **Remove** button. This will remove the next pending `LEAVE` event, effectively removing one busy server.

The **Execute** and **Remove** command buttons at the bottom of the **Edit Vertex** dialog box are useful for executing an event or removing an event from the future events list during a run. Since the executed event can itself schedule or cancel other events, this gives complete run-time control over the future events list.

It is good practice to include an isolated empty vertex, like the `INPUT` vertex in this example, to make changes to a variable during a run. You could use the `ASK{}` function discussed in Chapter 7 to do the same thing. However, that function is more for interactive games, where you want to prompt the model user to make a decision during a run.

> ➢ **Note:** *Change the values of variables during a run to feasible values. For example, you can change* `QUEUE` *to a negative number if you wish; however, it makes no sense to have a negative number of customers in line.*

6.6.2 Changing Edges and Vertices During a Run

Now try double-clicking on the self-scheduling edge for the `ENTER` event. You can change the time between arrivals by editing the delay time in the **Edit Edge** dialog box. The changes you enter will take effect as soon as you press **OK**. You make changes to vertices in a similar fashion, just as if the model were not running. Changes take effect the next time the vertex is executed in the run, or you can force the vertex to execute immediately by clicking on **Execute** in the dialog box. In this manner you can ask "what-if" questions concerning changes in demand rate and number of servers *while the model is running.*

6.6.3 Adding and Deleting Edges and Vertices During a Run

Deleting edges is done by clicking once on the edge and pressing [Delete]. (Be careful, since you are now changing the model logic, not just the values of variables.) Delete vertices the same way, by clicking once on the vertex you wish to delete and pressing [Delete]. You will be asked to confirm that you want to delete a vertex.

> ➢ **Caution:** *Adding or deleting edges or vertices during a run will change the model logic.*

You can connect a vertex to a running model or create a new edge. First click on the vertex that is to serve as the origin of the new edge. Next, click the *right mouse button* to get into **Create Process** mode. (The mouse cursor will have a circular shape.) Then click where you would like to have a new vertex created. (Click on an existing vertex if you want only a new edge.) Continue clicking if you would like to spawn a series of new vertices and edges off an existing vertex. Press the *right mouse button* again to return to **Select or Edit** mode. Click on the new edges or vertices to open their dialog boxes. You will generally alternate clicking the right and left mouse buttons as you add and edit new vertices to a running model.

> ➢ **Note:** *You should not delete a vertex while there are grouped vertices in the model. See Chapter 8 on animation for a discussion of vertex groups.*

6.7 Model Enrichment and Logic Checking

SIGMA has the most powerful simulation model enrichment and logic checking features of any simulation environment. This is because you can change your model while it is running, as discussed in Section 6.6.

6.7.1 Setting Up the Logic Checking Environment

One of the most important things to check before you start to verify a simulation model is that all the edges have enough attribute expressions for each of the parameters of the scheduled vertex. The *most* common error is to not have enough "initial attributes" in the **Run Options** dialog box for the parameters of the first vertex.

A model verification session will progress as follows. Start a SIGMA session and open the model to be checked. (Here we will again use `CARWASH.MOD`.) Open the **Run Options** dialog box in the **Run** menu and set the **Run Mode** to **Single Step**. Next, make the run very short by setting the **Stop Time** to a small number (10 will do). This is to initialize data tracking. Start the run by clicking **OK & Run**. Press [←Enter] several times or click on the **Single Step** tool to execute some events. Press [F5] to stop the run. Click **Yes** when asked to view the output file.

At this point you should have three windows tiled in your SIGMA session: an output window for the output file listed in your **Run Options** dialog box (`CARWASH.OUT`), the simulation graph, and the simulation plot.

Click once on the simulation graph window to activate it. Next, click on **View Output/Text File** under the **File** menu and then click on `CARWASH.MOD`; this will open the ASCII text file for your model. (If you don't see `CARWASH.MOD`, press the drop-down list under **List Files of Types** and click **Other Files**.) Under the **Window** menu select **Tile**. You should now have four windows showing: a simulation graph, a simulation plot, an output file, and a model text file. Activate the simulation graph window and set the **Stop Time** in the **Run Options** dialog box to a very large number, so your model will continue to run as you verify its logic. Press **OK**.

6.7.2 A Logic Checking Run

Press [F5] to start the run. Make sure you are again in **Single Step** mode and step through your model by pressing [←Enter] or clicking on the **Single Step** tool in the **Single Step Window**. Note that every time the "Refresh" arrow [↓] (near the upper left corner of `CARWASH.OUT`) is pressed during the run, the output trace will be updated and new data added to the output file.

If you have an edge that is not scheduling a vertex as you expected, click on the scheduling vertex (while the model is running) to open the **Edit Vertex** dialog box and set some **Display Variables** that are tested on the bothersome edge. (Enter the names of the variables separated by commas.)

If you activate the simulation plot window and click on the **New** command under the **File** menu, you can open a copy of the simulation plot. This plot can be double-clicked to change its plot type. In this manner, you can view several plots at once. For example, one could show a histogram and another a scatter plot. Only one plot will be updated during a run; the others are used to record snapshots of the run history.

6.8 Exercises

The models referred to in these exercises are on your SIGMA *disk. Exercises identified as mini projects are more extensive and may take considerably longer than the typical exercise.*

6.8.1 Event Execution Priorities

Modify `CARWASH.MOD` so that arrivals occur exactly every 2 minutes and make the execution priorities on every edge the same. Run the model for 50 minutes; then look at the output. What happens when an `ENTER` event and a `LEAVE` event take place simultaneously? What event should be executed first if there is an `ENTER` event and a `START` event scheduled at the same time and `QUEUE=1`?

6.8.2 Pre-emptive Vertex Execution

Using pre-emptive vertex execution, modify the model `CARWASH.MOD` so that the logic of the simulation does not change but the number of events scheduled on the future events list is minimized. (Hint: Make some of the edge delay times equal to `*`; you will in effect incorporate the `START` vertex into *both* the `ENTER` and the `LEAVE` events.)

Why might the output from a model that uses pre-emptive vertex execution be different from the output of the same model where pre-emptive execution is not used—i.e., all `*` delays are changed to 0? Why might the outputs be different even if the two models are logically equivalent in a probabilistic sense (output sample paths have the same probability of occurring)?

6.8.3 Pre-emptive Vertex Execution with Parameter Passing

Using pre-emptive vertex execution (edge delay times set equal to `*`), modify the multiple server queue, `BANK2.MOD`, so that the logic of the simulation is not changed but a minimum number of events is scheduled on the future events list.

6.8.4 System Reliability

Consider two systems, each with 50 identical components. System `A` is a serial system that fails when the first component fails. System `B` is a parallel system that fails when the last component fails. The times until failure, `T`, for the components are independent and have beta distributions with parameters 0.5 and 0.2. System B is obviously more reliable; however, differences between the times until system failure for the two systems are of interest.

(a) Model both systems and then estimate the difference between the failure times of the two systems.

(b) Would the variance of the sample difference generated in part (a) be biased? If so, in what direction?

6.8.5 A Drive-in Bank Window (Mini Simulation Project)

A drive-in window is added to the side of the bank being modeled by `BANK2.MOD`. This window is serviced by the same tellers as before. The tellers rotate in serving customers at the drive-in window. Each teller will serve one drive-in customer and then return to service the line in the bank. If there are no customers at the drive-in window when a particular teller's turn comes up, s/he will miss a turn at the window.

Drive-in customers arrive according to the same pattern as the customers who arrive on foot (as described in the text) except that during the noon hour (12:00 to 1:00 P.M.) drive-in customers arrive at the rate of 2 per minute. Drive-in customers will balk if there are three or more cars waiting for service at the drive-in window. Of the balking drive-in customers, 80% will try to park their cars in the bank parking lot and walk inside for service. Once a former drive-in customer parks and walks inside, s/he will not balk unless the line has more than 20 customers in it.

The bank rents parking spaces in an adjacent parking lot for its customers. Currently the bank rents spaces for 10 cars. Customers desiring parking will wait only 30 seconds in a full lot before balking. Assume that it takes between 2 and 3 minutes (uniformly) for a customer to travel from the lot to the bank and vice versa (including time to park).

To better serve their customers, the bank is considering hiring additional tellers. Each teller costs the bank $1500.00 a month in salary and fringe benefits. As an alternative, the bank is considering renting additional parking spaces at $150.00 a month each.

Experiment with your simulation to advise the bank if they should hire tellers or rent parking spaces (or both). State your decision criteria and any additional assumptions that you need to make (e.g., tellers absent from work). Evaluate each of your assumptions. (Are the assumptions conservative? Are they realistic? Can you confirm them with real-world data?)

6.8.6 Variability and System Performance

The model `FLOWSHOP.MOD` on your SIGMA disk is a simulation of a flow shop where there are several parallel machines at each of `N` sequential stations. A part needs to be processed by only one machine at each station. Run the system for three stations in a series where there are 5 machines at the first station, 3 machines at the second station, and 4 machines at the third station. The mean processing times (in hours) at each station have uniform distributions with means of 0.2 for each machine at the first station, 0.1 at the second station, and 1.5 at the third station. The processing time range is ±0.05 for all machines. Run several 8 hour shifts and increase the processing time range to see the effect of variability on the performance of the system.

6.8.7 A Queue with Service Breaks

Modify the model `BANK2.MOD` to more accurately simulate a ticket line at a major airport. At the ticket counter there are three agents. The time it takes an agent to serve a single passenger has an Erlang (3) distribution with a mean of 15 minutes (`5*ERL{3}`). Every hour each agent takes a 5 minute break. They rotate breaks so one agent goes on break every 20 minutes. When an agent's break time is due, s/he will immediately stop whatever s/he is doing and go on break. If the agent is busy at the time, the passenger must wait until the agent returns from the break. An agent will finish the remaining service of a customer when s/he comes off break. Customers may not change agents once they start service even if the agent goes on break; the agent has their ticket. All passengers arrive at this departure desk in a taxi. The time between taxi arrivals has an exponential distribution with a mean of 1 minute. Passengers sometimes arrive in groups to share the taxi fare. Each taxi carries between 1 and 4 passengers. The likelihood of a group size of 1 is 0.6, the likelihood of a group size of 2 or 3 is 0.15, and the likelihood of 4 passengers arriving in a taxi is 0.1. Customers arrive in groups but each customer is processed alone. Run your model and watch the queue build up. Do you think the queue length will ever stabilize or do you expect it to continue to grow in an unbounded manner?

6.8.8 Project Management

In the project management model in Section 5.6, assume that the activity times have beta distributions with both parameters equal to 0.5 (see Section 7.8) and scaled to be between the limits given in the following table.

Activity	Must Follow Activities	Number of Workers	Time Range
A	None	1	1–3
B	A	1	1–5
C	None	1	2–4
D	B and C	2	3–7
E	B and D	1	2–4
F	C	2	4–6

(a) Run the simulation of this project 100 times and estimate the probability that the project will take longer than 14 days.

(b) Assume that there are only 3 workers and a task needs the number of workers specified in the table above. (Tasks cannot be done partially; they must be completed once started.) Modify the model to account for this resource constraint. (PUT activities in a queue when their precedence constraints are met but not enough workers are available to start; GET tasks from this queue when activities finish. For more on this, see Chapter 7.)

7

Using SIGMA Functions

A number of predefined functions have been incorporated into the SIGMA simulation environment. They include functions for reading data files, changing the value of expressions during a run, bookkeeping, mathematics, keeping the size of arrays small, modeling priority ranked queues, generating random variables, and gathering statistics. A summary of SIGMA functions is presented early in the chapter, followed by a more thorough discussion of some selected functions.

7.1 Summary of SIGMA Functions

Effort has been made to keep the number of predefined functions small. This section presents a brief overview of all SIGMA functions.

Functions can be placed in expressions, which can be used in state changes, edge conditions, edge priorities, and edge attributes. The functions are treated just like any state variable. These functions can be nested and used as arguments for each other and as arguments for `USER` variables (executable functions). For example, `-6*LN{RND}` can be used to approximate an exponentially distributed random variable with a mean of `6`, as shown in Section 9.10.1. Any of the expressions in these functions can, of course, be replaced by real constants, which are rounded down if integers are required. Note that you cannot use an array as an argument for a function. For example, you should break the function `BET{X[I;J];Y}` into the two statements `Z=X[I;J],BET{Z;Y}`.

> ➢ **Note:** *Arguments of* SIGMA *functions are in braces* `{}` *and multiple arguments are separated by semicolons.*

The functions currently defined in SIGMA include:

ASK{X} will display the value of expression X during a run and ask if you wish to change it. You can type in a constant or another expression, or you can press [←Enter] to leave the value of X unchanged.

AVE{X} is the cumulative average of the traced variable, X.

BET{X;Y} generates a pseudo beta random variate with nonnegative parameters given by the values of expressions X and Y.

CLK is the current simulated clock time (which is automatically updated to the time of each event occurrence).

COS{Y} gives the cosine of the expression, Y, in real format.

DISK{F;I} reads the Ith number from disk file F where I is any valid SIGMA expression (If I=0, the file is read sequentially).

ERL{X} generates a standard pseudo Erlang random variate with shape parameter given by the value of expression X rounded down to the nearest integer. This is the sum of X exponential random variates each with mean 1, so M*ERL{1} is a pseudo exponential random variate with mean M.

GAM{X} generates a pseudo gamma random variate with fractional shape parameter given by the value of expression X with 0<X<1.

GET{O;L} gets values for the ENT[] array from list L according to option O. The options include:

FST "first" removes and places the contents of the first entry of list, L, into the ENT[] array

LST "last" removes and places the contents of the last entry of list, L, into the ENT[] array.

KEY "key" uses the current value of ENT[0] to search for a match in list, L. If a match is found, KEY removes the entry from list, L, and places its contents in the ENT[] array.

LN{Y} gives the natural log of expression Y in real format.

MAX{Y;X} gives the maximum of expressions Y and X in real format.

MIN{Y;X} gives the minimum of expressions Y and X in real format.

MOD{Y;X} gives the integer remainder when the value of expression Y is divided by the value of expression X.

NOR{M;S} generates a pseudo normal random variate with mean given by the expression M and standard deviation given by the expression S.

PI is defined to be 3.14159 and is used with the SIN{} and COS{} functions.

PUT{O;L} places all of the current contents of the ENT[] array in the list identified by the integer expression or constant L according to a ranking criterion given by the option O. The options are:

FIF "first-is-first" places the current contents of the ENT[] array after the last entry of list L.

LIF "last-is-first" places the current contents of ENT[] before the first entry of list L.

INC "increasing" places the current contents of ENT[] in list L by increasing ranking of the value of ENT[RNK[L]], where RNK is the ranking array for the lists.

DEC "decreasing" places the current contents of ENT[] in list L by decreasing ranking of the value of ENT[RNK[L]].

EVN "even" places the current contents of ENT[] ranked by increasing values of ENT[0] and then by attribute ENT[2] to break ties. This function is actually used to place events on the future events list, where ENT[0] is the time of the event and ENT[2] is the event execution priority used to break time ties.

RND gives the multiplicative congruential pseudo-random number generator, lcg(), to produce approximately "independent uniformly distributed" numbers strictly greater than 0 and less than 1. You choose an initial seed to start the generator in the **Run Options** dialog box. The source code for the function, lcg, is given in the C library, CSIGLIB.C on your SIGMA disk. Instructions for using other generators are given in Chapter 11.

SET{N} resets all SIGMA variables to zero and the random number seed to the integer N. If no argument is given, the original random number stream continues to be used. This is used to reset counters after a run has warmed up or to batch several runs in a designed experiment into a single run.

SIN{Y} gives the sine of the real-valued expression Y.

STS{X} is the area under the standardized time series for the traced variable X.

TAV{X} is the time average for the traced variable X.

TRI{X} generates a pseudo triangular random variate between 0 and 1 with a mode given by the expression X, with 0<=X<=1.

VAR{X} is the cumulative variance for the traced variable X.

7.2 Reading Data from Your Disk

DISK: The DISK{} function is used to read data files. This function has two arguments: The first argument is the full name of the data file (including the drive and path if necessary), and the second argument is an integer-valued expression telling which entry is to be read. When the index is zero, the file is read sequentially. If the end of a file is reached, reading data continues at the beginning of the file; this is called wrapping around a file. The data file should contain numbers separated by at least one blank. Extra spaces and lines are ignored.

Use an ASCII text editor such as Notepad (found in the **Accessories** file in Windows) to create your data file. It is important that you not use a word processor, since its default data format will likely not work. Type in your values for the data you have collected. Each value needs to be separated by at least one space, not a comma. Commas are not recognized by the `DISK` command in SIGMA. Also make sure that your data represents values. You can use variable names or expressions, but they must have values at the time they are read by your model. Comment lines can be placed in data files by starting the line with `\\`.

Use the **Save** command (under the **File** menu) to save your data with the `.DAT` extension (i.e., `JUNK.DAT`). Make sure to note where the data file has been saved. You can view this output file in SIGMA by selecting **View Output/Text File** under the **File** menu. Select `*.DAT` or simply type in the name of the file. A new window with your file name will appear. You can edit the data from this window.

Some examples: a data file, named `DATA`, on your disk might look like the following:

```
.06   5   4.0   .3   2.   1
```

This is equivalent to the file

```
.06   5   4.0
.3
     2.   1
```

For a real-valued variable, `X`, eight successive evaluations of

```
X=DISK{DATA;0}
```

would in turn assign the eight values of `0.06`, `5.0`, `4.0`, `0.3`, `2.0`, `1.0`, `0.06`, and `5.0` to `X`. After reaching the end of the file, reading would start again at the beginning of the file. The expression `X=DISK{DATA;4}` would assign a value of `0.3` to `X` since `.3` is the fourth entry in the file. Finally, if `I=4`, `X=DISK{DATA;2*I}` would assign a value of `5.0` to `X`. (We wanted the `2*I=8`th entry in the file, and wrapping around occurred.)

As another example, consider the following state change:

```
QUEUE=QUEUE+DISK{SIZE.DAT;RND*5+1}
```

This statement will randomly select one of the first five entries in the file, `SIZE.DAT`, and add it to the value of the variable `QUEUE`. The second argument of this `DISK` function is an index that is a random integer (rounded down) between 1 and 5 inclusive. The above expression can be used, for example, to model arrivals of randomly sized groups of customers to a simulated service facility such as a bus station. The possible group sizes will be listed as five numbers in the disk file named SIZE.DAT. One of the five different group sizes will be selected at random each time the above state change is executed.

7.3 Interactive Execution

ASK: ASK{X} allows you to change the value of the expression X during a run. SIGMA will prompt you for the change; you can enter any expression. Pressing [←Enter] without entering an expression results in no changes being made.

Suppose you wanted to set a value for the variable QUEUE from the keyboard whenever a customer enters and the expression for the state change when a customer enters is QUEUE=QUEUE+1. If you enclose the right-hand side of this equation with the ASK function—i.e., QUEUE=ASK{QUEUE+1}—you can enter any valid expression or number for the new value of QUEUE that you desire. This is illustrated in the model ASKDEMO.MOD on your disk. Of course, you do not need to be prompted by the ASK function to change a running model in SIGMA. Just double-click on an edge or vertex and enter the changes in the dialog box.

Another use of the ASK function is illustrated in FUNCDEMO.MOD. Here, the ASK function appears as an edge attribute on the edge from the DISKFN vertex to the NEXT vertex. The ASK function here allows you to override the value just read in from the disk, if you desire.

Besides allowing interactive simulation (gaming), the ASK function is very useful in debugging a model. You can try various values of variables while your model is running and see when the logic breaks down. For example, in ASKDEMO.MOD, if the server is idle and you enter a value of zero when a customer ENTERs, you will have created a "phantom" customer arrival. This will subsequently cause the QUEUE to become negative when this customer (who did not join the QUEUE) later LEAVEs!

7.4 Bookkeeping Functions

SET: SET{N} resets your SIGMA variables to zero and the random number seed to N. If no argument is given—i.e., SET{ }—then the random number stream continues with its next number. The simulation clock, CLK, is also set to zero. SET{ } returns 1 if successful and 0 if it fails, so it can be used as an edge condition. (In a state change, it should appear only on the right-hand side of an equation.)

SET is useful for running full experiments in batch mode. The model FACTORAL.MOD on your SIGMA disk is a full 2 x 3 factorial experiment (normally requiring 6 runs) done in a single run with the SET function. SET{} does not translate to C or Pascal. A very simple way to replicate is shown in the model INVENTRY.MOD, where several replenishment cycles are replicated; a self-cancelling edge with an edge condition of SET{} is all it takes to shut off the previous cycle.

CLK: CLK is the current simulated time, which is updated automatically when an event occurs. You cannot change CLK.

7.5 Mathematics Functions

PI: PI is defined in SIGMA as 3.14159. Thus, the Ith value of a cosine function at frequency F is COS{2*PI*F*I}. Here the frequency, F, is in oscillations per observation and is a positive number between 0 and .5; otherwise, the cosine and sine functions have arguments in radians. The output spectrum plot in **SIGPLOT** can be examined for a spike at frequency F.

RND: The function RND imitates the sampling of randomly valued fractions called random numbers; they are the key to modeling randomness. Random numbers are assumed to be independent of each other and equally likely to occur anywhere on the interval strictly between zero and one. Random numbers are more properly called pseudo-random numbers since they are not truly random by any reasonable notion of randomness; they just look random.

For every run you make of a SIGMA model, you supply a "seed" (in the **Run Options** dialog box) for the random number generator that produces values of RND. Different seeds will produce different random number sequences.

Like the CLK function, you use RND as if it were an ordinary state variable. You also do not assign values to RND; they are given to you. We can use RND to model a random variable since every time RND appears in an expression it will have a different value.

Here are some examples: If X is defined as a real-valued state variable, then

X=2*RND and X=RND+RND

are not equivalent statements. X=2*RND takes a single random number and doubles it, producing a value for X that imitates a uniformly distributed random variable between 0 and 2. On the other hand, X=RND+RND takes two different random numbers and adds them. This produces a value of X that also falls between 0 and 2 but has a symmetric triangular-shaped distribution. The expression

```
X=M+R*RND
```

will produce artificial values of X that are independent and uniformly distributed with a minimum value of M and a range of R—i.e., between M and M+R. If you define X to be integer-valued, it will be rounded down to the nearest integer from M to M+R-1. We will discuss random numbers in more detail in Chapter 9, where using multiple random number streams in a single model is explained.

7.6 Cycling Using the MOD Function

MOD: MOD{X;Y} gives the integer remainder when the rounded down integer value of expression X is divided by the rounded down integer value of expression Y. If X takes on successive values of 0,1,2,3,4,5,6,7,..., then MOD{X;4} repeats the cycle 0,1,2,3,0,1,2,3,0,1,2,3,....

One common use of the MOD function is to keep track of individual transient entities in a model (if you do not want to use SIGMA's PUT and GET functions). Array sizes are kept small by recycling indices. Say you want to keep track of individual customer waiting times in a simulated queue. Let WAIT[ID] be the waiting time of the customer whose identification number is ID. Assume that no more than M customers will be in the system at one time and they exit in the same order that they arrive. When a customer arrives, make the following state changes in the corresponding ENTER vertex:

```
ID=MOD{ID+1;M},WAIT[ID]=CLK
```

When the customer departs, make the state change

```
WAIT[ID]=CLK-WAIT[ID]
```

Of course, the customer ID must be passed as an edge attribute throughout the graph to identify which customer is being served. If you recycle array indices in this manner, you must be careful not to reuse an index before it is released by a transient entity leaving the system.

It is important to check that the number of transient entities (customers) in the system never exceeds M. Even this will not ensure that entity IDs are not duplicated. This is another advantage of resident entity models. In effect, we are modeling a capacitated queue with finite waiting room for, at most, M customers. If M is large, this is not a serious issue.

As another example of how the MOD function can be used, consider a bank where there are three tellers (numbered 0, 1, and 2). Each teller takes a 5 minute break once every hour, with a different teller going on break every 20 minutes. If the variable NEXT is the teller that is next to go on break, then the statement NEXT=MOD{NEXT+1;3} would make sure that the breaks rotated properly by generating the sequence 0,1,2,0,1,2,0,....

As a final example, consider a sensitive machining operation where a 10 second recalibration is needed for every 5 parts produced. If the normal processing time was 7 seconds and N the part number, the resulting processing delay would be 7+10*(MOD{N;5}==0). The Boolean variable will be equal to 1 once every 5 parts, adding the 10 second recalibration time to the edge delay.

7.7 Using Ranked Lists

> **PUT** and **GET:** Ranked queues occur whenever the order of service might differ from the order of customer arrival. SIGMA has two functions that make it very easy to model priority ranked queues and lists: The PUT function puts entries onto lists and the GET function gets entries off of lists.

Two arrays, ENT[] and RNK[], are used by the PUT and GET functions. We will describe the purpose of these two arrays first.

The ENT[] array is used exclusively as a buffer for customers joining ranked queues using the PUT{} and GET{} functions described below. Attributes of individual transient entities (customers in a queueing system) can be assigned to the elements in the array ENT[]. For example, ENT[0] might be the customer arrival time, ENT[1] the class of service, and ENT[2] the amount of product to be purchased. The state change vector

```
ENT[0]=CLK, ENT[1]=CLASS, ENT[2]=DEMAND
```

might then model the relevant attributes of a customer.

The array RNK[LINE] contains the index of the element of the ENT[] array that is to be used in determining a customer's position in the line designated by the integer LINE.

The PUT{OPTION;LIST} function places the current contents of the ENT[] array in the LIST. The elements of the temporary buffer, ENT, are typically the values of attributes of customers that are joining the queue. LIST is a number, variable, or function that identifies the queue to be joined. PUT{}OPTIONs include:

1 or FIF (first-is-first)—inserts the new entity after the last record on the LIST.

2 or LIF (last-is-first)—inserts the new entity before the first record on the LIST.

3 or INC (increasing)—the LIST is ranked by increasing values of ENT[X], where X=RNK[LIST] is the ranking entity attribute.

4 or DEC (decreasing)—the LIST is ranked by decreasing values of ENT[X], where X=RNK[LIST] is the ranking entity attribute.

5 or EVN (even)—when the values of ENT[0] for two entities are even, the tie is broken by increasing values of ENT[2], with remaining ties broken by "first-is-first."

GET{OPTION;LIST} removes a record from the specified LIST according to the OPTION chosen and places its contents in the ENT[] array. GET{}OPTIONs include:

1 or FST (first)—removes the first entry of LIST.

2 or LST (last)—removes the last entry of LIST.

3 or KEY (key)—removes the first entry of LIST (if any) whose value of ENT[0] matches the current value of ENT[0].

Both PUT{} and GET{} return 1 if successful and 0 otherwise. These functions should not be used as part of an edge condition that might be false since PUT and GET are executed regardless. If used in a state change, they should appear only on the right-hand side of an equation, such as

QUEUE[N]=QUEUE[N]+PUT{FIF;N}.

This state change will increase QUEUE[N] (the length of the Nth queue) by 1 when the customer with attributes currently in the ENT[] array is put into this queue. The customer can be removed later (with attributes placed in ENT[]) with the state change

QUEUE[N]=QUEUE[N]-GET{FST;N}.

NOTES:

1. The list with the largest index is the future events list.
2. PUT{} and GET{} return 1 if successful and 0 if not.
3. Like other SIGMA functions, a semicolon is used between arguments.
4. Redundant options are for clarity. For example: either pair, (PUT{FIF;1} and GET{FST;1}) or (PUT{LIF;1} and GET{LST;1}), could be used for a first-come-first-served queue.
5. The models SORT.MOD and PRIORTYQ.MOD on thc SIGMA disk illustrate the use of PUT{} and GET{} to sort random numbers and model a priority queue.

7.7.1 Example: Time-Constrained Processing

The SIGMA ranked lists functions, PUT and GET, are illustrated with an example of time-constrained processing. Time-constrained processing is where two processes must be performed within a certain interval. Examples

Figure 7.1: Event Graph of a Time-Constrained Sequence

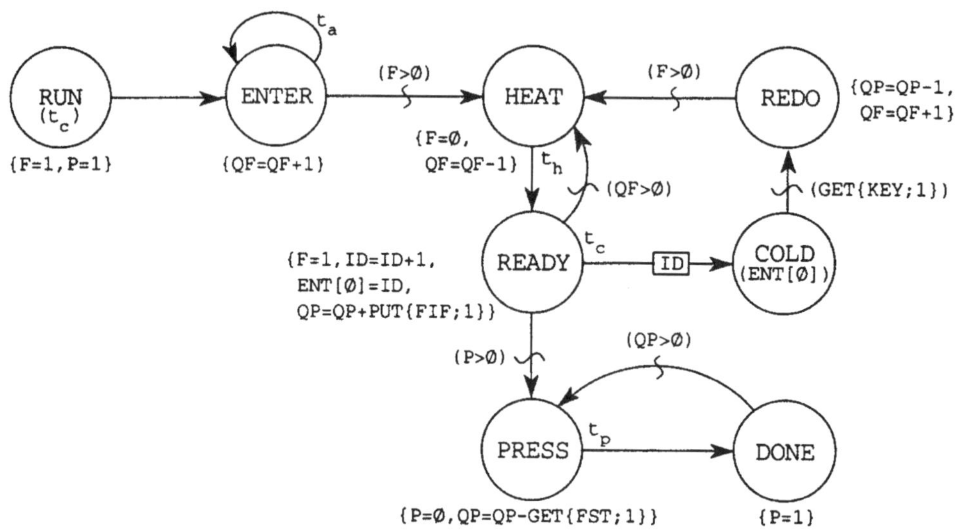

of time-constrained processes are common in semiconductor manufacturing, metal foundries, and where priming, preheating, or cleaning is required before performing a major processing step.

For this example, consider a heat and press sequence. Parts arrive every t_a minutes and must be heated in a furnace (for t_h minutes) before they can be pressed by a mold press machine (for t_p minutes). The interarrival times and both processing steps are somewhat random. The sequence is time-constrained because there is a maximum cooling time limit (t_c) after a part is heated during which the pressing step must start. If a part waits longer than t_c minutes after being heated before pressing starts, it must be returned to the furnace for reheating. We will identify each part waiting for the mold press with an ID number that is sequentially assigned after the part has been heated. F and P will denote the status of the furnace and press, respectively, (1=IDLE, 0=BUSY). QF and QP will denote the number of parts in the queue waiting for the furnace and press.

The event graph for this model, which is shown in Figure 7.1, is the complete simulation model. It might seem rather complicated at first glance; however, one of the most appealing features of event graph modeling is that the logic in each vertex, along with its exiting edges, can be verified in isolation. The graph naturally decomposes into vertices and sets of exiting edges that can be examined separately; the graph automatically ties everything together. We read the model in Figure 7.1 by examining one vertex at a time along with its set of exiting edges; ignore the rest of the graph as you read each of the following paragraphs. This model is called TIMEOUT.MOD on your SIGMA disk.

> The RUN vertex makes the furnace and press initially idle and requests a value for the cooling limit, t_c. The first part is then scheduled to ENTER the system.
>
> When a new part ENTERs the queue for the furnace, QF is incremented. If the furnace is idle (F>0), the part can be HEATed. The ENTER vertex also schedules successive new part arrivals.
>
> When HEATing starts, the furnace becomes busy (F=0) and the number of parts waiting for the furnace, QF, is decremented. After a heating time of t_h, the part is READY for pressing.
>
> When a part is READY for the mold press, the furnace is unloaded (F=1), an ID number is assigned to the part, and the part is PUT into the queue for the mold machine, QP. If there are more parts waiting for the furnace, the next part can be HEATed. If the mold press is idle (P>0), then the PRESS operation can begin immediately. Cooling starts as soon as the part is READY for the press. If part ID does not start its PRESS operation before t_c, it will become COLD and need to be sent back to the furnace.
>
> When the COLD event occurs, the cooling limit for part ID has been reached. The condition on the edge from COLD to REDO checks if the cold part is still waiting to be pressed using the GET function with the KEY option. If this part is not still waiting in the mold press queue (list 1), it must have already started its pressing step. In this case, the GET function will not find a match and returns a value of 0; this makes the edge condition false, and the REDO event will not be scheduled. Note that the ID value of the part is passed from the READY vertex to the COLD vertex as an edge attribute. This ID value is placed in ENT[0] to be used as the match KEY in the GET function to see if that particular part is still waiting for the mold press when it became cold.
>
> In the REDO vertex, if the cold part is still in the queue for the mold press (that is, part ID is still waiting in list 1), the part is removed from the press queue (QP=QP-1) and placed back in the queue for the furnace (QF=QF+1). If the furnace is idle, then HEATing can begin.
>
> The PRESS operation will GET a part out of the queue (if the COLD event has not already removed it) and make the press busy. After a pressing time of t_p, the part is DONE. If more parts are in

the mold machine queue (QP>0), the next part waiting (that has not cooled off) can begin its PRESS step.

(See TIMEOUTR.MOD for a model without transient entities.)

7.8 Generating Random Variables

There are several functions in SIGMA that can be used to generate random variables. These include BET{} for beta variates, TRI{} for triangular variates, ERL{} for Erlang variates, GAM{} for highly skewed gamma variates, and NOR{} for normal variates. The use of these functions and the generation of other types of random input are discussed in Chapter 9, on input process modeling.

7.9 Statistical Functions

Several functions have been included in SIGMA for statistical analysis. These functions are primarily for model diagnostics and are not included in the C, Pascal, or FORTRAN translations generated by SIGMA. More thorough statistical analysis of SIGMA-generated models in these languages is possible using the functions available in their corresponding libraries or using the **SIGPLOT** utility as discussed in Chapter 10. Note that the variables used as arguments in these functions must have been used as traced variables for at least one previous run in the current SIGMA session. The more commonly used statistical functions included in SIGMA are as follows:

AVE{X}, which is the cumulative average of the traced variable X,

VAR{X}, which is the cumulative variance of the traced variable X,

TAV{X}, which is the time average of the traced variable X, and

STS{X}, which is the area under the standardized time series for the traced variable X.

The *cumulative* average simply counts the recorded values of a variable and averages them, whereas the *time* average takes into account how much simulated time the variable spends at a particular value. These functions can be nested in creative ways. For example, VAR{AVE{X}} will be the variance of the average. This expression can be used, along with batching, to tell if the simulated run duration is long enough to obtain a desired relative or absolute precision of an estimator. Statistical analysis of simulation run output is discussed in Chapter 10. For examples of using these statistical functions see IIDNOR.MOD, which computes statistics from a sample of independent, identically-distributed, normal pseudo-random variates.

Table 7.1: Quick Reference to SIGMA Functions

Function	Action
`ASK{X}`	Allows expression to be changed during a run
`AVE{X}`	Cumulative average
`BET{X;Y}`	A pseudo beta random variate
`CLK`	The current simulated clock time
`COS{Y}`	The cosine function
`DISK{F;I}`	Reads data from disk files
`ERL{X}`	A standard Erlang random variate
`GAM{X}`	A fractional shaped pseudo gamma variate
`GET{O;L}`	Gets records from list L using option O
`LN{Y}`	The natural log
`MAX{Y;X}`	The maximum
`MIN{Y;X}`	The minimum
`MOD{Y;X}`	The modulus operator
`NOR{M;S}`	A pseudo normal random variate
`PI`	The constant 3.14159
`PUT{O;L}`	Puts records on list L using option O
`RND`	A pseudo-random number
`SET{N}`	Resets variables to zero and seed to N
`SIN{Y}`	The sine function
`STS{X}`	Standardized time series area
`TAV{X}`	Time average
`TRI{X}`	A pseudo triangular random variate
`VAR{X}`	Cumulative variance

Some of the more commonly used SIGMA functions are summarized in Table 7.1.

7.10 Exercises

7.10.1 A Priority Serving System

(a) The system administrators of a mainframe computer have devised a method of partitioning processing time. Every job submitted to the mainframe is assigned a priority: urgent and not urgent. When two jobs have the same priority, the first one submitted is processed first. However, when two jobs are of different priority, the job with the higher priority is always processed first. Urgent jobs arrive at a rate uniformly distributed between 3 and 5 hours and have required processing times uniformly distributed between 1 and 10 hours. Jobs that are not urgent arrive at a rate uniformly distributed between 30 minutes and 1 hour and have processing times uniformly distributed between 15 minutes and 2 hours. Model the mainframe queue assuming every job, once it is started, is finished without pre-emption.

(b) Now model the mainframe queue where jobs can be pre-empted by priority. In other words, if a job is submitted to the mainframe while a job of lower priority is processing, the lower priority job is discontinued until the job of higher priority finishes. When a pre-empted job returns to the mainframe, it does not need to be entirely reprocessed. It is processed only for the required time remaining when it was pre-empted. Use the `PUT` and `GET` functions in modeling this system.

7.10.2 Empirical Distributions

How can the function `DISK{FILE;I}` be used to generate a random variable from an empirical distribution function with data in the disk file `FILE`? (Hint: Consider a random index, `I`.)

8

Building Animations

Animations created with SIGMA are fundamentally different from those using other simulation animation software. Most simulation modeling environments have a separate program for the simulation and an add-on program for animation; in SIGMA the simulation and the animation are identical. The event graph model becomes the animation. Animating a SIGMA model is extremely simple; you are limited only by your imagination and the speed and memory of your computer. In the tutorial that follows, we will develop a simple animation, use it to find an error in our model, and then fix the error.

8.1 Perspective and Basic Principles

Animations are one of the more entertaining aspects of simulation modeling. However, it is important to keep them in perspective. Animations are most useful during model development and testing. Their main strength is in helping to find gross logic errors in a model. Once a model is developed and experiments are being run, animations have almost no practical value. Output plots and spreadsheet statistics are the major tools for analysis. Finally, after a study is completed and different systems are being demonstrated, animations once again become very useful.

While animations are useful verification and demonstration techniques, there are some disadvantages to keep in mind. Animations have little analytical value. Modifying a system based on the experiences of a few minutes or even a few hours of animated operations is not wise. As a demonstration, the time spent by managers watching even the most carefully crafted animation is typically several minutes. The requirements for an animation will almost always force you to develop a more cumbersome model than necessary, with many details that are added simply to support the animation. Take, for example, a system with 100 machines processing thousands of parts an hour.

We can *simulate* this system with an event graph having only three or four vertices. If one hundred machines are added, the model does not change. To *animate* the system, a different representation will be needed for each machine. This is true regardless of the particular simulation software you are using. However, it is easy to add the detail necessary for an animation to an event graph by connecting additional subgraphs.

Animating a SIGMA model is simple. The balls that represent event vertices are replaced by two types of pictures: one image appears when the vertex executes (active), and the other appears after the vertex executes (inactive). These two pictures are in the form of bitmaps that are selected from the **Edit Vertex** dialog box by clicking on the **Active Picture** or **Inactive Picture** button. For fancy animations, the pictures can be actual scanned photographs or pictures from a digital camera. They can also be simple drawings created by a drawing program. In our tutorial, we will use pictures created with the **Paintbrush** utility that comes with Windows.

Each individual picture used in SIGMA cannot be larger than 64,000 bytes; however, you can use as many pictures as your computer's memory or version of SIGMA will allow. Hint: If you are creating pictures using Windows **Paintbrush**, limit the picture sizes to less than two or three inches square using the **Options/Attributes** menu item. Save them as 16 bit pictures using the **Save As** option.

The fancier the pictures, the more impressive the animation will be. However, remember that others will probably not spend more than a few minutes looking at your animation.

8.2 Classes of Animated Objects

To get started, it will be helpful if we think of the physical entities in a system as belonging to one of three classes:

1. *Static resident entities* (such as halls and windows in a building): These entities do not change their appearance when the state of the system changes during a simulation run.
2. *Dynamic resident entities* (such as machines): These entities may change their appearance when the state of the system changes, but they remain at the same location.
3. *Transient entities* (such as parts, customers, and cars): These entities may change both their appearance and location while a simulation is running.

The three classes of physical entities are represented by different combinations of active and inactive pictures. For static resident entities, the active and inactive pictures are identical.

Figure 8.1: Strings of Vertices Added to `ENTER` and `LEAVE` Events of `CARWASH.MOD`—Cars Entering and Leaving Facility

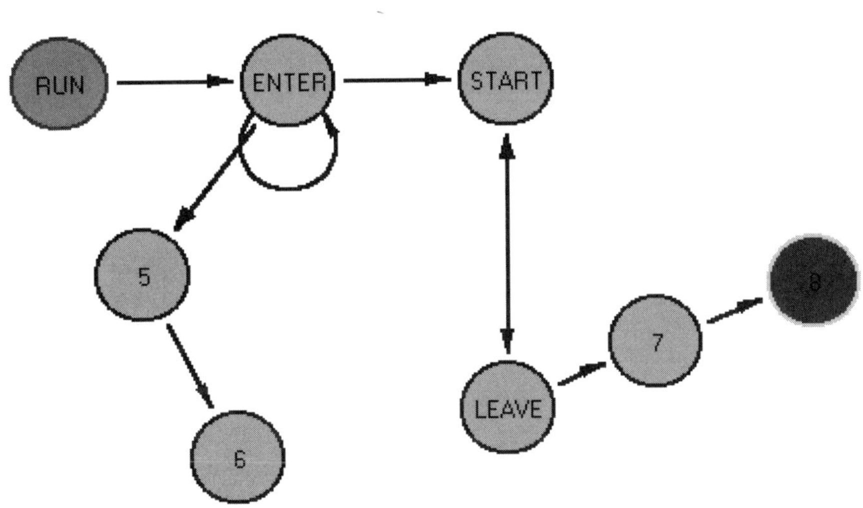

Dynamic resident entities typically will have different active and inactive pictures; the active picture represents a transitional state, and the inactive picture represents the state immediately after the vertex executes. Furthermore, a dynamic resident entity will often have several vertices stacked (or "grouped") on top of each other so that only the picture of the current state of the entity is showing. You can think of the inactive pictures for the grouped vertices associated with a dynamic resident entity as the frames of a video of the entity and the active pictures as transitions between these video frames that smooth out the motion.

Transient entities will have an active picture that is a representation of the entity and an inactive picture that is blank. Some of the vertices in our original event graph might trigger some movement of a transient entity. For example, in the carwash model, the `ENTER` event might trigger a dirty car to enter the carwash and a `LEAVE` event might trigger a clean car to depart from the carwash. This movement would be represented by a string of vertices along the transient entity path of motion triggered by the event. For example, Figure 8.1 shows our original carwash model with a string of vertices attached to the `ENTER` and `LEAVE` events.

When the active pictures are represented by clean and dirty cars and the inactive pictures are represented by blank pictures the size of the cars, the result will be like Figure 8.2. (The **Select All** button in the **Edit** menu was pressed to show all the animation elements.)

Figure 8.2: Strings of Vertices Added with Active Pictures Showing—Represents Cars Entering and Leaving the Carwash Facility

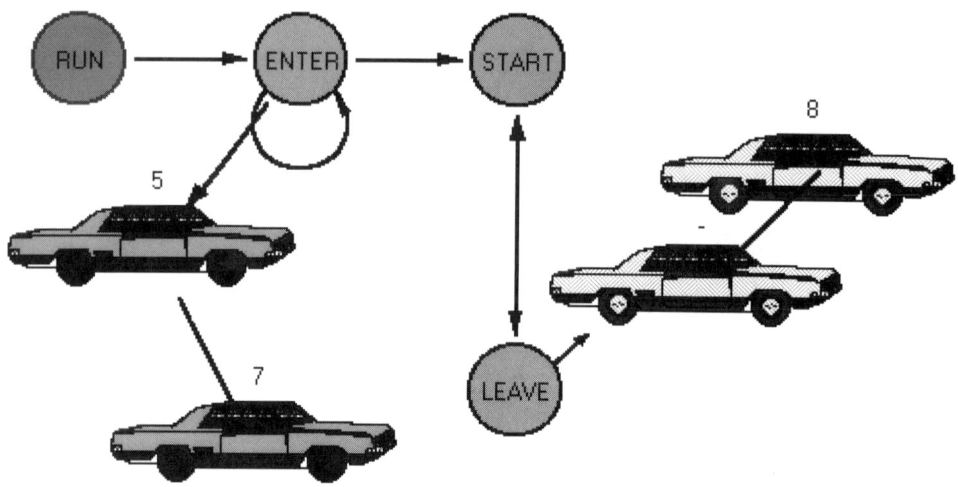

These paths of motion are very easy to create. Simply use the **Create Single Edge** tool to create the first vertex in the string. Edit the active picture for the new vertex so that it is a bitmap of the transient entity; have the inactive picture be a *blank* bitmap the same size as the transient entity. Next select the **Create Process** tool and click a string of vertices that can later be moved along the desired path of motion. (The string of vertices will have the previous pictures as defaults.)

Bitmaps of the proper size are easily created using the Windows **Paintbrush** utility and sized using the **Image Attributes** command in the **Options** menu. Clipping scanned photographs of the transient entity will make the animation look more like a video movie.

The delay times on the edges between these transient entity motion vertices can be set to represent actual move times, including acceleration and deceleration. The **Time Steps** run default mode along with a `TIMER` vertex should help make the motion smoother. (A "timer" is a self-scheduling vertex

Table 8.1: Physical Entities and Picture Representations for Animations

Physical Entity	Active Picture/ Inactive Picture	"Groups" of Stacked Vertices
Dynamic Resident Entity	Transition/ Ending State	Yes
Static Resident Entity	Same Picture for Both	No
Transient Entity	Picture/Blank	No

with an edge delay time of one time unit.) If you have a slow computer, you might change some of the edges between the transient entity motion vertices to be pre-emptive edges (`delay=*`). However, have no more than four or five pre-emptive edges execute in a sequence. If there are more than five in a sequence, increase your Windows stack to avoid a stack overflow.

The three types of entities are summarized in Table 8.1.

8.3 Tutorial: Animating Resident Entities

We will animate a simulation model from the SIGMA disk, `BRKDN.MOD`. This model represents a single machine, with periodic failures, that processes parts that arrive at random times. We will use each of the three basic types of animated objects discussed earlier, beginning with dynamic resident entities. The event graph for `BRKDN.MOD` is shown in Figure 8.3. Follow along on your computer as we animate this model.

Figure 8.3: Event Graph of `BRKDN.MOD`

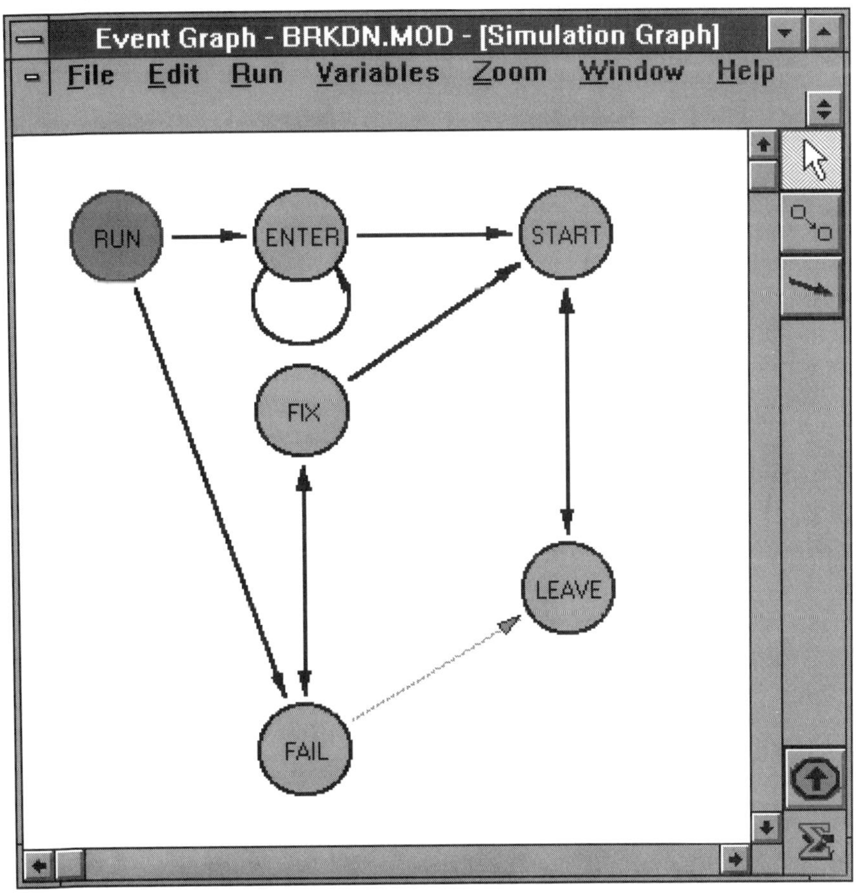

Start a SIGMA *session.*

Open the model BRKDN.MOD.

To represent the states of the queue (a dynamic resident entity), we will use a subgraph on your SIGMA directory called QSIZE.MOD. You should minimize the current SIGMA window and open a *separate* SIGMA session from the Windows **Program Manager**. Read QSIZE.MOD into this new SIGMA session. The event graph should look like Figure 8.4.

Click the **Minimize** *button on the* BRKDN.MOD SIGMA *session.*

Return to the **Program Manager** *and double-click on the* **SIGMA** *icon to open a second session.*

Click the **Open** *command under the* **File** *menu, locate* QSIZE.MOD, *and double-click on it.*

Figure 8.4: Event Graph for QSIZE.MOD, with Inactive Pictures Showing

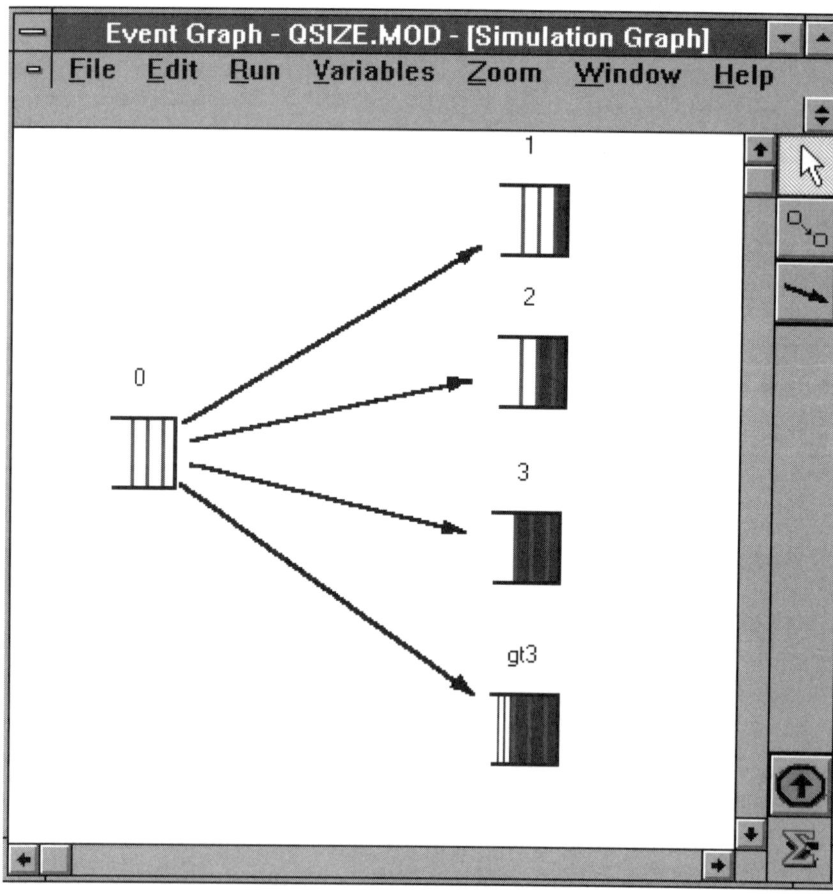

In `QSIZE.MOD`, simple active and inactive pictures drawn with the Windows **Paintbrush** utility represent the different states of a queue. Vertices represent `0`, `1`, `2`, `3`, and `>3` customers in the queue. The variable `QSIZE` represents the current size of the queue. If you explore `QSIZE.MOD` a bit, you will notice that vertex `0` has `QSIZE` passed to it as a parameter. Also note that the values of `QSIZE` are tested on each of the edges to see which picture is appropriate. Click on the vertices and edges to see how `QSIZE.MOD` works. It is very simple and serves no purpose other than animation. Do not "save" `QSIZE.MOD` if you change it, but rather "read" it into your SIGMA session again.

The next step will be to copy `QSIZE.MOD` and paste it into your other SIGMA session with the model `BRKDN.MOD`.

For `QSIZE.MOD`*, click the* **Select All** *command under the* **File** *menu.*

Click the **Copy** *command under the* **Edit** *menu.*

Click the **Minimize** *button on the* `QSIZE.MOD` *simulation window.*

Double-click on the `BRKDN.MOD` **SIGMA** *icon to maximize that event graph.*

Click on the **Paste** *command under the* **Edit** *menu for* `BRKDN.MOD`.

Hold the mouse button down on one of the newly copied vertices of `QSIZE.MOD` and drag the entire subgraph off to the side. (You might have to re-select these vertices by holding [↑Shift] and clicking on them to drag the selected subgraph out of the way.) If your screen looks something like Figure 8.5, the transfer was successful, and you can close the SIGMA session with `QSIZE.MOD`. The model in Figure 8.5 is called `BRKANIM1.MOD` in your SIGMA directory.

Drag the `QSIZE.MOD` *subgraph off to the side of* `BRKDN.MOD`.

Click the **Minimize** *button on the* `BRKDN.MOD` *event graph.*

Double-click on the `QSIZE.MOD` **SIGMA** *icon, and then press* [Alt-F4] *to close the* `QSIZE.MOD` **SIGMA** *session.*

Double-click on the `BRKDN.MOD` **SIGMA** *icon.*

Now we will simply wire the new `QSIZE.MOD` subgraph into our model by drawing two edges: one edge from the `ENTER` event to the `0` vertex of `QSIZE.MOD` and the other edge from the `START` event to the `0` vertex of `QSIZE.MOD`. These two edges should pass the attribute value of `QUEUE` (into the `QSIZE` parameter of vertex `0`) to let the subgraph know the current number of parts in the system. The delay time for these edges should be zero (`delay=0`), and they should be unconditional (`Condition:1==1`). Next, select all of the vertices in `QSIZE.MOD` and stack them on top of each other. This model is `BRKANTM2.MOD` in your SIGMA directory.

Figure 8.5: BRKANIM1.MOD After Pasting QSIZE.MOD into BRKDN.MOD

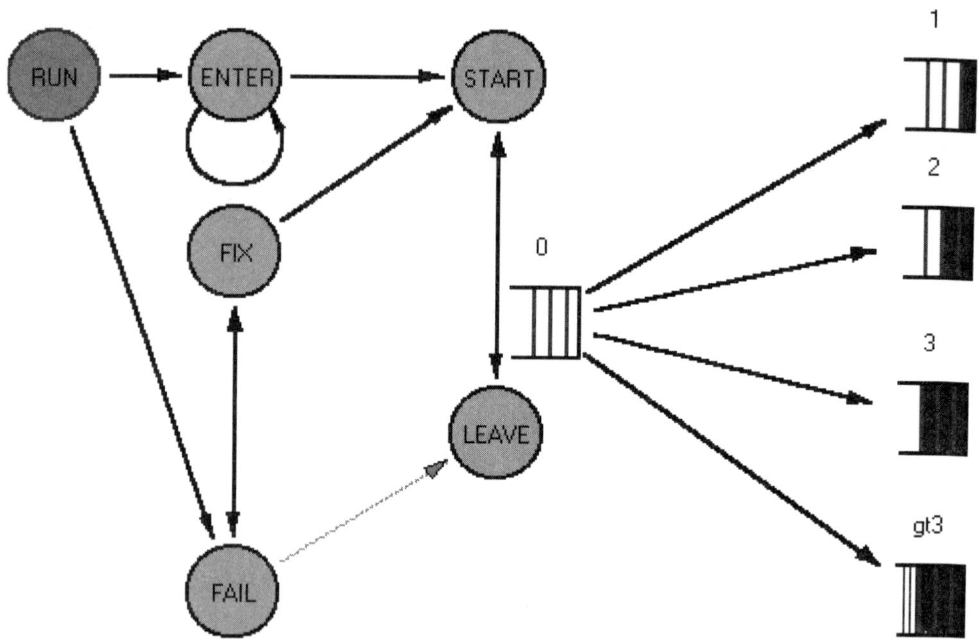

Click on the **Create Single Edge** *tool.*

Create an edge from the ENTER *vertex of* BRKDN.MOD *to vertex* 0 *of the* QSIZE.MOD *subgraph with* QUEUE *as its attribute value.*

Create another edge from the START *vertex of* BRKDN.MOD *to vertex* 0 *of the* QSIZE.MOD *subgraph with* QUEUE *as its attribute value.*

Highlight the QSIZE.MOD *subgraph by lassoing the vertices or pressing* [↑Shift] *and clicking the mouse.*

Click the **Group Vertices** *command under the* **Edit** *menu.*

Now we will assign pictures to the other vertices according to Table 8.2. Note that the *static resident entity* of the track is represented by the RUN vertex and has the same active and inactive pictures. The ENTER vertex represents a *transient entity* (part) entering the system; it has a blank bitmap for its inactive picture. The four vertices (START, LEAVE, FAIL, and FIX) represent various events for the machine, which is a *dynamic resident entity.* These vertices have transitional bitmaps as their active pictures; their inactive pictures represent the state of the machine immediately after the event occurs. The resulting model is BRKANIM3.MOD in your SIGMA directory.

Table 8.2: The Assignment of Bitmaps to Active and Inactive Pictures for BRKANIM3.MOD

Vertex	Representing	Type of Entity	Active Picture	Inactive Picture
RUN	A Section of Track	Static Resident	TRACK.BMP	TRACK.BMP
ENTER	A Customer	Transient	CUSTOMER.BMP	BLANK.BMP
START	Machine Working (Yellow)	Dynamic Resident	START.BMP	BUSY.BMP
LEAVE	Machine Available (Green)	Dynamic Resident	LEAVE.BMP	IDLE.BMP
FAIL	Machine Broken (Red)	Dynamic Resident	FAIL.BMP	BROKEN.BMP
FIX	Machine Available (Green)	Dynamic Resident	FIX.BMP	IDLE.BMP

Double-click on the RUN *vertex to open the* **Edit Vertex** *dialog box.*

Press the **Inactive Picture** *button to open a dialog box with a list of bitmaps.*

Scroll through the list until TRACK.BMP *is located; double-click on it.*

Press the **Active Picture** *button, locate* TRACK.BMP, *and double-click on it.*

Press the **OK** *button at the bottom of the dialog box.*

Repeat this process with all the vertices, using the active and inactive pictures specified in Table 8.2.

Next, we will group the four vertices that represent the various states of the machine (START, LEAVE, FAIL, and FIX) and then combine the objects on the screen. The resulting animation, BRKANIM4.MOD, looks something like Figure 8.6.

Highlight the START, LEAVE, FIX, *and* FAIL *vertices using* [↑Shift] *and the mouse.*

Click on the **Group Vertices** *command under the* **Edit** *menu.*

Click on the **Select All** *command under the* **Edit** *menu.*

Next, click the **Hide Selected Edges** *command also under the* **Edit** *menu.*

Drag the objects to locations similar to those in Figure 8.6.

You should load BRKANIM4.MOD and run it to see what happens. The simulation has become the animation. An add-on animation program would add an unnecessary layer of software between you and your model. Try clicking on some of the objects in BRKANIM4.MOD; you can use the **Ungroup**

Figure 8.6: Event Graph for BRKANIM4.MOD, a Resident Entity Animation of BRKDN.MOD

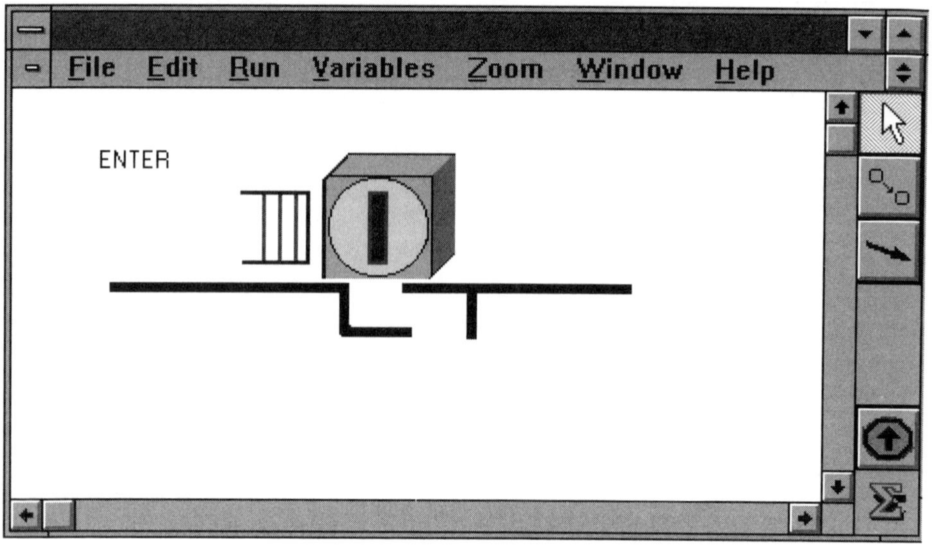

Vertices and **Show All Edges** commands under the **Edit** menu. You can double-click on vertices or edges and change their behaviors.

You will soon notice that the animated model, BRKANIM4.MOD, is a bit dull. This is because we have not yet added transient entities to our animation. It is the transient entities that move across the screen and bring our animations to life.

8.4 Tutorial Continuation: Animating Transient Entity Motion

Adding transient entity motion is quite simple in SIGMA. As discussed earlier, you simply attach a string of vertices to an event that will represent the path of motion for the transient entity when the event occurs. The active picture for transient entity vertices is a picture of the entity. In our example a simple colored bitmap of a bar is used to represent the part moving to and from the machine. Transient entities have a *blank* inactive picture the same size as their active picture. The active picture flashes at the current location of the transient entity. This picture is then blanked out when the transient entity moves on. The vertices in such a string will typically have no state changes associated with them and are connected with an unconditional edge with preemptive or high priority execution (delay=*). Figure 8.7 illustrates adding a transient entity leaving the machine after the LEAVE event. (The **Select All** command was clicked to show the active pictures of the new vertices.).

Figure 8.7: Adding a String of Vertices to Represent the Movement of a Transient Entity

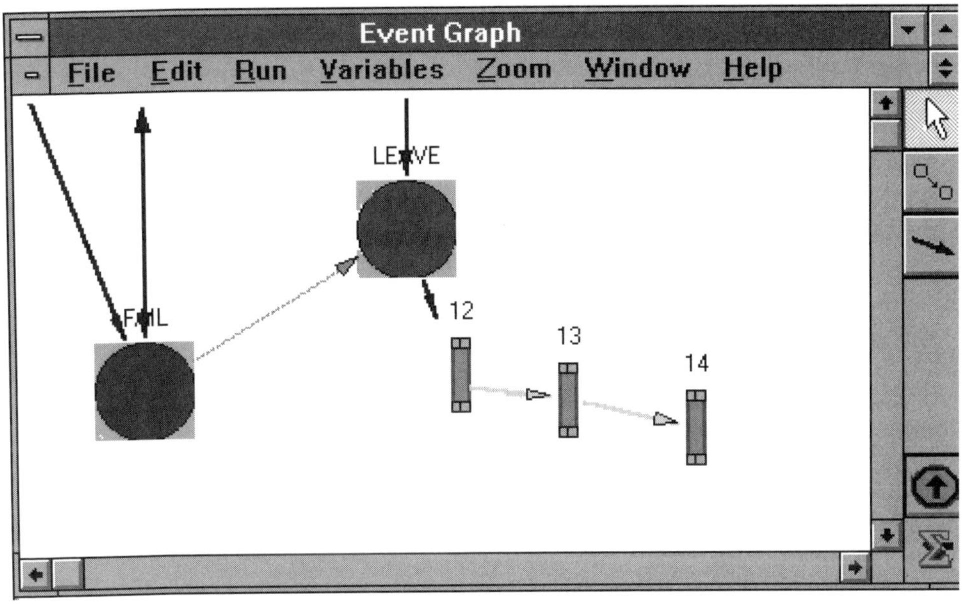

> ➢ **Important:** *Do not connect more than four or five vertices in a row with edges that have a delay of *. Insert an edge with zero delay to avoid a stack overflow condition.*

- *Open* `BRKANIM4.MOD` *or continue with the model you have been developing.*
- *Click once on the group of vertices represented by the box. This will be the starting point for the path followed by a transient entity.*
- *Since the starting point of the transient entity must be a vertex, click the* **Ungroup Vertices** *command under the* **Edit** *menu to ungroup these vertices.*
- *Click the right button to get into* **Create Process** *mode; click the left mouse button on the location of the first point of the transient entity path.*
- *Note that the vertex you create will be a duplicate of the last vertex created when building the model.*

- *Double-click on this new vertex.*
- *Assign* CUSTOMER.BMP *to the* **Active Picture** *and* BLANK.BMP *to the* **Inactive Picture**. *Press the* **OK** *button in the dialog box to incorporate the new images into the event graph.*
- *Check to see whether this is successful by clicking on a blank space; the transient entity image should disappear.*
- *Click again under the number of the new vertex; the transient entity image should reappear.*
- *Click on the right button to get into* **Create Process** *mode.*
- *Click several times along the path to be followed by the transient entity. (All you should see are the edges of the transient entity path.)*
- *Press the right button to get into* **Select or Edit** *mode.*
- *Click on the* **Select All** *command under the* **Edit** *menu.*
- *Click on the* **Hide Selected Edges** *command under the* **Edit** *menu.*
- *Click on any blank space to deselect the vertices. All the transient entities should disappear, leaving just the numbers of each break-point in the path of motion.*
- *When you run the simulation, the numbers at the break-point vertices along the transient entity path will disappear.*
- **Hint:** *Put a very high execution priority (low number) on each edge along the transient entity path if you want the transient entity to complete its movement before any other vertex executes.*
- *Press the* **Start Run** *tool to see the transient entity path in motion.*

A string of vertices was added to the ENTER event to show the part entering and to the FAIL event to show a part being discarded. The model is BRKANIM5.MOD in your SIGMA directory and is shown in Figure 8.8. Again, the **Select All** option was clicked to show all parts of the animation.

You should load and run BRKANIM5.MOD and observe how it works. The local display variables, INPUT, GOOD, and BAD, were added to the model, in addition to QSIZE, to show where each part went.

With the animation, it is rather easy to see that there is an error in the model; the count of discarded bad parts is increased even if the machine fails when it is not working. Since what goes into the system must go somewhere, the following equation should hold:

INPUT = GOOD + BAD + QSIZE + SERVER.

Increasing the number of BAD parts discarded even if the machine failed when empty will cause this balance equation to be invalid. Adding a vertex to

Figure 8.8: BRKANIM5.MOD with Strings of Vertices Representing Transient Entity Paths Added

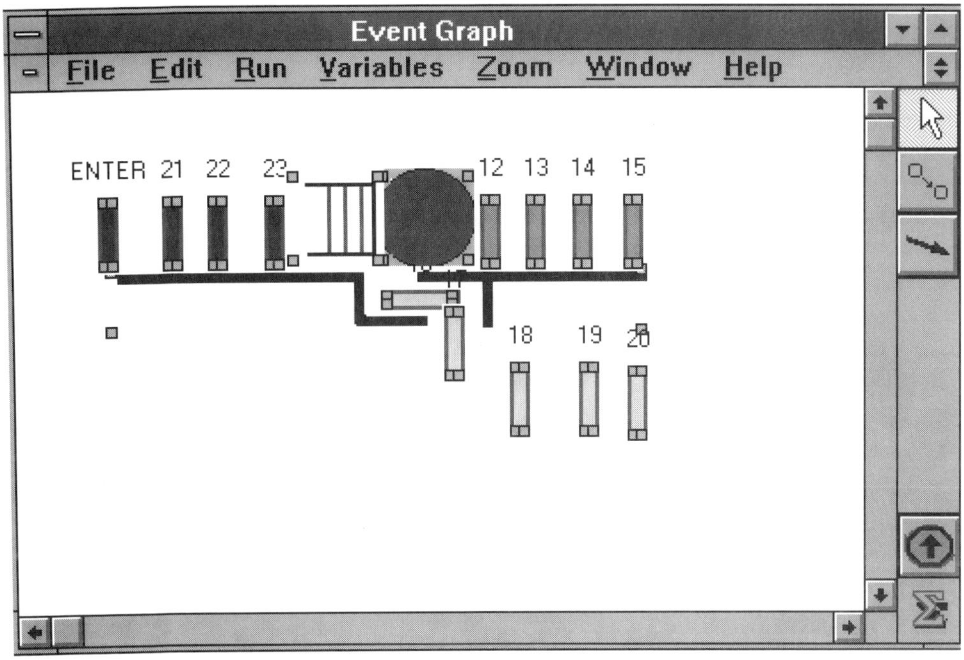

indicate if the machine fails when empty or loaded solves this problem. (See BRKANIM6.MOD on your SIGMA directory.) Note that a puff of smoke is added when the machine fails, using the same technique for adding transient entities.

Our final animation, ANIMATE.MOD, has a machine body with a fancier bitmap and is shown in Figure 8.9. Here we added an animated hammer hitting the machine to fix it.

Other examples of animations have been included on the SIGMA directory, including one with the ubiquitous carwash, ACARWASH.MOD. Also see GPSS.MOD for an animation of a process-oriented simulation language. ROBOT.MOD is an actual animation of a loading robot used in semiconductor manufacturing.

ROBOT.MOD uses the *marionette* animation technique. Here, the simulation event graph is moved out of the visible part of the screen. Connected to the original simulation model is a second graph, which does little but show the animation. The simulation controls the animation subgraph by edges, like the strings to a marionette. To see how this is done, open ROBOT.MOD and click on the **Show All Edges** command in the **Edit** menu. You should also look at some of the bitmaps used in ROBOT.MOD (e.g., POS1.BMP) to see that these are merely rectangular cutouts of a scanned drawing of a robot.

Figure 8.9: An Animation Using Slightly Fancier Bitmaps

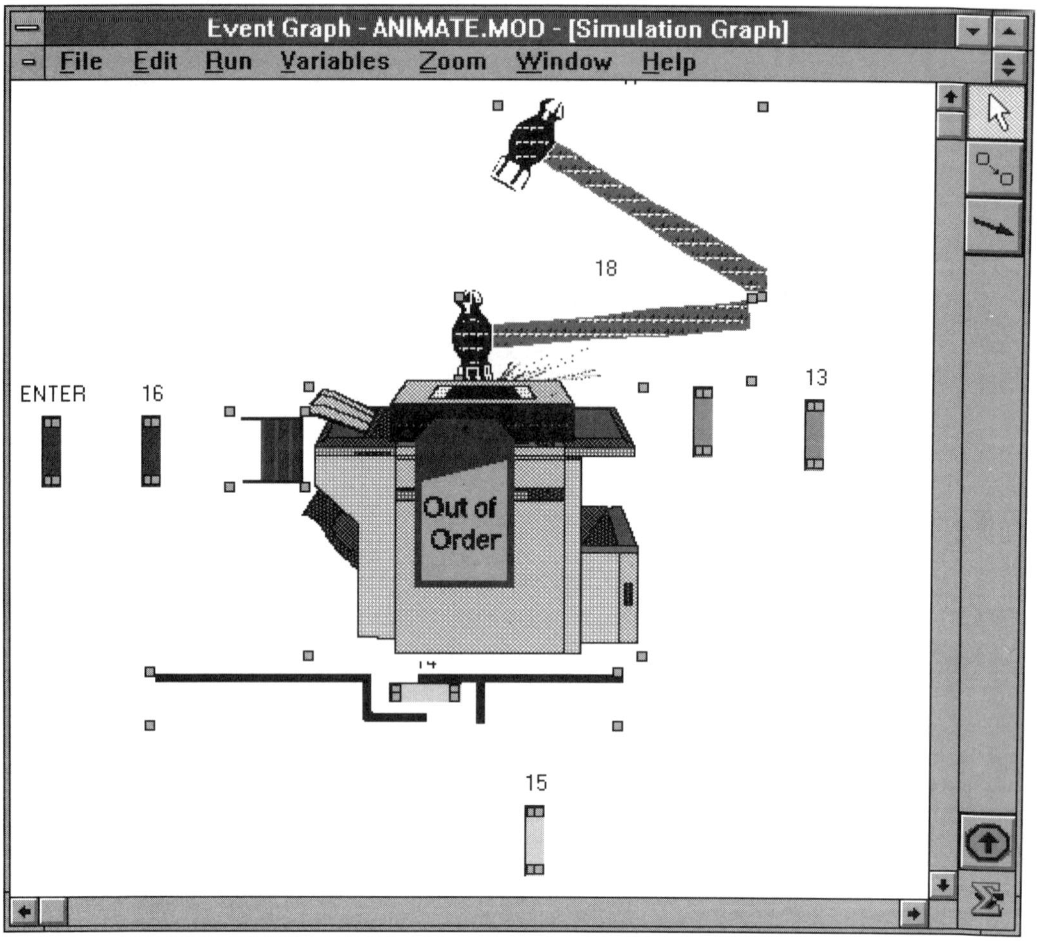

A final note about dynamic resident entities: in some cases it may be necessary to offset some of the pictures in a group representing a dynamic resident entity. For example, we may want to have a robot arm sticking out the side of a machine. The robot arm is part of the resident entity representing the states of the machine (the arm would be represented by a vertex that is grouped with the other machine state vertices). However, it has a blank inactive picture so that the arm would appear to retract. The arm is moved off to the side of the rest of the vertices in this group by slowly clicking on the group (so that it is not interpreted as a double click) until the arm appears. It is moved to the side, down, or up using the arrow keys. The other vertices in the group remain in their previous positions. Using the arrow keys to move a single vertex in a group can also give a sense of realism in animations of living things.

(See TOUCAN.MOD in your SIGMA directory, where the body of the bird was moved slightly using the arrow keys to make it appear to "wiggle.") Moving only one of the vertices in a group with the arrow keys is a powerful animation technique. The saved model has vertex groups listed at the bottom of the file. This shows the group members with their "offsets" from the center of the group.

9

Modeling Input Processes

Discrete event simulations are typically both dynamic (they change over time) and stochastic (they are random). So far, we have concentrated on learning to model the dynamics of a system. In this chapter we will review some of the considerations and techniques for generating random input processes to drive a simulation. Random numbers, trace-driven simulations, parametric input distributions, and empirical input distributions are discussed. The exponential autoregressive process is used to illustrate dependence in the input process. Various sources of data with which to model input processes are presented. A discussion on reusing random number seeds to reduce variance in the output is also included. The chapter closes with some techniques for generating random variates, including the generation of nonhomogeneous Poisson processes. These processes are useful models for generating exogenous events to drive a simulation model.

9.1 Randomness

Although there is much literature in this area, here we will be brief. This is due in part to the fact that simulation modelers rarely write code for this part of their programs. Algorithms for imitating random sampling are well developed, and reliable codes are readily available. Furthermore, while the dynamics of most simulation models are unique, the stochastic logic tends to be the same. Almost all of the simulations we have discussed have had at least one random process in the model. For instance, our carwash model was driven by customers arriving at randomly spaced intervals. We modeled the car arrival process by assuming that the intervals between arrivals were independent and had a uniform probability distribution. Realistic situations can be quite a bit more complicated: cars might arrive at a higher rate during rush hour, on weekends, or on days with nice weather.

Broadly speaking, there are three popular approaches to modeling input processes: using prerecorded data, using sample probability distributions, and using mathematical probability models. Prerecorded data is also called a process "trace," a sample probability distribution is also called an "empirical" distribution, and mathematical probability models are sometimes referred to as theoretical or "parametric" models. All but trace-driven simulations require the use of random numbers.

9.2 Trace-Driven Simulations

In a trace-driven simulation, whenever a value for a random variable is needed by the simulation, it is read from a data file. When it is practical, this input file contains actual historical records. In our carwash example, the trace might be a file of the intervals between successive car arrivals recorded while watching the system. Sometimes only a portion of the input is trace driven. In a fire department simulation, the times and locations of calls might be read from a file with data from a dispatcher's log book while other inputs, such as equipment repair status and travel times, might be generated as they are needed using techniques discussed later in this chapter.

Trace data is simple to read into SIGMA using the `DISK{}` function. Recall that the `DISK` function has two arguments. The first argument is the full name of the data file (with drive and directory path if necessary); the second is an integer index telling which entry is to be read. When the index is zero, the file is read sequentially, wrapping around to start at the beginning again when the end of the file is reached.

We could place the values (separated by at least one space) of times between customer arrivals at our carwash in a data file called `ARRIVAL.DAT`. We then could use the function `DISK{ARRIVAL.DAT;0}` as the delay time on the self-scheduling edge for the `ENTER` vertex that generates successive customer arrivals. If `ARRIVAL.DAT` contains only five observations and looks like the following

```
.32  2.6
.78  4.3  .85
```

then the sequence read by the `DISK{ARRIVAL.DAT;0}` would be

`.32, 2.6, .78, 4.3, .85, .32` (wrapped around) `2.6, ...`

There are some distinct advantages to having the values of random processes read from a data file. Foremost, there is less concern with the validity of the trace input data than when the inputs are artificially generated. Furthermore, trace data captures the dependencies between different input processes or within the same input process. (We will reexamine the question of dependent input later in this chapter.)

When attempting to validate that a model accurately represents the behavior of a real system, there is probably no better test than to simulate previous system behavior using past input data. All discrepancies between the performance of the model and the real system can then be attributed to model assumptions or errors in the simulation code. Accurate representation of the past is a reasonable minimal expectation. However, just because a model closely imitates last year's performance with last year's input data by no means makes the model correct or even useful. Driving a simulation with an artificial data trace rather than historical data is a useful technique for debugging the logic of a model. Specific sequences of otherwise random events can be forced to occur in a model that is being tested or enriched.

Many of the disadvantages of trace-driven simulations are more or less obvious; some are not. While historical data traces provide a valuable source of simulation input when developing or changing a model, traces are not a good general approach to driving a simulation model when it is being used for analysis. Trace-driven simulations require storage space for the data buffers, or they can be very slow due to the significant overhead of reading input files. Historical data that is detailed enough to drive a simulation is probably not available and would be time-consuming and expensive to collect. Actual data is also subject to errors in observation or may be invalid merely due to the intrusion of the observer. Even if detailed data is readily available, the simulation still could not be independently replicated or run for a longer period than the interval for which actual data was collected. In using trace input, we are giving up two of the major advantages to simulation modeling: time compression and independent replication.

Using a historical data trace as input when considering alternative policies or designs is typically not valid. Most trace-driven simulation models are *closed* systems; that is, the laws governing the input processes are not dependent on the state of the simulation. On the other hand, the actual system most likely is an *open* system that influences its environment. All statements about the effect of a change are based on the implicit assumption that the change has no influence on the environment in which the system operates. For example, assuming that a system operates in an inelastic economy; demand is not altered by supply, price, quality, etc. Although they are run all the time, trace-driven, "what if" simulation experiments are often not appropriate. What we most likely want to know is how sensitive the new system might be to changes in the input. It is difficult to do input sensitivity analysis with trace input.

Another disadvantage concerns rare but important events (i.e., a single, very long repair time at a service center). Since an unusual event is, by definition, unlikely to be on any given historical data trace, we may never see its influence in our simulation runs. Perhaps worse, if such a rare event happens to be in our trace, it will occur in every alternative system we simulate. We might choose an alternative that handles this rare event well but is too expensive or does not perform well in more typical situations.

9.3 Random Number Generators

At the heart of stochastic modeling are random numbers. We define random numbers as positive fractions whose values are assumed to be independent of each other and equally likely to occur anywhere between zero and one. Random number generators are algorithms that imitate the sampling of random numbers. In SIGMA, `RND` has its values generated by such an algorithm. The source code for `RND` is given on your disk in the `CSIGLIB.C` file. The algorithm simply takes an integer that you supply as the "seed" and recursively multiplies it by a fixed constant, divides by another constant, and uses the remainder as the next "seed." This remainder is also scaled to lie strictly between zero and one and used as the current value for `RND`. The random number generator we are using originated with Lewis, Goodman, and Miller (1969).

We will forgo a discussion of the philosophy of random number generation. Suffice it to say that, by most common notions of what we mean by randomness, it is impossible to "generate" random numbers. Indeed, there have been some widely used algorithms that generate numbers that look far from random. Perhaps with the exception of the seed you give it, there is nothing whatsoever truly random in the values of `RND` or the outputs from any other random number generator; they just "look" random if you are not overly particular. Any random number generator that has passed all statistical tests for randomness simply has not been tested enough. Nevertheless, modeling random number generators as producing true random numbers has been amazingly successful.

It is very easy to modify the SIGMA-generated source code in C to include multiple random number input streams. This is discussed when we introduce correlation induction techniques used in variance reduction in Section 9.8.

9.4 Using Empirical Input Distributions

With this approach to input modeling, a sample of observations of an input variable is used to estimate an empirical probability distribution for the population from which the sample was taken. The customary estimate of the empirical probability distribution is to assign equal probability to each of the observed values in the sample. If the sample contains `N` observations, then the empirical probability distribution will assign a weight of `1/N` to each of these observations.

Suppose that a trace of interarrival times of customers to our carwash is in the data file `ARRIVALS.DAT`. Sampling from the empirical distribution is equivalent to reading a randomly chosen value from this file. This is like shuffling and drawing from a data trace. In SIGMA this is done by making the index of the `DISK` function a random integer from `1` to `N`. For example, the file `ARRIVALS.DAT` may look like the following:

```
.3    .42    .2    .54    .79
```

A delay time of `DISK{ARRIVAL.DAT;1+5*RND}` will result in one of these five numbers (chosen at random) being used. Wrapping around the data file will not occur here since the index is never greater than 5. A considerably more efficient but perhaps less flexible approach is to place the data in an array and generate the index of the array uniformly. If the data is in the array `X`, then `X[1+5*RND]` would select one of these values with equal probability. In SIGMA the index is automatically rounded down to the nearest integer.

Similar to using historical data traces as input, the big advantage to using sample distributions to generate input is that there is less concern over validity. However, with sample distributions we can replicate and compress time. The disadvantages to using the empirical input distributions are similar to the disadvantages to using trace input: the data might not be valid, sensitivity analysis to changes in the input process is difficult, we cannot generalize the results to other systems, and it is hard to model rare events. The one major advantage trace input has over empirical distribution sampling comes in modeling dependencies in the input processes. The trace will capture these dependencies, whereas the empirical distributions will not.

9.5 Using Parametric Input Distributions

Efficient algorithms have been developed for imitating the sampling from a large number of parametric families of probability models. In Chapter 7, we saw some SIGMA functions for artificially generating samples that behave very much as though they were actually drawn from specific parametric distributions.

The values of parameters for these models determine the particular characteristics of the sample. This ability to easily change the nature of the input by changing a few parameter values is the primary advantage of using these models to drive a simulation. The variate generation algorithms in common use are fast and require very little memory. Furthermore, you can easily run replications, compress time, and generalize the results to other systems having the same structure. The major drawback to using parametric input distributions is that they can be difficult to explain and justify to people who have no background in probability and statistics.

Devroye (1986) provides a very complete reference on variate generation algorithms. The article by Leemis (1986) catalogs the relationships between dozens of probability laws.

There are several obvious classifications of probability models: finite or infinite range, continuous or discrete values. On a practical level we can also classify probability models as primarily providing good models for input processes or good models for output statistics.

Most of the common distributions that are used to model output statistics are derived from the normal (also called the Gaussian) distribution. In SIGMA the function `NOR{M;S}` will imitate sampling from a normally distributed population with a mean of `M` and a standard deviation of `S`. `M` can be any real-valued expression, and `S` can be any positive real-valued expression. Samples from other distributions such as the *t, F,* and *χ-square* can easily be derived from their relationship to the standard normal distribution (Leemis, 1986).

A selection of parametric distributions that are good for input modeling are provided as SIGMA functions. The C source code for these functions appears in the `CSIGLIB.C` file.

The function `BET{P;Q}` imitates sampling from a beta random variate with parameters given by the positive real-valued expressions `P` and `Q`. This is a standard beta on the interval from 0 to 1 and can be scaled to the interval (`C,C+D`) in the usual way as `C+D*BET{P;Q}`. The beta distribution is one of the most useful in simulation input modeling because of the richness of shapes it can take with simple changes of its two parameters. Figure 9.1 provides a convenient "matrix" of beta distribution shapes for various values of its parameters.

`ERL{M}` will give a sample imitating an *M*-Erlang random variate. The parameter, `M`, can be any positive integer-valued expression. Multiplication by a real number, `A`, will move the mean from `M` to `A*M`. Since the *M*-Erlang is the sum of `M` independent exponentially distributed random variates with mean 1, `A*ERL{1}` will be an exponential random variate with mean `A`.

If you want a sample that is even more highly skewed than one having an exponential, the function `GAM{A}` will imitate sampling from a gamma distribution with a fractional parameter. Here the shape parameter, `A`, is a real variable strictly between 0 and 1. The result can be multiplied by a scale parameter to give a variety of distribution shapes. For integer values of `M`, *M*-Erlang random variates have the same distribution as gamma variates.

The function `TRI{C}` will imitate sampling from a triangular shaped distribution over the range from 0 to 1. The mode (peak) of the distribution

Figure 9.1: Array of Beta Distributions

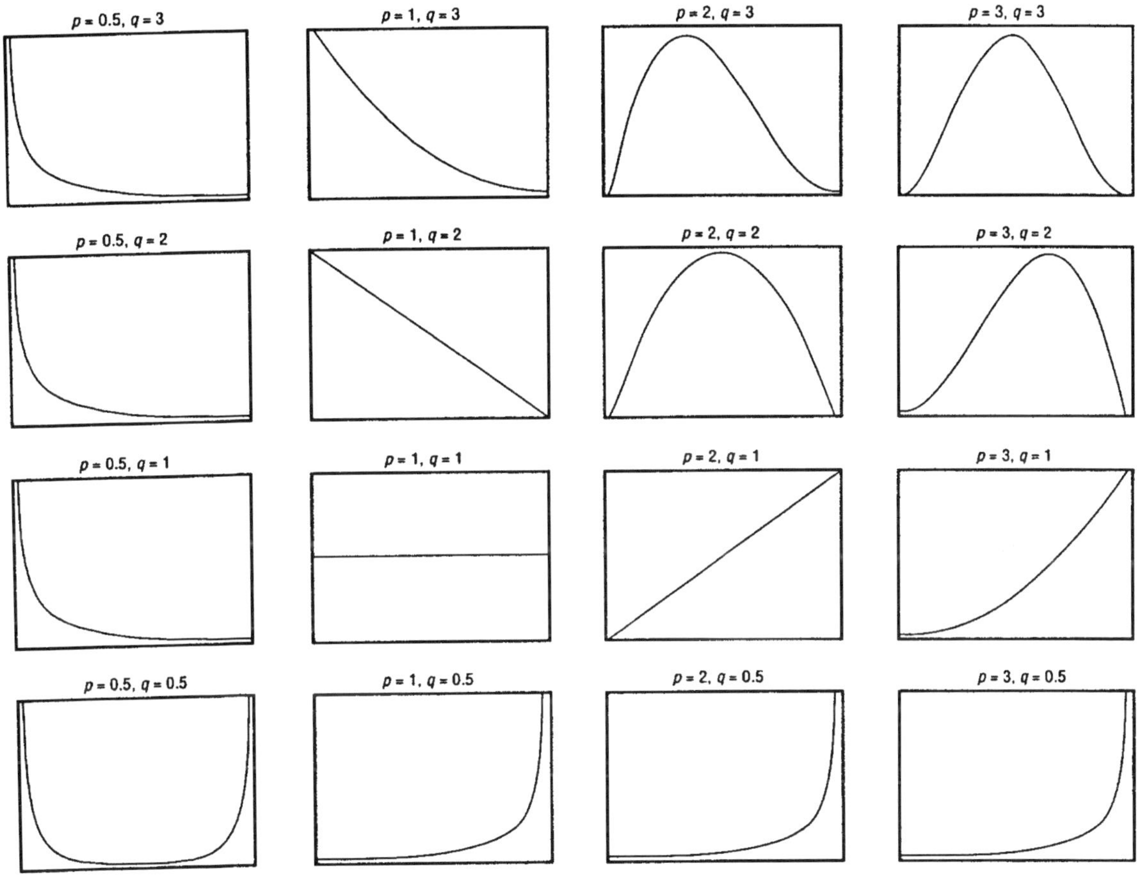

$$\text{Beta Densities: } f_x(x) = \frac{\Gamma(p+q)}{\Gamma(p)\Gamma(q)} x^{p-1}(1-x)^{q-1}, \quad x \in [0,1]$$

is at the value of the real-valued expression, C, which is between 0 and 1 inclusive. The linear function

```
A+(B-A)*TRI{(D-A)/(B-A)}
```

imitates a sample from a triangular distribution between A and B with a mode at D.

It is easy to code other probability models with SIGMA. We will illustrate this with two very useful models, the multinomial and the lambda. The multinomial probability law models independent sampling, with replacement, where there are only `K` possible mutually exclusive outcomes. The simplest example of multinomial sampling is drawing a numbered ball from a jar, returning the ball to the jar, and drawing again. While there are more efficient algorithms available, multinomial sampling is easily done in SIGMA using the `DISK` function. To illustrate, suppose that there are only three possible outcomes from our experiment. We will see a 1 with a probability of 1/2, a 2 with a probability of 1/3, and a 3 with a probability of 1/6. We simply set up a data file called `MULTINOM.DAT`, which has the following entries:

```
1  1  1  2  2  3
```

The statement `X=DISK{MULTINOM.DAT;1+6*RND}` will assign the values of `X` with the given probabilities. The index of the above `DISK` function is a randomly chosen integer from 1 to 6 (rounding the index down is automatic).

The lambda (more properly, the "generalized" lambda) distribution is like the beta in that it can take on a wide variety of shapes. This distribution is discussed by Ramberg et al. (1979). The major difference between the lambda and the beta is that the lambda can take on an infinite range of values, whereas the beta is restricted to take on values only within a specified interval. There are four parameters to the lambda that can be estimated using subjective data. Generation of a lambda variate is very easy. Suppose that you have defined real-valued state variables, `X` and `R`, along with the four lambda parameters, `L1`, `L2`, `L3`, and `L4`. The statements `R=RND`, `X=L1+(R^L3-(1-R)^L4)/L2` will give values of `X` that imitate sampling from the lambda.

You should exercise caution when using Erlang, exponential, gamma, lambda, and normal distributions for input modeling. Variates from these families can take on unrealistic values. You need to check and/or control for reasonableness. For instance, if you are using an exponential (`ERL{1}`) variate to model the service time at a store, it is not reasonable for the service time to exceed some upper limit. No one is going to wait years for service. Truncating these distributions at some upper bound is advised. To illustrate, a vertex with the state changes

```
X=ERL{1},
X=X*(X<5)
```

would produce a sample from an exponential variate truncated to be strictly less than 5. The truncated probability (the likelihood that an exponential variate exceeds 5) is added to the probability of zero occurring. Proportionally rescaling an exponential variate after truncating is shown in Section 9.10.1.

9.6 Modeling Dependent Input

The book by Johnson (1987) along with the articles by Lewis (1981) and McKenzie (1985) are devoted primarily to the generation of dependent input processes. To illustrate the critical importance of recognizing and modeling dependence in the input processes for a simulation, we will use a simple process called the exponential autoregressive (EAR) process (Lewis, 1981).

Successive values of an EAR process X with mean M and correlation parameter R are generated from the recursion

```
X=R*X+M*ERL{1}*(RND>R)
```

with an initial value of X given by the exponential M*ERL{1}. The values of this process will have an exponential distribution, but they are not independent. The correlation between two values of an EAR process that are k observations apart is R^k. At the extremes when R=1, the Boolean variable (RND>R) is always equal to zero and the above expression reduces to X=X. The process never changes value, so the serial correlation is a perfect 1. When R=0, (RND>R) is always equal to 1, and independent (zero correlation) exponential random variables are generated as X=M*ERL{1}. The EAR process is easy to use since its serial dependency can be controlled with the single parameter R. Although histograms of the values of this process look like a simple exponentially distributed sample, the line plots of successive values of an EAR process look rather strange. As is obvious from the EAR process equation, the value of X takes large randomly spaced jumps and then decreases for a while.

To see the effects of dependent input, consider our simple queueing model, CARWASH.MOD, where we change service times. We will use an EAR process with mean M and a correlation parameter of R. This model is called EAR_Q.MOD on your SIGMA disk. If you run EAR_Q.MOD with the same M but very different values of R, you will see a radical difference in the output series. Dependence in the service times has made the two systems behave very differently. When building this model, if we had looked only at the histograms of service times and ignored the serial dependence on service times, we might have had a very poor model.

9.7 Sources of Data

One of the most common excuses given for not successfully completing a simulation study is the lack of "real-world" data with which to model the input processes. While real data is valuable in establishing the credibility of a simulation, lack of data is not a good excuse for not proceeding with the study. You should be trying a wide range of reasonable input processes to assess

Table 9.1: Sources of Data

Source	Cost	Validity	Information	Insight Provided
Physical Constraints	Low	High	Static	Design
Subjective Opinions	Low	Low	Static	Behavioral
Aggregate Reports	Low	Moderate	Static	Performance
Artificial Data (MTM)	Moderate	Moderate	Dynamic	Policy
Direct Observation	High	High	Dynamic	Operational

system performance sensitivity to changes in the environment. Furthermore, there are many sources of data that should not be overlooked when planning and conducting a simulation study. Each source of data has different associated costs, risks, and benefits.

At the least detailed level, there are physical constraints of the system being modeled, such as space limitations for a waiting line. This is reliable, low-cost information that gives design insight. It tells a great deal about the rationale for the way a system was designed. Unfortunately, it is static information and is of little help in modeling the system dynamics. At the next level of detail, there are the subjective opinions of persons involved with the system. This is low-cost (but unreliable), static data that provides behavioral insights about the people involved with designing, operating, and managing the system. Increasingly detailed information can be obtained from aggregate reports on system operations such as labor, production, and scrap reports. This is low-cost, verifiable, static data that can provide performance insight. Information that is useful in modeling the dynamics of the system can sometimes be obtained from artificial data, classical Industrial Engineering MTM methodology. MTM (Motion Time Measurement) tables give standard times (with allowances for fatigue) for performing different manual operations in a system. The cost of this information is moderate, and you do not need to have access to the actual system to obtain it. However, its validity depends on the skill and experience of the person doing the analysis. This data uses detailed motion analysis and provides policy insights in how the system managers and designers *intend* people to perform their jobs. Finally, the most expensive source of data is direct observation. The validity of this data depends on the skill of the observer and the relationship between the observer and the person being observed. Direct observations of a system's operations might be collected manually with time studies or mechanically with sensors. This data provides the operational insights needed to accurately model system dynamics. These sources of data are summarized in Table 9.1.

Alternate sources of information are sometimes overlooked. For example, part routing sheets can be used to verify traced job flows in a factory.

Production records might be used to augment and validate data on the reliability of machines. Knowing the number of machine cycles in a particular time period from production records along with the total number of failures from maintenance records permits estimation of the probability that a machine will fail on a given operation cycle. It is unlikely that these failures are independent; however, at least you have a starting place for your sensitivity analysis and a potential consistency check for verifying more detailed machine failure testing data.

When deciding on what types of and how much data are needed for a simulation, sensitivity analysis is of great value. If you change the values of an input parameter to your simulation, does the measured system output change significantly? If not, you do not need a better estimate of that parameter. On the other hand, if the output is highly sensitive to variations in a particular input parameter, you had best devote some effort to estimating the true value or range of that parameter. Sensitivity is only one key factor in determining a need for more information about an input process. The other is the degree of control that you might have over the process. If the process is essentially beyond your control, detailed data collection of the current behavior of the process is probably not worthwhile. For example, customer arrivals at your carwash are not under your direct control. Knowing a great deal about the current demand is not critical. Hopefully, the demand for your carwash will increase dramatically from its present level once the improvements from your simulation study are implemented. You should run any prospective design against both high and low demand.

Finally, one needs to be alert for communication problems when collecting data. You might think that the data is about one thing when it is really about another. Or the data might have been translated, scaled, or simply recorded incorrectly. Fortunately, these are not fatal problems in carefully conducted simulation studies. We are going to change the values of the input data during our sensitivity analysis experiments anyway.

To help keep the relative importance of real-word data in perspective it may be useful to remember the following *Five Dastardly D's of Data.* Data can be

1. *Distorted:* The values of some observations may be changed or not consistently defined. For example, travel times may include loading and unloading times, which would tend to overestimate the value of a faster vehicle, or product demand data may include only backlogged orders, ignoring customers who refused to wait.
2. *Dated:* The data may be relevant to a system that has been or will be changed. Perhaps factory data was collected for an older process or using last year's product mix.

3. *Deleted:* Observations may be missing from the data set. This might be because the data was collected over an interval of time, and events such as machine failures simply did not occur during the study period. Medical trial data might be censored by patients dropping out of the study for various and unknown reasons.
4. *Dependent:* Data may be summarized (i.e., only histograms or daily averages are reported). This may remove critical cycles or other trends in a data sequence or hide relationships between different sequences. For example, data from a surgical unit might give very accurate estimates of the distributions of preparation, operation, and recovery times. However, it may fail to capture the fact that some surgical procedures will tend to have large values for all three times while other procedures may tend to have all small values.
5. *Deceptive:* Any of the above four data problems might be intentional.

9.8 Variance Reduction

It is often possible to obtain significantly better results by using the same random number streams for different simulation runs. For example, you might want to compare the performance of two different systems. When doing so, it is a good general experimental technique to make "paired" runs of each system under the same conditions. In simulations you do this by using the same random number seed in a run of each system. This technique, called using common random numbers, extends to more than two alternative systems. You would reuse the same seed for a run of each system. To replicate, choose another seed and run each system again with the same new seed. This technique reduces the variance of estimated differences between the systems.

Another example where reusing random number seeds can help reduce the variance of the output applies when making two runs of the same system. As before, you use the same seeds for both runs in the pair. However, for the second run, use `1-RND` wherever `RND` was used before. If `RND` is a random number, then `1-RND` is also. Furthermore, there is a perfect negative correlation between `RND` and `1-RND`. If `RND` is a small random number, `1-RND` will be large; if `RND` is large, `1-RND` will be small. The pair of runs using `RND` and `1-RND` are called antithetic replications. The hope is that the negative correlation between the input streams will carry over to the output. If one run produces an output that is unusually high, its antithetic run will have an output that is unusually low. When the antithetic replicates are averaged, a run with an unusually high result is canceled by its antithetic replicate having an unusually low outcome, and vice versa.

Reusing random number seeds falls under the general category of variance reduction techniques. For a discussion of common and antithetic random numbers as well as some other techniques (which tend to be much less successful in practice), see the text by Bratley, Fox, and Schrage (1987).

The chances that the beneficial results of correlated input streams carry over to the output are greater if the runs can be synchronized as much as possible. That is to say, we want any unusual sequence of random numbers in a run also to be used in the same manner in its commonly seeded replicate(s). For example, if one run in a queueing simulation has an unusual sequence of long service times that causes the system to become very congested, we would like its antithetic replicate to have an unusual sequence of short service times that reduces congestion in the system. We would like all systems using common random numbers to have the same experiences. Synchronization of runs is generally improved if we use different random number streams exclusively for different stochastic components of our simulation. For example, in a queue we might use one stream to generate interarrival times and another stream to generate service times. Thus, we will want to use more than one sequence of random numbers in our simulation. Perfect synchronization of different components of an event graph is possible using simultaneous parallel replications as discussed at the end of Section 12.2.

9.9 Using Multiple Random Number Streams

Function definitions in C make it very easy to change your SIGMA random number stream to a "vector" of random number streams. We discuss how to generate C simulation programs in Chapter 11. In your SIGMA-generated C code, replace `RND` with `RND(I)`, where `I` is an integer indicating which stream you want to use. For example, to draw a random number from stream 3, replace `RND` with `RND(3)`. Then "vectorize" your library functions by replacing `rndsd` with `rndsd[i]` and `RND` with `RND(I)` in `CSIGLIB.C`. Note that `RND` is now a function and `rndsd` becomes an array. If you are using three different random number streams in your model, you would make two changes in the library header file for your C compiler (`CSIGLIB.H`). The two replacement lines would be

```
long rndsd[3];  /*makes rndsd a vector*/
#define RND(j) ((float) (rndsd[j]
=lcg(rndsd[j]))*4.656612875e-10)
```

Like before, you still would have to read in the seeds for each stream when you run your model. The SIGMA-generated Pascal models use the generator supplied with the Pascal compiler.

Figure 9.2: The Cumulative Distribution Function of a Discrete Random Variable

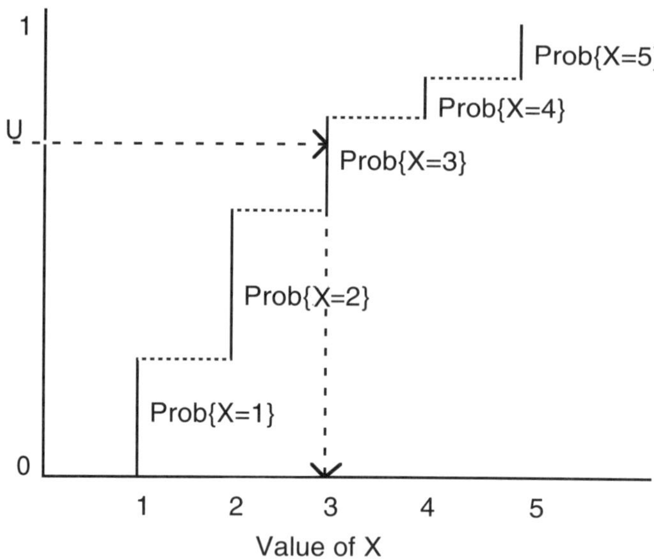

9.10 Methods for Generating Random Variates

In this section, techniques for generating random variates are presented. Included among the techniques is the generation of nonhomogeneous Poisson processes.

9.10.1 Distribution Function Inversion

The cumulative distribution function $F_X(x)$ for the random variable X is the probability that the value of a random variable will be less than or equal to the function argument

$$F_X(x) = \text{Prob}\{X \leq x\}.$$

Discrete-valued random variables can be generated by partitioning the interval between zero and one into sections whose widths are equal to the probability of each value. The value of the random variable is determined by the interval in which a pseudo-random number, U, falls. The probability of U falling in an interval is equal to the width of the interval, which in turn is the probability of the corresponding value occurring. This is equivalent to inverting the cumulative distribution function as illustrated in Figure 9.2.

The same technique can be applied to continuous-valued random variables. For example, the cumulative distribution for an exponential random variable is

$$y = F_X(x) = 1 - e^{-x/\mu}$$
$$\Rightarrow F_X^{-1}(x) = -\mu * ln(1-y).$$

So, the inverse distribution function of a uniform random number will generate an exponential variate as

$$X = F_X^{-1}(U) = -\mu * ln(1-U) \approx -\mu * ln(U).$$

It is easily seen that a proportionally rescaled exponential variate that has 20% of its lower tail truncated can be generated as

$$X = -\mu * ln(.8 * U).$$

When the cumulative distribution function is easily inverted, this technique is recommended. Unfortunately, not very many of the more commonly used probability distributions have easily inverted cumulative distribution functions. Exceptions that are particularly useful are order statistics from a sample of uniform random variables.

Order Statistics: Order statistics are sorted samples; the minimum order statistic is the smallest value in a sample. Suppose we want to know the first time that one of several identical independent components will fail. We could generate the lifetime of each component and sort them to find the shortest. If there are many components, it would be easier to generate the minimum order statistic from the lifetime distribution.

Order statistics can be generated by evaluating an inverse cumulative distribution function at the corresponding uniform order statistic. The *i*th smallest of *K* uniform random variables has a beta distribution with paramcters *i* and *K-i+1*. A common special case is where we want the smallest of *K* independent values of a random variable. The cumulative distribution function of the smallest of *K* independent uniform random variables is

$F_X(x)$ = Prob{smallest of K independent Uniforms $\leq x$}
= 1-Prob{smallest of K Uniforms $> x$}= 1-Prob{all K Uniforms $> x$}
$= 1-(1-x)^K$

Therefore,

$$F_X^{-1}(U) = 1-(1-U)^{1/K}$$

If the lifetime of each of *K* independent components has an exponential distribution, the distribution of the time until the first component fails is equal to

$$X = -\mu * ln(1 - (1 - (1 - U)^{1/K}))$$
$$= -\mu * ln\{(1 - U)^{1/K}\}$$

9.10.2 Other Methods

Other methods for generating random variates include acceptance/rejection, composition, and special relationships. As with inversion, it is not always possible to use these other methods in their pure form, and special algorithms that combine these methods have been invented. The reference by Devroye (1986) contains many of these algorithms.

Acceptance/rejection involves bounding the probability density and generating a point uniformly within this bounding area. If the generated point falls below the density function, the horizontal value of the generated point is used as the random variate. If the point falls outside the density function, the generated point is rejected and a new point is tried. This is continued until an accepted point that falls under the density function is found. This is analogous to throwing uniform points onto the bounding region and accepting those points that fall below the probability density. The algorithm for generating beta variates, `beta_fn`, in the SIGMA C library, `CSIGLIB.C`, uses an acceptance/rejection algorithm due to Cheng (1978).

Composition involves breaking the probability distribution into regions from which it is relatively easy to generate variates. One of these regions is selected with the probability in that region and the variate is generated from that region.

Special properties exploit relationships between different types of random variables. Some commonly used relationships include generating an Erlang variate as a sum of exponentials, generating a geometric variate as the integer part of an exponential, generating a chi-square variate as the sum of squared normal variates, and generating a Poisson as the count of exponential variates whose sum falls within an interval. (When the Poisson rate is large, there are better methods for generating Poisson variates, given in the references.)

9.10.3 Generating Nonhomogeneous Poisson Processes

Random arrivals to a service system can often be modeled using a Poisson process. This process has proven to be a rather good model for many processes that occur naturally. It is also used for other types of exogenous events that drive a simulation model, such as equipment failures or flaws occurring in a piece of fabric. The parameter for a Poisson process is its rate, λ, expressed in the number of events per time unit (e.g., customer arrivals/hour or flaws/square foot).

There are numerous methods for generating Poisson processes that exploit different properties of these processes. The fact that the *times between*

Figure 9.3: Nonhomogeneous Poisson Arrivals to Our Carwash Model

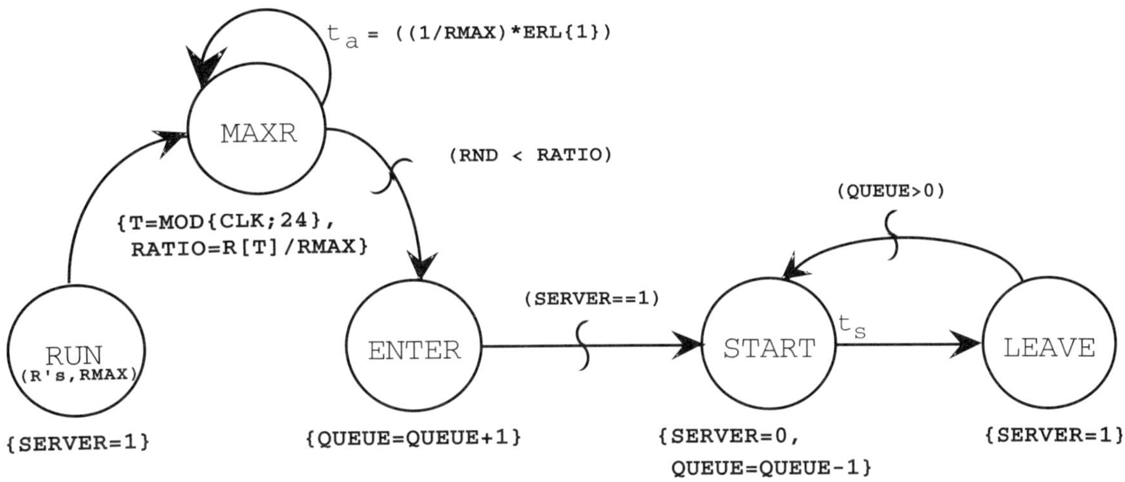

Poisson events have exponential distributions can be used to simply make the delay time for a self-scheduling edge have an exponential distribution with a mean equal to the inverse of the Poisson rate. For example, if the arrivals to a queue are going to be modeled as a Poisson process with a rate equal to `RATE`, then the edge delay time for the self-scheduling edge that models sequential arrivals would have a delay time of `(1.0/RATE)*ERL{1}` (recall that Erlang-1 and exponential distributions are the same).

If we know the total number of Poisson events that occur in an interval of time, we can better match the process by conditioning on this knowledge. We do this using the fact that the distribution of the times of *K Poisson events in an interval have the same distribution as K uniform random numbers on the same interval.* Say we know that K Poisson events occurred in an interval between 0 and T. We can generate the minimum order statistic of K uniforms over the interval for our first event time, T_1. The second event time will be the minimum of the remaining K-1 uniforms distributed over the remaining interval between T_1 and T. The rest of the K events in the original interval can be generated in this manner.

Unfortunately, processes in the real world do not often occur with a constant rate. The arrival rate may be relatively high during a rush hour and slack (or zero) late at night. A Poisson process with a changing rate is called a *nonhomogeneous* Poisson process. An easy way to model a nonhomogeneous Poisson process is by a technique called "thinning" (Lewis and Shedler, 1979). Here we simply generate Poisson events at the maximum rate and keep them with a probability proportional to the current rate. To illustrate: assume we know that during a 24-hour day, customers will arrive at our carwash with the following hourly rates: `R[0]`, `R[1]`,. . ., `R[23]` (the rate can be zero if the facility is closed). Let `RMAX` be the maximum of these rates. The event graph to generate Poisson arrival events according to this daily demand cycle is shown in Figure 9.3 and is `NONPOIS.MOD` on your SIGMA disk.

9.11 Exercises

The models referred to in the exercises are on your SIGMA *disk.*

9.11.1 Chaos

A simple example of a so-called chaotic system is the recursive equation

```
X=R*X*(1-X)
```

If you start off with a particular value of `X`, if `R` is set high enough, it becomes impossible to predict the value of `X` very far into the future. Starting the system with `X=0.2`, try values of `R=0.5`, `1`, `2`, and `4`. Does the system behave differently for different values of `R`? Does "chaos" describe the behavior? (Do you think chaotic systems might make good pseudo-random number generators?)

9.11.2 Generating Discrete Random Variates

(a) Consider the probability distribution function

`P(X=i)=i/6` where i `=1, 2, 3`

i. Create an event graph using `RND` to generate 25 random variates of this distribution.

ii. Create an event graph using `DISK{}` and a data file to generate 25 random variates of this distribution.

(b) What is the probability distribution function of `X`?

```
U=RND
X=(U>0.2)+(U>0.5)
```

9.11.3 Generating Continuous Random Variates

(a) Let `A` and `B` be two random variables uniformly distributed between `0` and `1`. Let `X` be the larger of `A` and `B`. Create an event graph that generates 20 values of `X` (try to be clever).

(b) Consider the following probability distribution function:

$$f(x) = x/8 \qquad 0<=x<=4$$

Create an event graph using RND to generate 25 random variates of this distribution.

(c) What does the probability distribution function of X look like if X is given by the following?

```
U=RND
X=(2*RND)*(U<0.5)+(4+RND)*(U>=0.5)
```

(d) If U is a random variable with a uniform distribution between zero and one, what is the distribution of V=1/2-U/2?

(e) What will the following state changes do in SIGMA to the value of X? That is, give the value(s) of X and tell how the(se) value(s) might occur. [Assume that all variables are REAL valued (i.e., floating point).]

```
X=(RND<0.2)+(RND<0.5)*2+(RND<0.7)*4
```

(f) What does the following Sigma state change do?

```
X=(RND>0.5)*1+(RND<=0.5)*2
```

(g) How can you generate a proportionally rescaled exponential variate with 80% of its upper tail truncated?

9.11.4 Generation of Minimum Statistics

There are 100 identical components operating independently in a system. Each component has a lifetime, X, that has an exponential distribution with a mean of 6 days. Generate the time until the first component fails from a single uniform random number, RND. (Hint: The minimum of N uniform random variables is given by RND^N, and X=-M*LN{RND} is an exponential random variable with mean M.)

9.11.5 Testing Variate Generators

SIGMA has built-in generators for uniform (RND), gamma (GAM), and normal (NOR) random variates. Using the methods in texts referenced in this book (Bratley, Fox, and Schrage and Law and Kelton), perform at least three tests of these functions (at least two of the tests should be quantitative). Program and test generators for lambda variates.

9.11.6 A Variance Reduction Technique

Two runs are made of a simulated queue. The random number stream that was used to generate interarrival times in the first run is used to generate the service times for the second run. The random number stream that was used to generate service times in the first run is used to generate the interarrival times for the second run. Will the average customer waiting times from these two runs tend to have zero, positive, or negative correlation? Explain why.

9.11.7 Dependent Processes

Run `CARWASH.MOD` where the interarrival times and service times are exponentially distributed with the same means as before but now follow `EAR` models with lag-1 correlation of $p = 0.7$. Compare this system with `CARWASH.MOD` having deterministic service and `CARWASH.MOD` having *independently* distributed exponential service.

9.11.8 A Simple Recursion for Queue Times

Generate 90% confidence intervals for the average waiting time, `E[W]`, in an `M/M/1` queue with traffic intensity of 0.9. Use the recursion

`W=MAX{W+S-A;0}` starting with `W=0`,

where

`S` is the service time of the `i`th customer (exponential with mean = 1) and
`A` is the `i`th customer interarrival time (exponential with mean = 1/0.9).

9.11.9 Dependent Input Data

You are building a model for a chain of automatic carwashes. These carwashes have deterministic service rates. A sample of car arrivals indicates that the time between car arrivals has an exponential distribution. Unfortunately, the people collecting the demand data simply tabulated a histogram of the interarrival times rather than recording the actual sequence of arrival times.

(a) What problem(s) do you anticipate this might cause in getting a valid model for the customer arrival process? Specifically, what information are you missing that you wish you had? Why?

(b) What if you are also told that the lag-1 serial correlation between successive interarrival times is 0.7? Given that an arrival event just occurred and the simulated time is `CLK`, how can you generate the time of the next car arrival (call this time `T`) using all of the information you have?

(c) Why might your approach not be acceptable to the people who own this chain of carwashes?

9.11.10 Generating Points in a Plane

Generate a sample of N independent points uniformly scattered over the area in the two-dimensional region in the plane bounded by the horizontal axis and an arbitrary function.

10

Graphical & Statistical Output Analysis

In keeping with our philosophy of utilizing pictures whenever possible, several graphical methods of presenting simulation results have been incorporated into the SIGMA software. The graphical output plots available to you while in SIGMA are line plots, step plots, scatter plots, histograms, autocorrelations, and standardized time series. These plots, along with the frequency spectrum to analyze cycles in an output series, are also available using the separate **SIGPLOT** utility that is included with SIGMA. The **SIGPLOT** utility is for the statistical and graphical analysis of large data sets such as those produced when running SIGMA-generated simulations in C code. This chapter discusses these graphical output plots and the **SIGPLOT** utility. The chapter concludes with an explanation of standardized time series.

10.1 Keeping a Perspective

It is easy to become overwhelmed by the information produced by a simulation model. Different types of simulation output are most useful during different stages of a simulation study. Animations, graphs, and statistics all have their appropriate roles to play.

During the initial development and testing of the simulation model, animating the simulation logic while running SIGMA in **Single Step** or **Graphics** run mode is the most valuable. The logical animation in SIGMA is different from the physical animation of a system. Physical animations are useful in selling the simulation to prospective users and for catching gross logic errors in the simulation model. Physical animations using SIGMA are discussed in Chapter 8.

Table 10.1: Typical Phases of a Simulation Project and Predominant Form of Output

Phase of the Study	Predominant Form of the Output
Model building and validation	Logical animations and English descriptions
System evaluation	Charts and plots
Detailed design	Statistics
Implementation	Physical animations

The **Translate to English** feature of SIGMA (found under the **File** menu) is an extremely effective tool for catching program logic errors or communicating the details of a model to persons not familiar with simulation. If the SIGMA-generated English description of your simulation is nonsense, it is likely that the logic in your model will not make sense either.

When evaluating alternative system designs at a high level, plots of the output are most useful. Here we are comparing the performance of very different systems (e.g., manual operations versus automated ones). Plots of the output offer information not only on overall system performance but also on the dynamics of the system. We can see, for example, if the manner in which we initialized the variables in our simulation has an inappropriate influence on the output. We will say more about the bias caused by initializing variables later in this chapter.

Once a particular design has been tentatively selected, it is important to do detailed sensitivity analysis and design optimization before a final recommendation is proposed. Here we are going to run a great many replications with different settings of the factors and parameters in our model. It is neither fun nor particularly informative to watch hundreds of different animations or look at hundreds of output plots. In the detailed design phase of a simulation study, numerical summaries of system performance in the form of output statistics are the most appropriate form of simulation output.

Finally, once a design has been finalized, the most effective form of output is a physical animation that lets people more fully understand the changes being suggested. Plots, statistical summaries, and the English description of your model can also be effective in helping you sell your ideas. The above discussion is summarized in Table 10.1.

10.2 Elementary Output Plots

The **Output Plot** dialog box is discussed in detail in Section 4.2.8 of this book. In SIGMA there are four basic output plots and two plots for advanced analysis. The four basic plots are:

Figure 10.1: Queue Length as a Function of Customer Number

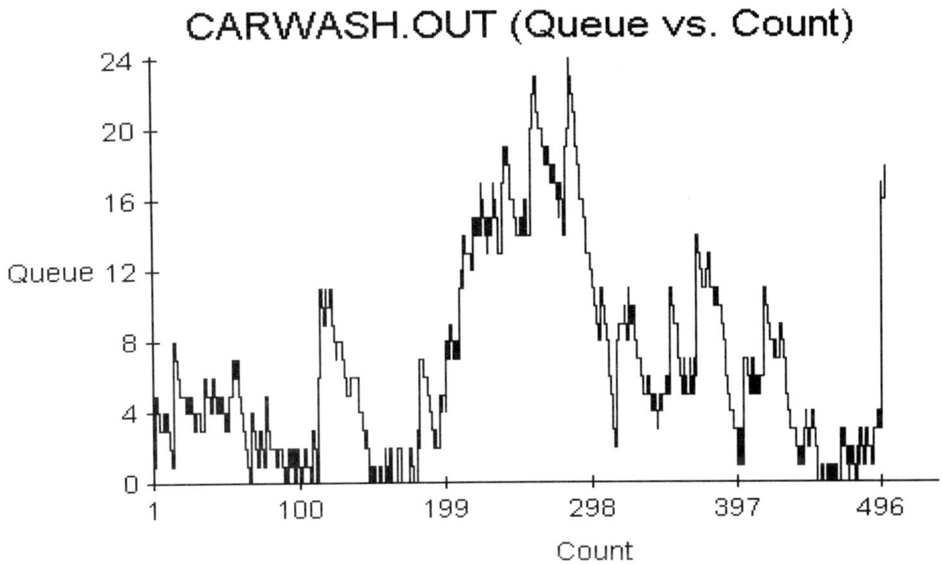

1. Step plots, which show the values of traced variables during a simulation run.
2. Line plots, which are similar to step plots except straight lines are drawn between successive data points.
3. Scatter plots, which show the relationship between pairs of traced output variables.
4. Histograms, which count the relative frequencies at which different values of a variable occur.

More advanced output analysis is possible using the following plots:

5. Autocorrelation functions, which show dependencies in the output.
6. Standardized time series (STS), which can be used to detect trends.

In addition, the **SIGPLOT** utility has frequency spectra plots, which can be used to detect cycles in the output.

10.2.1 Step and Line Plots

Step plots and line plots (also called index plots) are by far the most common form of graphical simulation output. Here we see how one variable changes

Figure 10.2: Scatter Plot of Waiting Time and Line Length in a Bank

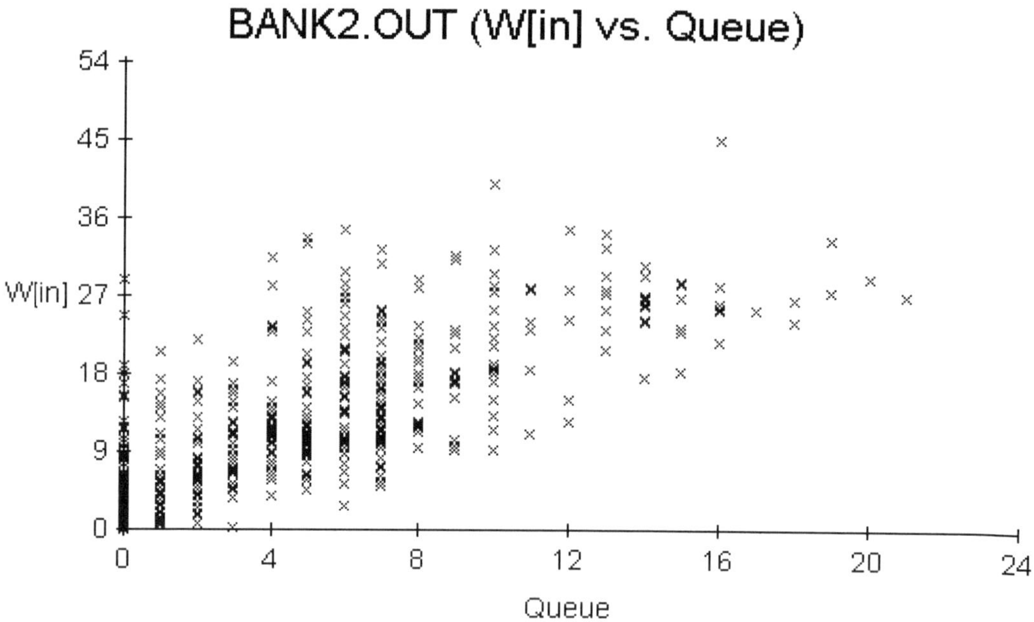

during the simulation run. The variable of interest is chosen for the vertical axis of the plot and an indexing variable is chosen for the horizontal axis. The indexing variable is often simulated time, but other variables (such as customer identification number) might be used. Figure 10.1 shows a line plot of the queue length in our simulated carwash (exponentially distributed service times were used here).

10.2.2 Scatter Plots

When two variables are of equal importance, they can be chosen as the two axes of a scatter plot. A point is plotted for every observed pair of values for these variables. If the points tend to fall along a line with a positive slope, the two variables are likely to be positively correlated. (Small values of one variable are observed along with small values of the other variable, and large values are observed with large values.) Similarly, if the points in a scatter plot tend to fall along a line with a negative slope, negative correlation between the variables should be suspected. Figure 10.2 shows a scatter plot of the waiting time of each customer for our simulated bank in Chapter 5 and the number of customers in line when each customer departed; the expected positive correlation is evident.

Figure 10.3: Histogram of Number of Customers in Carwash Queue

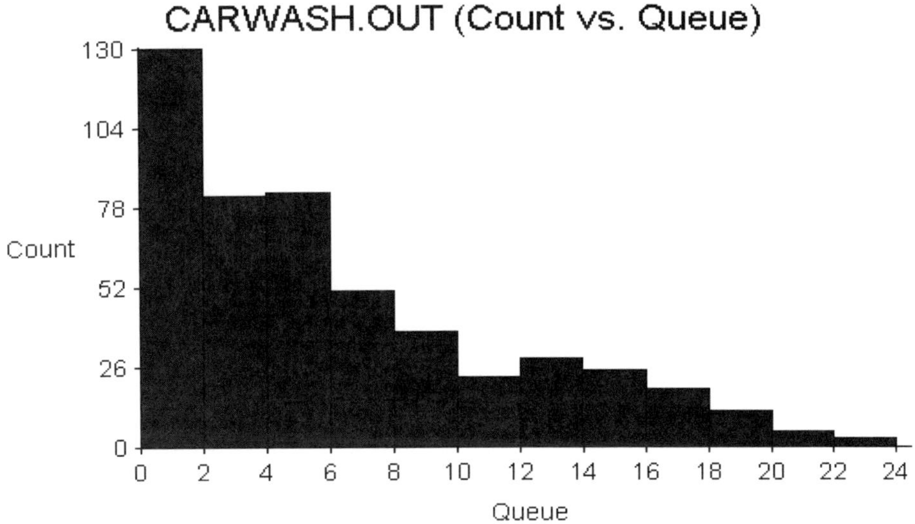

10.2.3 Histograms

Histograms show counts of the number of times the observed values of a variable fall within a specified interval. These counts show the relative frequency at which values of a variable are observed. Figure 10.3 shows a histogram of the number of customers in the carwash model with exponentially distributed interarrival times.

10.3 Advanced Graphical Analysis

10.3.1 Detecting Trends Using Standardized Time Series

Using a standardized time series (STS) plot, it is possible to detect trends in the output that might not otherwise be visible. The STS plot should appear to be symmetric about zero if there is no trend in the data. When there is a trend, the STS plots will be pulled either above (increasing trend) or below (decreasing trend) the zero line. STS can also be used for other types of inference such as confidence interval estimation. The STS plots in SIGMA are the unscaled standardized time series for the selected output measurement. The best way to learn how to use STS plots is to look at a few simple output series. Try generating a sequence of independent random variables, say, with the state change `X=NOR{0;1}`. Look at the line plot of the successive values of `X` and the

Figure 10.4: STS Plot Indicating a Downward Trend in the Data

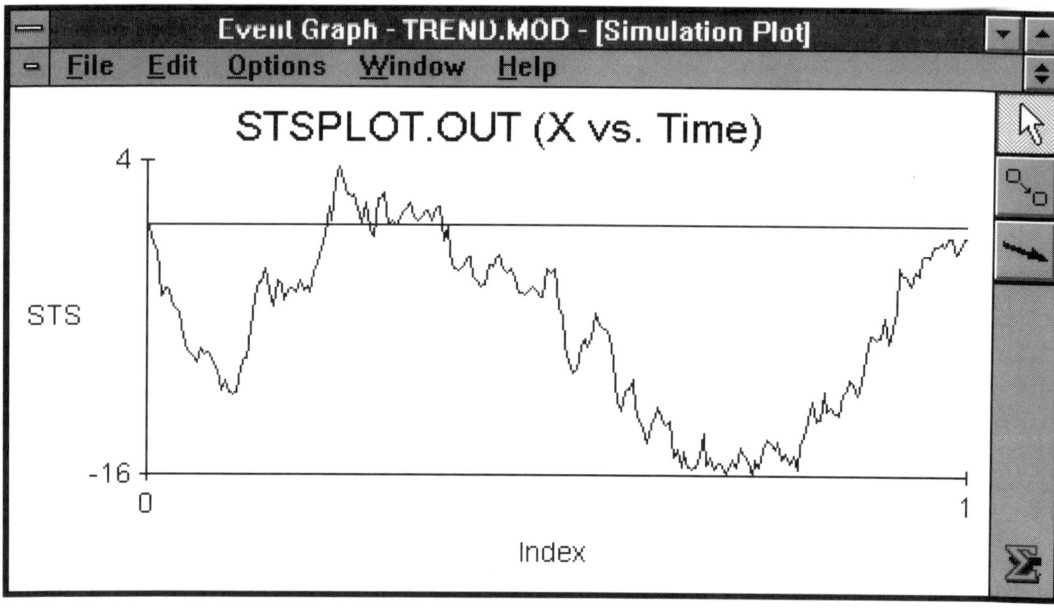

corresponding STS plot. Now add a trend to the data, say, `X=CLK*NOR{0;1}`, and look at the differences in the same two plots. Do this for some more interesting and subtle trends (exponential decay, quadratic, sudden shift, etc.) and see how the STS behaves. You will find that familiarity with the behaviors of STS plots is a valuable visual tool for output analysis.

Standardizing a time series is similar to the familiar procedure of standardizing or normalizing a scalar statistic. Standardizing a scalar statistic, such as a sample mean, involves centering the statistic to have a zero mean and scaling its magnitude to generic units of measurement called standard deviations. Limit theorems can be applied that give us the asymptotic (large sample) probabilistic behavior of correctly standardized statistics under certain hypotheses. This limiting model for scalar statistics is typically the standard normal probability distribution. This model can be used for statistical inference such as testing hypotheses or constructing confidence intervals. Here we extend this concept to the standardization of an entire time series. More information about STS can be found in Section 10.5.

The value of standardizing time series comes from the fact that the same mathematical analysis can be applied to series from a variety of sources.

Figure 10.5: Plot of the Raw Data Series for the STS Plot of Figure 10.4

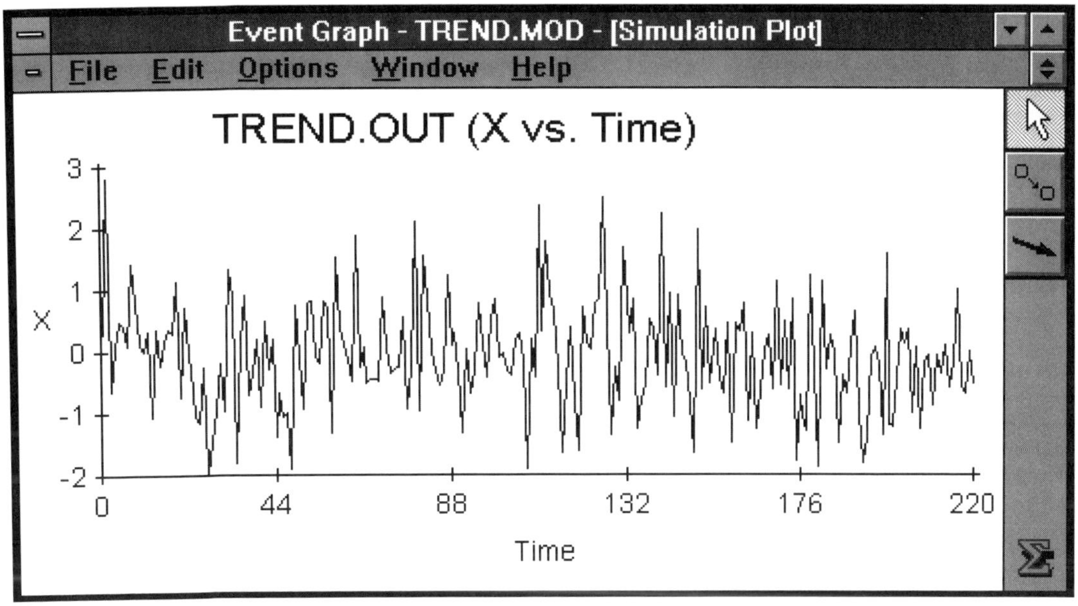

Thus, the technique of standardization serves as a mathematical surrogate for experience with the data under study. No matter what the original time series looks like, the standardized time series will be familiar if certain hypotheses are correct. An unusual appearance of a standardized time series can be used to conclude that these hypotheses are not valid. The statistical significance of these conclusions can be computed in the same manner as with standardized scalar statistics.

To illustrate using STS plots to detect trends, consider first the STS plot in Figure 10.4. Since this plot is mostly negative, a clear downward trend in the data is evident. A line plot of the actual data is shown in Figure 10.5, where the downward trend indicated by the STS plot is at best only marginally apparent.

Figure 10.6 is an STS plot that indicates the presence of a strong increasing trend in the data. The STS plot is pulled in the positive direction by this positive trend in the data. Figure 10.6 should be compared with Figure 10.4, where a negative trend was indicated. The raw data for the STS plot in Figure 10.6 is plotted in Figure 10.7, where the increasing trend in the data is again only slightly detectable.

Figure 10.6: An STS Plot Indicating an Increasing Trend in the Data

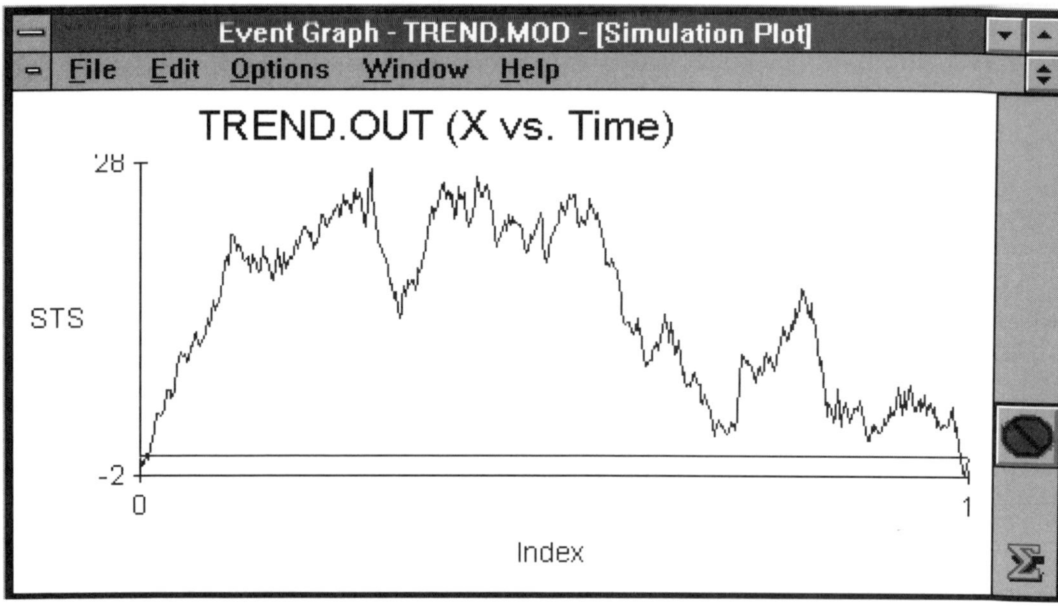

Figure 10.7: Raw Data for the STS Plot in Figure 10.6

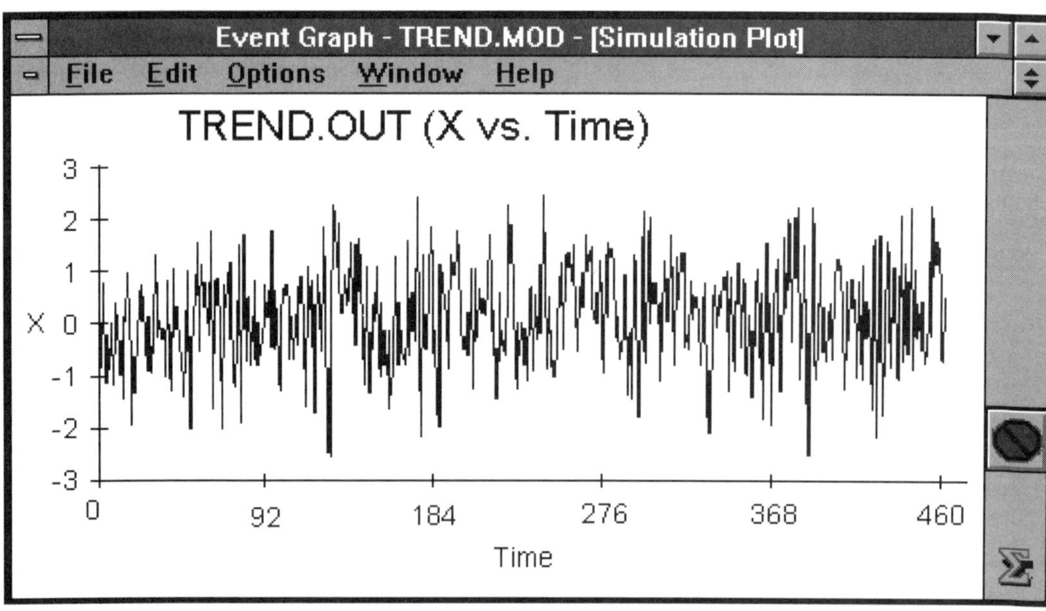

The sensitivity of STS plots to trends has a down side: STS plots can indicate a trend that may disappear as more data is collected. However, given the potential seriousness of initialization bias causing an artificial trend in the simulation output, it seems better to be able to detect trends easily at the risk of falsely indicating a nonexistent trend.

10.3.2 Dependencies

The autocorrelation function is a plot of the correlation between two observations in the same output series as a function of how far apart (lag) the observations are. For example, the lag 1 autocorrelation function is the sample correlation between two adjacent output measurements. The autocorrelation function should drop off sharply at a lag of 1 if the observations are not correlated. This would indicate that the batch size is large enough to remove correlations between successive batched means and initial transient output observations have been truncated. Crude 95% confidence bounds at $\pm 1.96/\sqrt{n}$ can be used as a very rough guide (Brockwell and Davis, 1987).

The standardized time series (STS) plots can also be used to visually assess whether or not there is significant positive serial correlation in an output series. The more jagged the STS plot appears, the less serial dependency in the output. If the STS plot is smoother than you are typically used to seeing, you can suspect either a serious trend in the data or significant positive serial dependency between successive observations of the output.

10.4 Using the SIGPLOT Analysis Program

The plots discussed earlier in this chapter as well as the frequency spectrum to detect cycles in the data are available through the **SIGPLOT** utility that is included with SIGMA. **SIGPLOT** also computes several advanced statistics. You should use a spreadsheet or **SIGPLOT** to analyze data from a SIGMA-generated simulation in C.

10.4.1 Running SIGPLOT

Note that **SIGPLOT** does not have mouse support. You select choices from various text menus by highlighting them with the arrow keys and pressing [←Enter]. You must exit all of the **SIGPLOT** menus before you can close the **SIGPLOT** window and return to SIGMA.

For speed, these plots share intermediate computations. The tree in Figure 10.8 shows how to find a particular plot within **SIGPLOT** (respond by entering **Yes** to prompts for intermediate plots).

Figure 10.8: Tree of **SIGPLOT** Output Plots

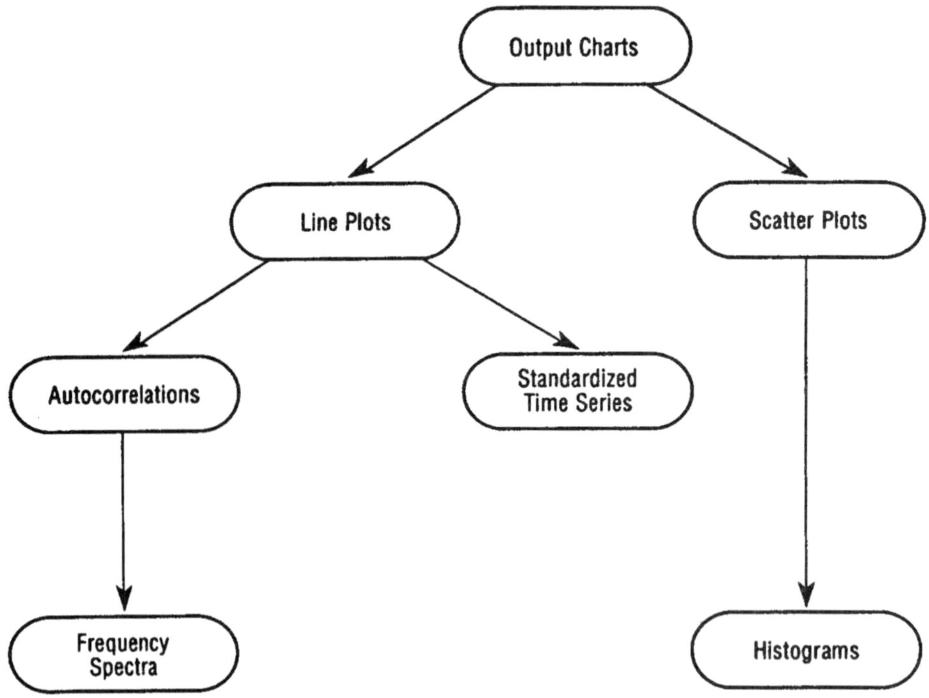

You can print the plots produced by **SIGPLOT** by first copying them to the Windows clipboard (using [Alt-Print Screen]). The plot can then be copied into several other Windows applications, such as a word processor or the **Paintbrush** accessory that comes with Windows. From there it can be printed by selecting the **Print** command under the **File** menu.

After clicking on the **SIGPLOT** icon, you will be asked to enter the name of the SIGMA output file that you wish to analyze. You then will be asked to enter an initial data truncation point and a batch size.

The *truncation point* is the number of initial observations that you wish to discard to let the system "warm up." It is a good idea to look at the untruncated output and examine the initial transient period of a simulation run. If you wish to consider output that is not biased by the initial warm up period, truncate at a point where you think the initialization bias has dissipated. (See the section on detecting trends earlier in this chapter.)

Batching is where nonoverlapping, adjacent, equal-sized groups of data are averaged. The resulting series of batched means will often be more independent, less erratic, and have an approximately normal distribution. If there are about 20 batches, there is a sufficient number of degrees of freedom for

Figure 10.9: Plot of Unbatched 1000 Observation EAR (0.50 output series)

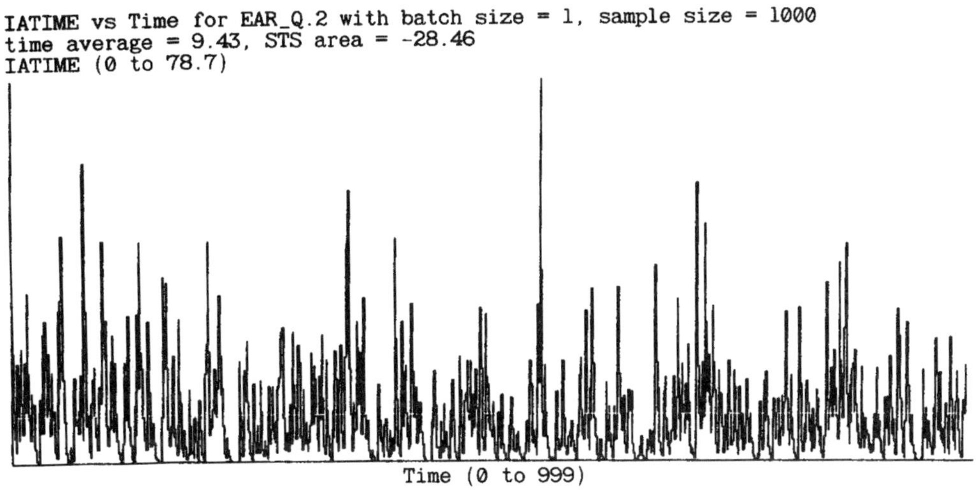

most inferences (Schmeiser, 1983). Batched means are computed after truncation. From within **SIGPLOT**, you are limited to 10,000 batches of output data.

10.4.2 Using Statistics

In the margins of each plot are sufficient statistics and maximum likelihood estimators for common inference. The assumptions behind the statistics are probably more important than the numbers themselves and should be understood before too much faith is placed in their values. This is part of the reason only sufficient statistics are given for the computations. When looking up the simple formulas, you can review the assumptions. Do not let an unfamiliarity with statistics prevent you from looking at the plots.

The time average (line plots) and sample average (scatter plots) give two sample means; the time average takes into account how long a variable spends at each value, whereas the sample average just counts and averages each observed value.

Averages of squares (scatter plots) are sufficient for batched means confidence interval estimation and other inferences. Approximately 20 to 30 large batches are recommended (Schmeiser, 1983). Batching tends to make the output better approximate an independent sample from a normal distribution.

To illustrate the effects of batching, 1000 observations of the EAR (ρ = 0.5) process discussed in Chapter 9 were simulated. The mean of the process, μ, was 10. The raw output, before batching, is plotted in Figure 10.9. The sample mean from Figure 10.9 is seen to be 9.43. The autocorrelation func-

Figure 10.10: Plot of Unbatched EAR Autocorrelation Function

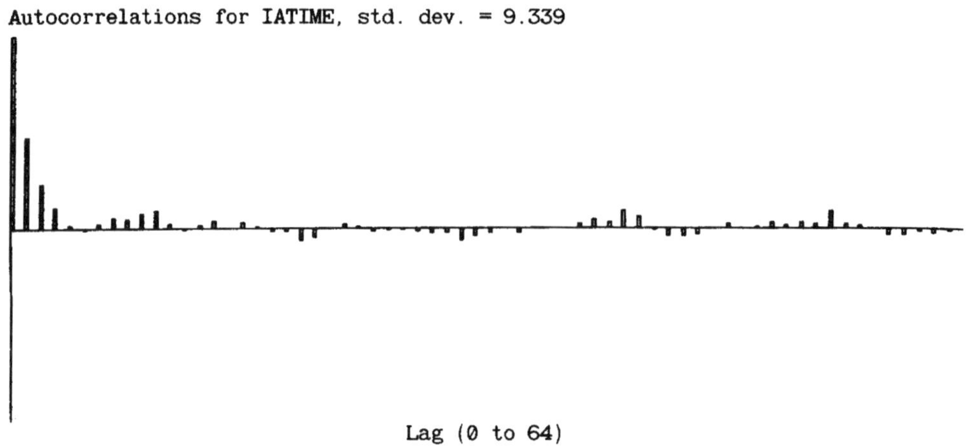

tion of this process in Figure 10.10 and the histogram in Figure 10.11 show us that this output series does not appear to be independent nor does it have the characteristic "bell shaped" distribution function expected of normally distributed observations. From Figure 10.10, we see that the correlation between the observations appears to slowly decrease as the lag (time interval) between the observations increases. There appears to be significant correlation between neighboring observations at lag 1. The sample standard deviation is

Figure 10.11: Plot of Unbatched EAR Histogram

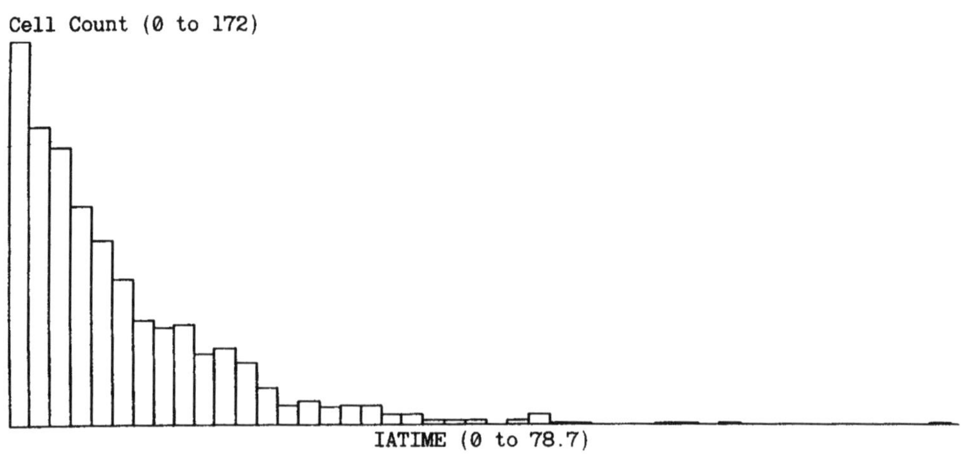

Figure 10.12: Plot of Batched EAR (0.5) Observations, n=500

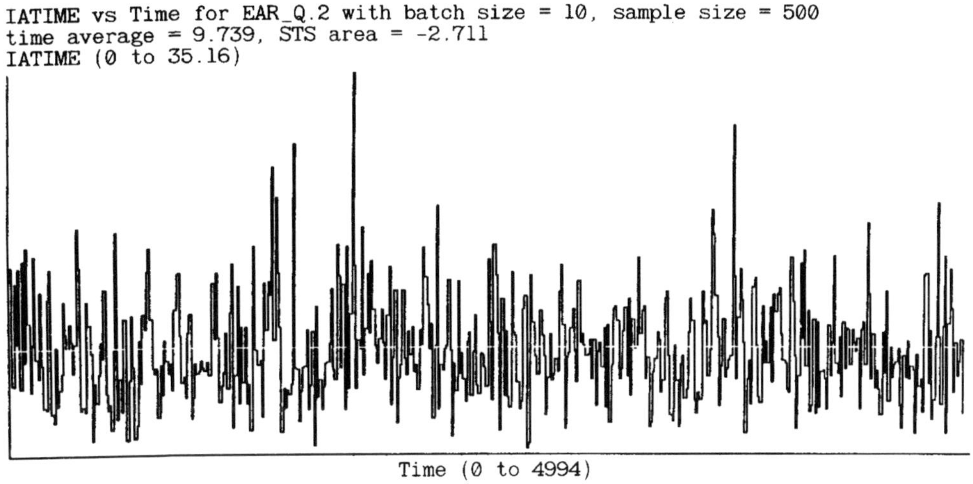

seen in Figure 10.10 to be 9.339. (This is approximately equal to the sample mean, as expected from exponential data.)

To see the effects of batching, we averaged groups of 10 observations in a sample of 5000 from the same process. The 500 resulting batched means are plotted in Figure 10.12. The sample mean of the batched process is given in that figure as 9.739.

Figure 10.13: Plot of Batched EAR Autocorrelation Function

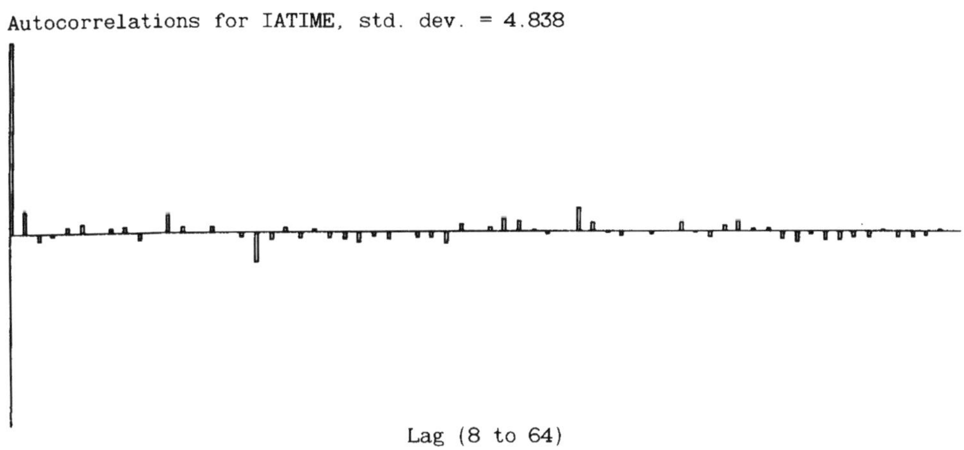

Figure 10.14: Plot of Batched EAR Histogram

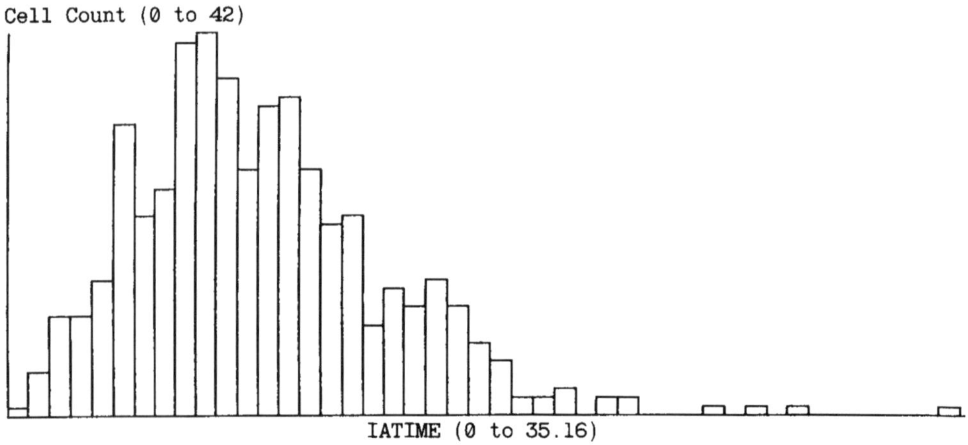

Even with a batch size as small as 10, we can see from the autocorrelation plot in Figure 10.13 that the data appears now to have very little serial correlation. From Figure 10.13 we see that the sample standard deviation is 4.838. The histogram of the batched means in Figure 10.14 shows that the data is beginning to look like it came from a normal, bell-shaped distribution (as expected from the Central Limit Theorem of statistics). With averages of only 10 observations from a highly skewed dependent exponential distribution, we begin to approximate an independent normal data set. The mean and variance of the batched process can safely be used to form a batched means confidence interval for the mean of the process, based on the usual *t*-statistic with 499 degrees of freedom. (We can use the normal approximation to the *t* distribution for such a large degrees of freedom parameter.) For example, a 90% confidence interval for the process mean, μ, is found to be

$$\overline{X} - t_{499,0.95}\frac{S}{\sqrt{n}} \leq \mu \leq \overline{X} + t_{499,0.95}\frac{S}{\sqrt{n}}$$

Substituting the statistics from Figures 10.12 and 10.13 into the above interval estimation formula, we get the following confidence interval for the true mean of the process:

$$9.739 - 1.645\frac{4.838}{\sqrt{500}} \leq \mu \leq 9.739 + 1.645\frac{4.838}{\sqrt{500}}$$

$$9.383 \leq \mu \leq 10.09$$

The true value of $\mu = 10$ was within this confidence interval, as it was for the wider 90% confidence interval of $9.696 \le \mu \le 10.763$ constructed with 1000 unbatched observations.

In addition to averages, time averages, and standard deviations, the **SIGPLOT** utility provided with SIGMA also includes average products for regression and regeneration analysis as well as STS statistics.

The average product statistic (scatter plots) is used in the estimation of covariance (and for OLS regression as well as regenerative confidence interval estimation if the data is sampled accordingly).

The STS area, `A`, given in the line plots can be used for confidence intervals as described by Goldsman and Schruben (1984). For *large* samples, `A` might behave like the standard deviation times a chi-square random variable with 1 degree of freedom independent of the sample mean. (Use independently seeded replications to increase the degrees of freedom.)

The (unscaled) STS maximum, `M`, located at the `K`th of `N` batches might behave like the standard deviation times `(N-K)K/N` times a chi-square random variable with 3 degrees of freedom if `N` is very large (and the batch size is moderate). See Goldsman and Schruben (1984). This can be used for computing the STS maximum confidence interval estimator.

In addition to the plots discussed earlier, the **SIGPLOT** utility will plot the frequency spectrum. The frequency spectrum estimator used in **SIGPLOT** is the Tukey windowed cosine transform of the autocorrelation function. At high resolution, the plot can be used to help detect cycles in the simulation output. Cycles will cause bumps or spikes to appear in the smoothed sample frequency spectrum. The value of the frequency spectrum at zero might also be used for confidence interval estimation (Heidelberger and Welch, 1983).

10.5 Standardized Time Series

As a guide to standardizing a time series, we will first review the procedure of standardizing a scalar statistic. We will use the familiar *t*-statistic as an example. The data will consist of n observations

$$Y_1, Y_2, \ldots, Y_n$$

that are independent and have identical normal distributions. We wish to make inferences about the unknown population mean, μ. The average of the data sample

$$\bar{Y} = \frac{1}{n}\sum_{i=1}^{n} Y_i$$

will be the statistic used for these inferences. The population variance, σ^2, is an unknown nuisance parameter.

Standardization involves the following steps.

1. *Center the Statistic:* The population mean, μ, is subtracted from the sample mean giving the random variable, $\overline{Y}_n - \mu$, which has an expected value of zero. (Strictly speaking, this difference between the average and the mean would not be called a "statistic" since it includes the parameter, μ.)
2. *Scale the Statistic Magnitude:* Since statistics can come in an almost endless variety of measurement units, we will need to express the statistic in a common unit of measurement called a standard deviation. The magnitude of the statistic is scaled by dividing by $\sqrt{\sigma^2/n}$. Our statistic is now

$$Z_n = \sqrt{n}\left(\overline{Y}_n - \mu\right) / \sigma$$

which is our standardized statistic. Standardized sample means will all have the same first two moments. The unknown scaling parameter, σ, can be either estimated or cancelled out of a ratio statistic; the cancelling out of this parameter in a ratio statistic is the more common approach and is followed here.

3. *Cancel the Scale Parameter:* The data is aggregated or batched into b exclusive adjacent groups of size m (if necessary, discard data from the front of the run so that $b = \lfloor n/m \rfloor$). The average of each batch is denoted as $\overline{Y}_{(i,m)}$, $i = 1, \ldots, b$. The usual unbiased estimator of the variance of the batched means is

$$S^2 = \frac{1}{(b-1)} \sum_{i=1}^{b} (\overline{Y}_{(i,m)} - \overline{Y}_n)^2$$

Inferences about the parameter, μ, are based on the random t-ratio,

$$T_{b-1} = \sqrt{b}\left(\overline{Y}_n - \mu\right) / S$$

4. *Apply Limit Theorems:* The limiting distribution of T_{b-1} is known. As $n \to \infty$ (making $m \to \infty$ since b is fixed), the distribution function of $(b-1)S^2/\sigma^2$ converges to that of a χ^2 random variable with $b-1$ degrees of freedom. Also, as $n \to \infty$, $\overline{Y}_n$ will converge to the constant μ from the law of large numbers. Also, from the Central Limit Theorem of statistics, the distribution function of Z_b will converge to that of a standard normal random variable. Thus, the distribution function of the ratio T_{b-1} (being a continuous mapping) will converge to that of a t random variable with $b-1$ degrees of freedom. The unknown scaling constant, σ, is cancelled out of the ratio.
5. *Use the Limiting Probability Model for Inference:* The limiting distribution of T_{b-1} can be used for statistical inference and estimation.

The concept of standardization can be applied to an entire time series. The original series of observations is transformed into a standardized series of observations. We will hypothesize (and test) that the series is stationary. We also assume that there is some minimal amount of randomness in the process; however, we do not assume that the data is independent. The mathematical assumptions needed are given in a paper by Schruben (1983), where it is argued that many simulations on a computer will meet the imposed restrictions for applicability. Suppose we want to standardize the output from the ith run of a simulation, with i representing the run number. Let

$$\{Y_{i,j} : j = 1, \ldots, m\}$$

denote m stationary but perhaps dependent observations in the ith output time series. We will standardize the sequence of cumulative means up to and including the kth observations, given by

$$\overline{Y}_{i,k} = \left(\frac{1}{k}\right)\sum_{j=1}^{k} Y_{i,j}$$

Similar steps to those in standardizing a scalar statistic are followed in standardizing a time series. The steps in standardization are as follows:

1. *Center the Series:* For run i, the sequence given by

$$S_{i,m}(k) = \overline{Y}_{i,m} - \overline{Y}_{i,k}$$

will have a mean of zero if the series has a constant mean.

2. (a) *Scale the Series Magnitude:* The scaling constant for dependent sequences (independent of the run i) that we use is defined as

$$\sigma^2 = \lim_{m \to \infty}[m\text{Var}(\overline{Y}_{i,m})]$$

which is just the population variance in the special case of independent identically distributed data. Magnitude scaling is done by dividing $S_{i,m}(k)$ by $\sigma\sqrt{m}/k$. The scaling constant is again unknown but will cancel out of our statistics as before.

There is one additional step required that was not necessary in the scalar standardization case. Different time series can be of different length, so we must also scale the length of the series. Thus, we have the additional step:

(b) *Scale the Series Index:* We will define the continuous index, $t = k/m$. Our previous index is thus given by $k = \lfloor mt \rfloor$. We also add the starting point $S_{i,m}(0) = 0$ so that the standardized series is 0 at $t = 0$ and $t = 1$. The result is that all standardized time series have indices on the unit interval and start and end at zero. We now have what we will call a standardized time series given by

$$T_{i,m}(t) = \lfloor mt \rfloor S_{i,m}(\lfloor mt \rfloor) / (\sqrt{m}\sigma)$$

where $\lfloor \cdot \rfloor$ is the greatest integer function.

3. *Cancel the Scale Parameter:* There are several functions that might be considered for the denominator of a ratio that cancels σ. We will consider here only one such function, the sum or limiting area under the function $T_{i,m}(t)$.

$$A_{i,m} = \frac{\sigma}{m}\sum_{k=1}^{m} T_{i,m}(k/m) = m^{-\frac{3}{2}}\sum_{j=1}^{m}[\frac{m+1}{2} - j]Y_{i,j}$$

4. *Apply Limit Theorems:* The standardized series, $T_{i,m}(t)$, will converge in probability distribution to that of a Brownian Bridge stochastic process. Thus, the Brownian Bridge process plays the role in time series standardization that the normal random variable played in scalar standardization. An important feature of the standardized series, $T_{i,m}(t)$, is that it is constructed to be asymptotically independent of the sample mean, $\overline{Y}_{i,m}$.

   There are several functions of $T_{i,m}(t)$ that will also be asymptotically χ^2 distributed. The area, $A_{i,m}$, will have a limiting (as $m \to \infty$) normal distribution with zero mean and variance

$$V = \sigma^2/12$$

   Therefore,

$$A_{i,m}^2 / V$$

   will have a limiting χ^2 distribution with one degree of freedom.

   Now consider where each of b independent replications (or b batches of data) are standardized in the manner above. We can then add the resulting χ^2 random variables, $A_{i,m}^2 / V$, for each replication or batch to obtain a χ^2 random variable with b degrees of freedom.

5. *Use the Limiting Probability Model for Inference:* In a manner similar to the scalar case, the standardized (scalar) sample mean of all of the data is divided by the square root of $A_{i,m}^2 / V$ over b to form a ratio where the unknown scale parameter, σ, cancels. For large values of m, the distribution of this ratio can be accurately modeled as having a t distribution with b degrees of freedom. The resulting (1-α)100% asymptotic confidence interval for the mean μ is

$$\mu \in \bar{\bar{Y}} \pm t_{b,1-\frac{1}{2}\alpha}\left(\frac{12}{bn}\sum_{i=1}^{b} A_{i,m}^{2}\right)^{1/2}$$

where $\bar{\bar{Y}}$ is the "grand mean" of all of the data in all batches or replications. More complicated, but superior, confidence intervals can be obtained by weighting the standardized time series as in Goldsman and Schruben (1990). The SIGMA function `STS{X}` is equal to $A_{i,m}$ for the output time series of values of `X`; this function can be used with the other weightings given in the reference.

Also, each of the replication or batch means can be treated as a scalar random variable and standardized and squared, giving another χ^2 random variable. Due to the independence of $T_{i,m}(t)$ and the $\bar{Y}_{i,m}$'s, these χ^2 random variables can be added, giving a χ^2 random variable with *2b–1* degrees of freedom. This can be considered as a "pooled" estimator of σ^2, which we will denote as Q. The same types of inferences can be made for the dependent simulation output series as were applicable in the independent data case. The resulting "*t* variate" is given by

$$T_{b-1} = \left(\bar{Y}_n - \mu\right) / \sqrt{Q / n}$$

Theoretical properties of confidence intervals formed using standardized time series are presented by Goldsman and Schruben (1984), which compares the standardized time series approach to conventional methods.

Standardized time series has been implemented in several simulation analysis packages, most notably at IBM (Heidelberger and Welch, 1983), Bell Labs (Nozari, 1985), and General Electric (Duersch and Schruben, 1986). These packages typically control initialization bias (see also Schruben, Singh, and Tierney, 1983, and Schruben, 1982) and run duration as well as produce confidence intervals. Other applications of standardized time series have been to selection and ranking problems (Goldsman, 1983) and simulation model validation (Chen and Sargent, 1984).

The asymptotic arguments above require that the batch size, *m,* become large as *n* is increased. The common method is to allow the batch size to grow as the sample size increases and keep the number of batches, *b,* fixed. Fixing *b* at 10 or 20 seems reasonable in most applications as long as the sample size is large (see Schmeiser, 1983).

The limiting probability model of a *t* random variable has the virtue that it is widely tabulated and has been studied extensively. There exist other limiting models that might be used, but none have been developed to the extent of the *t* model.

11

Generating Source Code for SIGMA Models

One of the most powerful features of SIGMA is its ability to automatically generate source code for a simulation program from a graphical model. This chapter discusses the generation of source code in C, Pascal, and FORTRAN (SIMAN or SLAM). Only the C code generator is supported as a part of SIGMA; code generated in Pascal, SIMAN, and SLAM is intended only as limited prototypes. Also discussed are ways to use source code to build large models, run models on mainframe computers, replace SIGMA's pseudo-random number generator, and run large experiments using batch files.

11.1 Source Code Generation

SIGMA's ability to generate source code gives you the power and flexibility of using a common language compiler. Currently, there are options to generate source code in C, Pascal, and FORTRAN. SIGMA-generated C simulations have proven to be very portable. (These C programs have run with very little or no modification on a variety of hardware including Apple, DEC, IBM, and Sun.) FORTRAN simulations are created using a separate utility program called **TRANSLAT**. The FORTRAN prototype simulations use either SIMAN or SLAM libraries, which are proprietary (Pegden, 1987; Pritsker, 1986), and are included here only for illustration since FORTRAN-based models have distinct disadvantages in terms of speed, size, portability, and flexibility when compared with C. Pascal is not only slower than C, it is also much less standardized; SIGMA-generated Pascal code is limited and included only to help those familiar with Pascal bridge the gap to C.

Of course, SIGMA event graph models can be run directly from within SIGMA. Neither a compiler nor knowledge of C, Pascal, or FORTRAN is needed to use SIGMA. However, SIGMA executes models interpretively (translating code as it goes); this is necessary for interactive model debugging but slow compared with compiled code. In fact, experienced SIGMA users will often rough out the logic of a model graphically, translate the model to C source code, and work directly with the generated source code.

Unlike other simulation model building environments, SIGMA gives you the full and complete source code for your simulation (including library functions like the random number generator and list management routines). This code can then be ported to other machines that have appropriate compilers.

11.2 Generating C Programs from SIGMA Models

You create C simulations from your SIGMA event graph model simply by clicking your mouse on the **Translate** command under the **File** menu and selecting **C**. You are prompted for the name of the file that will contain your C program. A file name with the extension "`.C`" should be entered. The rest is automatic and very fast. SIGMA-generated C models typically can be compiled and run without any modification. The library of support functions, `CSIGLIB.C`, is used in running these programs. The source code for this support library is included on your SIGMA disk. We will discuss the library functions later in this section.

Since there is a commonly accepted standard for the C language, your SIGMA-generated C simulation will be relatively easy to compile and run on different computer hardware. An introduction to reading C programs is given in Appendix B. If you do not know C, you should read this appendix now and look at some SIGMA-generated C code. SIGMA-generated C code is heavily commented and very easy to read. All keywords in C are in lower-case characters. Code that you create in SIGMA that is specific to your model will be written using upper-case characters. It is easy to recognize the code that was taken from your event graph—just look for the upper-case characters.

> ➢ **Important:** *Code that you created that is specific to your* SIGMA *simulation will appear in upper-case characters. Generic C code is in lower-case.*

C is a very powerful language, and there are many features of C that are not used in creating SIGMA simulations. There are also a few features of SIGMA that do not translate easily into standard C code; these also are discussed in Appendix B.

SIGMA-generated C models also have been run with the object oriented C++ language. The author has used Borland C++, Microsoft C++, and Zortech C++ with SIGMA. As you become familiar with C and C++, it is recommended that you use your skills to streamline and enrich your SIGMA-generated simulation programs. SIGMA's intent is to give you a working simulation that is also reasonably fast; you can then modify your simulation according to your experience and programming skills. Even without modification, SIGMA simulations are often much faster than the same simulations written in other popular simulation languages. Learning to use C and C++ will allow you to bring a great deal of programming power to your simulations.

In addition to vastly improved execution speed, one of the major advantages of translating your SIGMA models into C source code is the ability to use data structures and pointers, which are not used in SIGMA. Arrays, pointers, and structures are introduced in Appendix B. While structures and pointers are not available in the FORTRAN-based SLAM and SIMAN languages or in SIGMA event graphs, they are used extensively in the SIGMA C and Pascal libraries. You can look at these libraries in the `CSIGLIB.C` and `PSIGLIB.PAS` files for examples.

11.2.1 Structure of SIGMA-Generated C Simulations

The C code generated by SIGMA has a very elementary structure. It also contains extensive comments. In fact, your descriptions of variables, vertices, and edges appear right in the C source code (in upper-case letters). You should look at a SIGMA-generated C simulation (e.g., `CARWASH.C`) while we discuss the different elements of the program.

The program starts with comments that give the model run defaults that were in effect when the SIGMA event graph was translated to C. This gives you a quick look at the events and variables that are being traced during the run (you can, of course, easily change this in the C code). This is followed by the two `#include` directives that insert the library function definitions and variable definitions into your code from two header files, with the code

```
#include "csigfns.h"
#include "csiglib.h"
```

If you want to change any of the size limits (number of queues, etc.), you can do so by modifying the definitions in the `CSIGLIB.H` file.

The program next lists the event functions and state variables for your model; as in SIGMA, these are global variables. If you want, you can add local variables to the functions for each event or you can create additional global variables, say, for statistics gathering. This is followed by the `main()` function in your program.

The `main()` program initializes the variables and files in your model by calling the `initialize()` function, which appears after the `main()` function. The `initialize()` function prompts you for an output file, a random number seed, stopping conditions, and initial values of the attributes for the first event vertex in your simulation. (Values for these attributes were needed in the **Run Options** dialog box to initialize your run in SIGMA.)

The `main()` function next schedules the beginning and end of the simulation run. The stopping conditions for your C simulation will match the choice you made for stopping your SIGMA event graph that generated this model. You should look at the C code generated from event graphs that have run options that specify stopping after a specific time (**Stop on Time**) or after a specific number of occurrences of some event (**Stop on Event**). Next, the start of your run is scheduled and the event execution loop is begun. This loop looks like the following:

```
while (!run_error)
  {
  /* Pull next event from event list */
  next_event = c_timing();
  event_count[next_event]++;
  /* Call appropriate event routine */
  switch ( next_event )
    {
    case 0: run_end();
            break;
    case 1: RUN();
            event_trace("RUN",event_count[next_event]);
            break;
    case 2: ENTER();
            event_trace("ENTER",event_count[next_event]);
            break;
    case 3: START();
            event_trace("START",event_count[next_event]);
            break;
    case 4: LEAVE();
            event_trace("LEAVE",event_count[next_event]);
    }
  }
```

The event execution loop is a `While` loop that runs as long as there is no run error. The `run_error` flag is set if there is an error during execution; otherwise, this loop will continue until a run error occurs or the `run_end()` function is executed. The event execution sequence follows the event execution outline given in Appendix A. The sequence is as follows:

1. Find the event number for the next event and advance the simulation clock (called `current_time`) using the `c_timing()` library routine in `CSIGLIB.C`.
2. Increment the `event_count` for the next event by one.
3. Execute a `switch` on the next event causing the appropriate event function to be called. If the event is to be traced, the `event_trace()` function is also executed.
4. The `while` loop returns to find the next event unless the `run_end()` function has executed or the `run_error` flag has been set.

If you have a source-level debugger like that in Microsoft Codeview, QuickC, or Borland C++, you should place a "break point" at the statement `next_event=c_timing();`. Next, step through the code. You can also step into the library functions in `CSIGLIB.C` and see how they work. Setting "watch" variables lets you know what is going on in your code. If you do not have a source-level debugger with your C compiler, you should get one. They are well worth learning to use and not very expensive.

The `event_trace()` function simply prints out the traced variable values in the same format used by SIGMA. You should be careful not to trace too many variables as this might make your output line too long for your compiler. Also, you should be careful not to trace too many vertices since this also might make your output file too long. In running a C simulation, most of your execution time typically is used in writing data to the output file in the `event_trace()` function. You can speed this up a great deal by using "virtual" disk drives for output and input files in your computer's main memory. See your operating system documentation for instructions on how to specify a virtual disk drive.

> ➢ **Hint:** *Replacing the* `event_trace()` *function with some data collection variables and arrays will speed up execution of your simulation considerably.*

Elements of the `transfer[]` array (called `ENT[]` in SIGMA) are used as temporary storage buffers for the values to be placed on lists. Note that in the `CSIGLIB.H` file, elements `0`, `1`, and `2` of the `transfer[]` array are redefined to equal the `event_time`, `event_type`, and `event_priority`, respectively. Also, in `CSIGLIB.H`, the general list filing function, `c_file()`, is renamed `schedule_event()`. These name changes in the `CSIGLIB.H` file are intended to make the SIGMA-generated C simulations more readable; they have no other effect.

The remainder of your simulation is made up of functions for ending the run (`run_end()`) followed by functions for each of the events in your simulation. For each vertex in your SIGMA graph there is an event function. The event functions have the following structure:

1. The description you gave for the vertex in your event graph model.
2. Definitions of some local variables for testing edge conditions (and any local variables you might want to add).
3. Assignment of values (from the `transfer[]` array filled in from the future events list) to the parameters for this vertex.
4. Execution of the vertex state changes.
5. Testing of conditions for all exiting edges.
6. Schedule (or cancel) destination vertices for the edges with conditions that test true by:
   (a) Setting elements of the `transfer[]` array to the values of attribute expressions for the edge.
   (b) Setting the event type, event time, and execution priority for the destination vertex of this edge.
   (c) Scheduling the event onto the list of future events using the `schedule_event()` function.

11.2.2 Compiling Simulations in C

The translated C file can be compiled and linked using almost any C compiler. The compiled simulation can be executed after the object code is linked with the simulation management utilities in the file `CSIGLIB.C`. The headers `CSIGFNS.H` for function declarations and `CSIGLIB.H` for use with the Microsoft compiler and QuickC should provide sufficient guidance for compiling and running SIGMA-generated C models with other compilers. The source files for `CSIGLIB.C` are given on your SIGMA disk. These files are very heavily commented, and descriptions of the functions will not be repeated here. The `CSIGLIB.C` file must be compiled and linked with the same compiler used for the SIGMA models you have translated to C.

The batch file, `CBUILD.BAT`, is provided to compile and link a translated model using Microsoft C. A sample project make file, `CARWASH.MAK`, for QuickC is also included on the SIGMA distribution disk.

11.2.3 C Library Functions

The source code for the functions that are needed to run your SIGMA simulations are in a file called `CSIGLIB.C` on your disk. A detailed description of how each function works is given as comments at the top of each function. The functions are grouped into different sets according to their purposes.

1. Functions for Input and Run Initialization

`c_initlk();`	Initializes all global variables and lists.
`c_initfiles();`	Initializes the file structures.
`c_disk_in();`	Reads from a disk input file (`DISK{}` in SIGMA).
`c_askme();`	Asks for new value for an expression during a run.

2. Functions for Modeling Dynamics and Lists

`c_timing();`	Finds next scheduled event on the events calendar.
`c_file();`	Places entity (or future event) on a list (`PUT{}`).
`c_remove();`	Removes entity (or future event) from a list (`GET{}`).
`c_cancel();`	Cancels a specified event on the events calendar.
`c_put();`	Places `ENT[]` into `transfer[]` and calls `c_file`.
`c_get();`	Calls `c_remove` and places `transfer[]` into `ENT[]`.

3. Functions for Modeling Randomness

`lcg(long);`	Pseudo-random number generator (`RND` in SIGMA).
`gamma_fnc();`	Gamma generator (`scale=1`) (`0<shape<1`) (`GAM{A}`).
`erlang_fnc();`	Erlang generator (`scale=1`) (`0<shape`) (`ERL{A}`).
`triangle_fnc();`	Triangle generator (0,1), peak at `A` (`TRI{A}`).
`norm_fnc();`	Normal generator (`NOR{MEAN;STD}` in SIGMA).
`beta_fnc();`	Beta generator on (0,1) (`BET{A:B}` in SIGMA).

4. Optional Statistical Functions

`c_rndint();`	Generates user-defined integer (`DISK{}` in SIGMA).
`c_expon();`	Generates exponential (`MEAN*ERL{1}` in SIGMA).
`c_unifrm();`	Generates a uniform variate on a,b.
`c_sampst();`	Computes state sampled statistics.
`c_timest();`	Computes time interval statistics.
`c_filest();`	Computes statistics on entity lists.

These last functions for statistics collection use special variables defined in the file `CSIGLIB.H`. The defined constant, `S_NUMSTVARS=40`, is the default maximum number of variables for which statistics are collected. You can change `S_NUMSTVARS` to a number greater or less than 40 if you so desire by editing the `CSIGLIB.H` file. Other statistics-gathering variables are defined in `CSIGLIB.H` as follows:

`s_max[S_NUMSTVARS]`	= Maximum of variables.
`s_min[S_NUMSTVARS]`	= Minimum of variables.
`s_sum[S_NUMSTVARS]`	= Sum of variables.

t_area[S_MAXLISTS+S_NUMSTVARS] = Area under curve.
t_max[S_MAXLISTS+S_NUMSTVARS] = Maxima observations for variables.
t_min[S_MAXLISTS+S_NUMSTVARS] = Minima observations for variables.
t_preval[S_MAXLISTS+S_NUMSTVARS] = Previous value given.
t_tlvc[S_MAXLISTS+S_NUMSTVARS] = Time last value collected.
t_reset = Time of last statistical reset.
s_nobs[S_NUMSTVARS] = Number of observations.

The comments in each of these functions in the source code in CSIGLIB.C give details and options for their use. In most applications, the operations of these functions can be ignored; however, they are there in case you need them or if you want to compile them on a different computer or operating system.

There are several additional defined constants used in SIGMA. These definitions also appear in the file CSIGLIB.H. Most of these defined constants are intended to make reading your program easier; however, some of them set limits on the size of various objects in your simulation. You can change these size limits by changing the defined values for the following constants in CSIGLIB.H. The following default definitions are set:

S_MAXATRIB = 15, maximum number of entity/event attributes.

S_MAXLISTS = 25, maximum number of lists (start with list 0).

MAX_VERTS = 50, maximum number of event types (SIGMA vertices).

NO_FILE = 20, maximum number of open disk-in files allowed.

Also, some variables are defined in CSIGLIB.H. These include the following:

ENT[S_MAXATRIB] = Values of entity attributes to be filed in lists.

transfer[S_MAXATRIB] = Temporary data buffer to be placed in files.

rndsd = Random number seed for run.

current_time = Simulated system time.

lrank[S_MAXLISTS] = Attribute by which each list is ranked.

lsize[S_MAXLISTS] = Length of list of entities.

maxatr = User defined number of attributes.

11.3 Generating Pascal Programs

Pascal is less standardized and much less flexible on variable types than C. Also, not all of the SIGMA functions translate to Pascal. Nevertheless, if you know Pascal, you might want to translate your SIGMA models into Pascal.

Translating SIGMA models into Pascal is also easy and fast. As with C, select the **Translate** command under the **File** menu. You generate Pascal source code by clicking on **Pascal**. The code generated uses the `PSIGLIB.PAS` support routines. Pascal source code for these routines are given on your SIGMA disk and are similar in function to the C library functions in `CSIGLIB.C` discussed earlier. Pascal compilers do not seem to be as standardized as C compilers. The Pascal code generated by this version of SIGMA is specifically tailored for Borland's TurboPascal (Version 5.5). If some other Pascal compiler is used, you may need to make minor modifications to the SIGMA-generated Pascal code.

There are several minor differences between SIGMA-generated C code and SIGMA-generated Pascal code that should be noted.

1. In Pascal, variables, functions, or models should not have the same names; for example, a model call `QUEUE.MOD` may not have a variable named `QUEUE`.
2. The Pascal pseudo-random number generator is different than the one used in SIGMA. Therefore, SIGMA and Pascal output will not match exactly. As discussed later, you can use your own pseudo-random number generators with SIGMA-generated models.
3. The SIGMA `MOD{A;B}` function will not translate into Pascal since `MOD` is a reserved word. You will need to change `MOD(A,B)` into `A MOD B` in your SIGMA-generated Pascal code if you use the `MOD` function. Similar action must be taken if you wish to divide integers using the `DIV` function in Pascal.
4. Pascal does not parse Boolean expressions like C or SIGMA. In Pascal, you will need to use "`if`" statements.
5. Some Pascal compilers do not automatically initialize variables to zero. This is done for you by a call to the `PSIGLIB.PAS` support routines.
6. The `#include` and `#define` statements in C are not supported in the same manner by Pascal as they are in C. TurboPascal Version 5.5 links other files with your program with the expression command "`uses...`" followed by the name of the file to be linked. The `PSIGLIB.PAS` file must be compiled to your disk.

11.4 FORTRAN Simulations Using SIMAN or SLAM

With the translate utility (invoked simply by exiting SIGMA and clicking on the **TRANSLAT** icon), you can also generate SIMAN and SLAM prototype FORTRAN code for your SIGMA models. Typically, with very few modifications, your program can then be run with those commercial languages. The event scheduling features of SIMAN and SLAM, while faster and more powerful than their network or block modeling components, are relatively difficult to use. Building your model in SIGMA before translating to SIMAN or SLAM makes it much easier to build event scheduling models with these languages.

You will probably find that these FORTRAN models have two distinct disadvantages: They are likely to execute more slowly than SIGMA programs in C, and they require proprietary library functions, for which you most likely do not have the source code. The SIMAN and SLAM prototyping utility is included primarily for people who want to run their simulations with these languages for reasons other than speed, size, portability, control, and flexibility.

Although every language has its merits, C and C++ have some significant advantages over Pascal and FORTRAN. They may be a bit more difficult to learn but are well worth the effort.

11.5 Building Large Models

A technique that will allow you to build very large SIGMA models is to create subgraphs of your model and translate these into C (or Pascal). The SIGMA-generated source code for the events can easily be appended into a large simulation. Of course, you must use consistent state variable names and event numbers for the main event execution loop. Be careful not to duplicate the names of events unless you want to change these in the source code later. When putting the events together, you will need to globally change the integer values assigned to each event type in the main timing loop and where events are scheduled or cancelled. This is a very simple task with most ASCII text editors.

11.6 Running SIGMA on a Mainframe Computer

Simulation models that have been translated automatically by SIGMA into C (as well as to Pascal, SIMAN, and SLAM) have been run on a variety of computers. C programs are both faster and more easily ported to other computers; therefore, C is by far the most popular language for moving your models to different computers. You need to ensure that the C code libraries (`CSIGLIB.C`) and header files (`CSIGLIB.H` and `CSIGFNCS.H`) are also copied over to the other computer along with your simulation model. Specifically, if you have named your simulation model `MYPROG.C`, you must have `CSIGLIB.H`, `CSIGFNCS.H`, `CSIGLIB.C`, and `MYPROG.C` available to your compiler. You will need to link the object files for `CSIGLIB` and `MYPROG` before execution. Most likely you will have to make some minor changes to the header file `CSIGLIB.H`. However, you need only do this once; thereafter, the rest of your SIGMA programs should transfer directly to your minicomputer or your mainframe computer without modification.

11.7 Replacing the SIGMA Pseudo-Random Number Generator

SIGMA uses the pseudo-random number generator function, `lcg()`, provided in the `CSIGLIB.C` file on your disk. Like all pseudo-random number generators, `lcg()` is not perfect. You might want to replace this generator in your SIGMA-generated source code with one of your own. Fortunately, this is easy to do. Simply add your function to `CSIGLIB.C` and globally change the calls to `lcg()` in the other `CSIGLIB.C` functions.

11.8 Running Large Experiments Using Batch Files

It is easy to use a SIGMA-generated C simulation to make a series of runs with different input settings and place the outputs in different output files. This allows you to run large experiments with many different input conditions without constant attention. You can let SIGMA execute the required runs while you do something else. Input specification files are sometimes called "experimental frames" in other simulation languages, and can be somewhat awkward to use. However, this is quite simple using SIGMA-generated C simulations because C allows the "piping" of input and output files. Piping is where keyboard input and screen output can be replaced with any devices or files you choose; we will see how this is done shortly.

To make our illustration concrete we consider a simple example: suppose that we want to run an experiment with our carwash simulation to study the effects of the initial run conditions. Recall that the only initial conditions in this model are the random number seed, the run duration, and the initial number of cars waiting when the carwash opens each morning (`QUEUE`). The simulation, `CARWASH.EXE`, was compiled from `CARWASH.C`, which in turn was generated by SIGMA from `CARWASH.MOD`. We run this simulation by entering the name of the executable file, `CARWASH`, at the DOS prompt and answering several questions at the keyboard, as in the following dialogue:

```
>[carwash]

OUTPUT FILE (Enter File Name with Path):
[carwash.out][←Enter]

WARNING: carwash.out will be written over and the old
   data lost! Is this O.K.?(yes/[no])
[y][←Enter]

RANDOM NUMBER SEED (Enter Integer Between 1 and 32767):
[12345][←Enter]

   STOPPING TIME (Enter number of time units until run
   termination):
```

[100][←Enter]

```
Enter initial value for QUEUE:
```
[5][←Enter]

Now, suppose we want to make six runs: three independently seeded replications with two initial values for `QUEUE`, 5 and 10. The duration of all runs will be 600 minutes. We will use common random number seeds for the runs made with each of the two initial conditions. (See Section 9.8 on variance reduction techniques for a discussion of commonly seeded replicates.) Rather than repeat the above dialogue six times, we can place the exact keyboard responses we would make in six ASCII text files. The first three files will be replications with `QUEUE` initially equal to 5 (we only change the output file name and the random number seed). In the second three files, `QUEUE` is changed to 10. Each of the following input files is on your SIGMA disk:

```
CARBAT1.INP:carbat1.out y 12345 600 5
CARBAT2.INP:carbat2.out y 21121 600 5
CARBAT3.INP:carbat3.out y 31756 600 5
CARBAT4.INP:carbat4.out y 12345 600 10
CARBAT5.INP:carbat5.out y 21121 600 10
CARBAT6.INP:carbat6.out y 31756 600 10
```

Before running our experiment, we will need to make a simple change in the SIGMA-generated simulation, `CARWASH.C`. We need to remove the statement "`fflush(stdin);`" everywhere it appears in our code (four times in the initialize function for this model). This statement was placed in your simulation in case you hit stray keys while running with keyboard input. Since our input is now going to come from (hopefully) correct input data files, we should not clear the input stream. This has been done in the model `CARBATCH.C` on your SIGMA disk, which was compiled and linked to produce the executable simulation `CARBATCH.EXE` on your disk.

> ➢ **Important:** *Remove the statement* `fflush(stdin);` *from your C simulations before running with piped input data files replacing the keyboard.*

The rest is simple; we can replace the keyboard input with a filename following a < each time we run `CARBATCH.EXE`. The use of > and < to redefine the input and output devices or files is further explained in Appendix B.

Our experiment is easily set up by placing all of the command lines in a batch file that looks like the following (called BATCHCAR.BAT on your SIGMA disk):

```
carbatch  <carbat1.inp
carbatch  <carbat2.inp
carbatch  <carbat3.inp
carbatch  <carbat4.inp
carbatch  <carbat5.inp
carbatch  <carbat6.inp
```

We can now make our six runs with the single keyboard entry BATCHCAR.

Now suppose that you have a simulation (called MYMODEL.EXE) that reads a disk file called INPUT.DAT using a DISK{} function. You want to run this simulation with two different input disk files. You can place the two input data files in two disk files, say, INPUT1.DAT and INPUT2.DAT. You need only copy these disk files into the INPUT.DAT file before each run. The following batch file will run both the experiments with the two input files:

```
copy input1.dat input.dat
mymodel <keyin1.inp
copy input2.dat input.dat
mymodel <keyin2.inp
```

KEYIN1.INP and KEYIN2.INP should be literal copies of keyboard responses when you run the simulation as in the previous example in this section.

11.9 Exercises

11.9.1 Translations

Translate any of the models in Chapter 5 into C (or Pascal) and run them.

Translate any of the exercises in Chapter 5 into C (or Pascal) and run them.

12

Advanced Programming Techniques

Chapter 12 contains numerous advanced techniques that allow you to get the most out of your simulation programs. Techniques include how to start a run with simultaneously executing vertices, how to stop an event graph model on any general condition, how to run several replications of the same model in parallel, how to use arrays with more than two dimensions, how to incorporate the "`USER`" function to call any executable program on your default disk, how to reduce the number of vertices in a model without changing the model's behavior, and how to use preemptive execution to eliminate the need to schedule some events.

12.1 General Starting and Ending Conditions

If several vertices are to be simultaneously executed or scheduled at the start of a run, create a start-run vertex (called, say, `RUN`) as vertex 1. Create edges from this vertex that schedule all the other vertices unconditionally with zero delay times and correct execution priorities.

To stop a run on any general condition, simply create a `STOP` vertex as the counted event. Add appropriate edges entering this vertex, conditioned by the desired halting criterion. In SIGMA, set the ending condition in the **Run Options** dialog box to **Stop on Event**, locate the `STOP` vertex in the drop down list, and click on it. The **Iterations** box should have a count of 1.

12.2 Simultaneous Parallel Replications

To assess the variability of a simulation output series, it may be desirable to run several independent replications of the same model. Parallel replication

Figure 12.1: Three Simultaneous Parallel Replications of a Queue

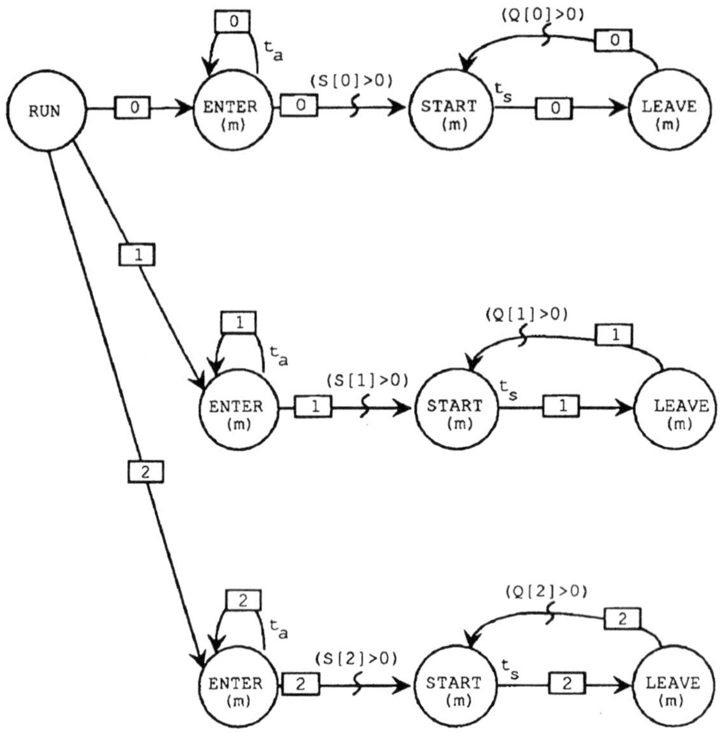

has a number of advantages, such as making the detection of initialization bias much easier.

With event graphs, it is very easy to run these replications simultaneously. Simultaneous replication of a model is another application of event parameters and edge attributes. It might be useful here to think of parallel replicated simulations as an array of identical event graphs that are to be run at the same time.

To set up parallel replications, simply add two state variables to the model: one variable to identify the replication to which a particular event occurrence belongs and the other variable to tell how many simultaneous replications are desired. The replication index is globally added to the end of all edge attribute and event parameter strings. Also, every one of the original state variables gets an added array dimension for this index.

Consider the model of the single server queue we saw in Figure 2.6. An event graph for running three simultaneous replications of this model is given in Figure 12.1. The problem with this model is that, in addition to being

Figure 12.2: Simultaneous Parallel Replications of a Single Server Queue

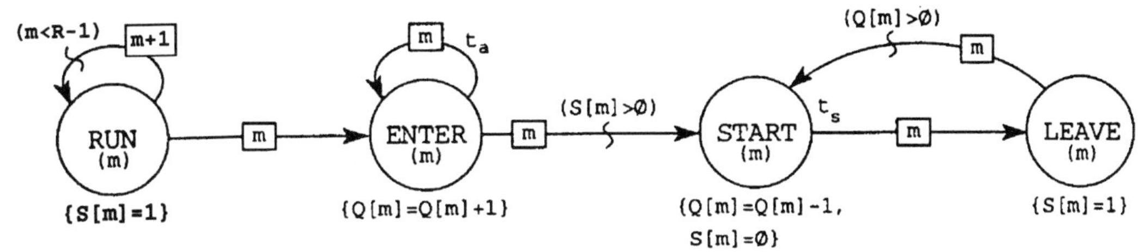

messy, each time another replicate is desired a new subgraph has to be appended. We can solve this easily by using parameterized events; define R as the desired number of replicates and M as an index to identify the replicate to which an event vertex belongs. The resulting parameterized event graph now looks like that in Figure 12.2. Finally, as a more complicated example, consider the model in Figure 5.14, where we kept track of transient entities. Our queueing simulation event graph is parameterized for R simultaneous replications in Figure 12.3. The event graphs in Figures 12.2 and 12.3 are complicated and good tests of your comprehension. Fortunately, event graphs for these models look almost the same as the simple model in Figure 2.4. In fact, these models were created from our basic queueing model by using an ASCII editor to globally add the parameter M to all edge attribute and vertex parameter strings and to make M an additional state variable dimension. The only other change needed was to set up a loop on the initial RUN vertex to start each replicate.

Figure 12.3: Simultaneous Parallel Replications of a Queue with Five Servers Collecting Customer Waiting Times

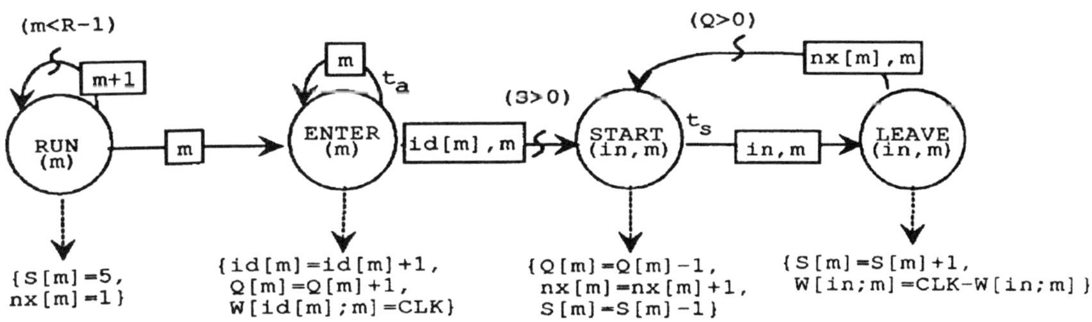

Notice that if the same arrival rate is used for all three replications, one ENTER event could be used to generate arrivals for all three replications. This would automatically implement the variance reduction technique of common random number streams discussed in Section 9.8. If our replicates represented small differences in some of the input parameter values, this technique could be used to estimate the gradient of the simulation response in a "single run" using finite differences between the averaged output series.

An implementation of parallel replications in SIGMA is given in the model REPLCATE.MOD on your SIGMA distribution disk. Here we set up our basic model, CARWASH.MOD, for simultaneous parallel replication. The SIGMA graph for this model looks identical to that for CARWASH.MOD in Chapter 3, with the single exception of the "do loop" for the RUN vertex. In the RUN vertex, each replication is STARTed and indexed by the value of M passed as a vertex parameter.

12.3 Event Graph Reduction

It is sometimes possible to reduce the number of vertices in an event graph without changing the behavior of the model. Simulations with few events will often run faster than models with more events although this is not always the case. An event graph with fewer vertices may lead to a more efficient simulation program; however, the graph may be more difficult to understand. Generally, models with a large number of very simple vertices will be easier to debug or modify than models with fewer but more complicated vertices.

It is possible, however, to increase the efficiency of a simulation without increasing the complexity. This is done by using preemptive vertex execution, a scheduling delay time for an edge given by an asterisk (*). Recall that a delay time of * means that the scheduled destination vertex is executed immediately, without being placed on the future events list. It preempts any other events that might be scheduled at the same time. This often results in a significant reduction in simulation execution time.

We will use our basic single server model to illustrate event graph reduction. The START vertex can be eliminated if we redefine Q (queue) to be the number of customers in the system, including any customers in service, rather than the length of the waiting queue. The resulting graph is shown in Figure 12.4. To get the same run time efficiency, the START vertex can be effectively eliminated without changing the graph except to make the delay times on the edge from ENTER to START and the edge from LEAVE to START asterisks (*) rather than zero. This would cause the execution of the START event to occur without ever scheduling it on the list of future events.

Figure 12.4: Event Graph without a START Event

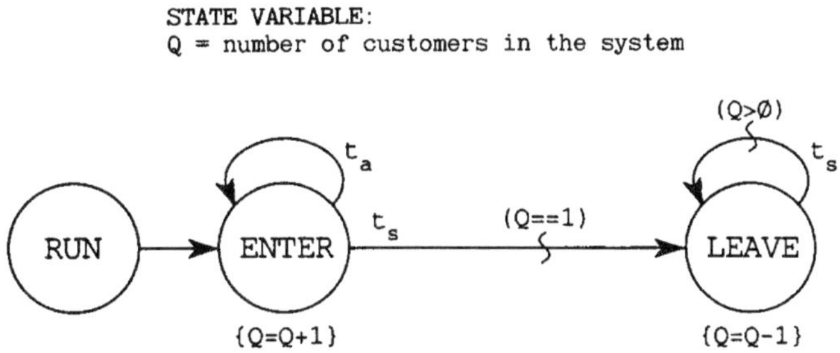

It is possible to eliminate all of the vertices in our model except the RUN vertex (which is executed only once anyway) and the LEAVE vertex. This would require that we generate the (random) number of arrivals to the queue during the time that a single customer is served. We will call this number of arrivals during a service interval A. In some simple cases, a value for A can be generated very easily (e.g., if the times between customer arrivals are exponentially distributed, A will have a Poisson distribution). The single-event model for our queue is shown in Figure 12.5. While the model in Figure 12.5 might run very fast, it is difficult to enrich; therefore, it is not as useful as some of our earlier models for this system.

It is possible to use edge attributes to assign values to vertex parameters rather than using state changes. At first glance, this might seem like a complicated way to do things, but it is useful. Sometimes edge attributes make the model clearer; sometimes they do not. We will illustrate this technique with

Figure 12.5: Single Vertex Model (RUN and LEAVE)

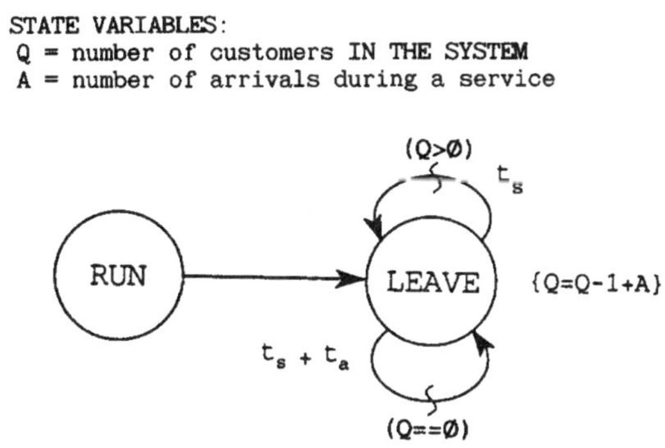

Figure 12.6: Event Graph That Uses Edge Attributes to Assign Values to Vertex Parameters

```
STATE VARIABLES:
Q = number of customers waiting in line
    (initial value set to zero, by default),
S = status of the server (0=busy/1=idle),
    (initially set equal to 1=idle).
```

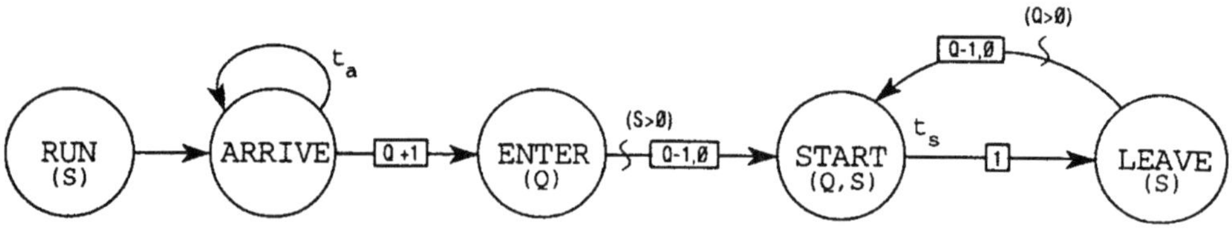

our single server queue, where the status of the server, S, and length of the waiting line, Q, will become parameters of the START and LEAVE vertices. The values of these parameters are passed as edge attributes. When an entering customer finds the server idle (S>0), the customer will begin service, making the server busy; the value 0 is passed as an attribute of the edge from ENTER to START into the START parameter, S. The result is the same as having the state change S=0 in the START vertex. Similarly, when the server finishes service, its status will change back to idle (1). This is done by passing the edge attribute value, 1, along the edge from START to LEAVE into the parameter, S, of the LEAVE vertex. This is shown in the event graph in Figure 12.6 (NOSTATEQ.MOD).

We can do this since there is no chance that the state variable, S, will change during the time intervals represented by the delay times of the edges from ENTER to START and from START to LEAVE. If we had more than one server in this system (S initially greater than one), we would not be able to do this since S might be changed by more than one instance of an event vertex.

12.4 Using Arrays of Arbitrary Dimension

Two-dimensional arrays will be sufficient to meet most simulation modeling needs. However, if you find it necessary to have higher dimensional arrays, the method discussed here is easily implemented. Assume that one is conceptually working with a two-dimensional (N by M) array, A. That is, the element in the ith "row" and jth "column" of this array is the value of the variable $A_{i,j}$. The equation $L = A_{i,j}$ written in SIGMA is L=A[N*J+I]. Recall that we start indexing arrays with zero, not with one.

Figure 12.7: Representing a Multidimensional Array as Elements of a One-Dimensional Array

K = 0

I \ J	0	1	2	3	4	5
0	0	4	•••			20
1	1	5	•••			
2	2	•••				
3	3					23

K = 1

I \ J	0	1	2	3	4	5
0	24	28	•••			44
1	25	•••				
2	•••				42	
3						47

This indexing scheme can be extended to more than just two dimensions. For example, element $B_{i,j,k}$ of an N by M by L array would be the element `B[N*M*K+N*J+I]` of a single dimensional array `B[.]`. The logical structure for a three-dimensional array of size (4,6,2) is shown in Figure 12.7. Each element of the single dimensional array `B[.]` is shown in a cell. In the figure, a 4 by 6 by 2 dimensional array is represented as elements `[24*K+4*J+I]` of a one-dimensional array. Thus, element `[2,4,1]` is `[24*1+4*4+2]` or `[42]`.

A more sophisticated array indexing scheme uses "ragged" arrays, which sometimes saves memory. Here the total number of elements in all rows strictly less than `I` is the value of the variable `M[I]`. The `i,j`th element of the ragged array, *A*, is given by the nested arrays `A[M[I]+J]`. When an element is added to the array, both the `M` and `A` arrays are updated (resulting in some additional computational overhead). Ragged arrays can be useful when

Figure 12.8: The Passing of Information Between SIGMA and a USER Variable Function

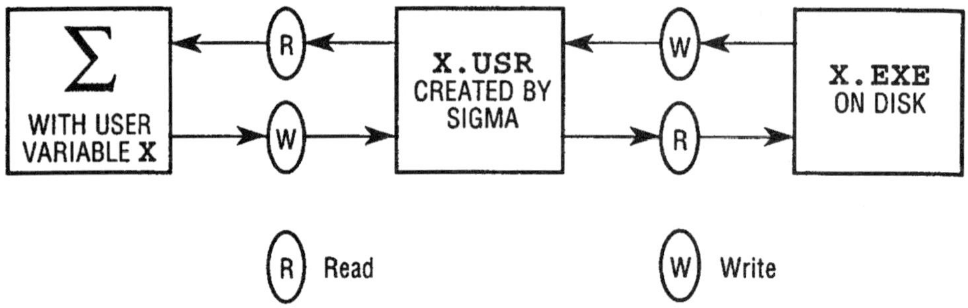

the rows of a matrix are of unequal length (for example, the `i,j`th element is some characteristic of the `i`th customer in the `j`th queue). The trade-off in using a ragged array is favorable when the rows (or columns) of the array are of significantly differing lengths.

12.5 USER Defined Functions

A variable type, perhaps unique to SIGMA, is the `USER` variable. A `USER` variable is actually a function call to an executable program on your default disk. These functions may be used in any expression where a state variable is used. A `USER` function can be written in any language (e.g., FORTRAN, C, BASIC, etc.) that creates an executable file. These files do not need to be linked with SIGMA. `USER` variables are followed with a string of arguments separated by semicolons and enclosed in braces. The arguments may themselves be floating point expressions computed from other state variables. SIGMA `USER` variables work well only where more than the conventional DOS memory is available, such as workstations.

Associated with a `USER` variable is an executable program that reads input (sent by SIGMA) and writes results (for SIGMA) using a file with its own name and the extension `.USR`. For example, if you have a `USER` type variable named `X`, the program `X.EXE` would use the file `X.USR` as its interface for communicating with SIGMA. This file is used to pass the values of function arguments from SIGMA to the executable function and for SIGMA to get the function value passed back from the executable program. A varying number of arguments can be passed, but a single result is returned. The passing of data between SIGMA and the executable function corresponding to the `USER` variable `X` is depicted in Figure 12.8 (where `R` means read and `W` means write).

To illustrate, let us suppose that your model has the USER variable called USERDEMO. An expression in which SIGMA might use USERDEMO could be X=USERDEMO{Y*3;RND-6;7}+Z. USERDEMO refers to an executable function on your default disk called USERDEMO.EXE. This expression will compute the value of X as follows: First, the values of the three arguments to USER are computed by SIGMA and written onto the temporary file USERDEMO.USR. Next, USERDEMO.EXE is executed reading the file USERDEMO.USR. The results of the computation in USERDEMO.EXE are written (over the previous data) onto the file USERDEMO.USR. SIGMA then reads the result, which is added to the value of Z and assigned to X. The skeleton of the corresponding program (in C) called USERDEMO.C would look like the following (comments /**/ are indented):

```
   /* This is a function that does nothing but change
      any input to the number 5.0. It is intended to
      demonstrate parameter passing through a file named
      userdemo.usr */
   /* Include some standard C header files */

#include        <stdio.h>
#include        <fcntl.h>
#include        <conio.h>
#include        <io.h>

main()
{
   /* Define a pointer to a buffer file to pass data to
      and from SIGMA. This file will have the same name
      as the function but with an extension of .usr. */
FILE *fp;
   /* Declared arguments of the user function are stored
      in the file, userdemo.usr, by SIGMA.*/
float arguments;
   /* Declarations for local variables for this function
      would be here.*/
   /* Open the buffer file, userdemo.usr, created by
      SIGMA for reading*/
fp = fopen("userdemo.usr","r");
   /* Loop to read the arguments written by SIGMA.*/
while (fscanf(fp,"%f",&arguments) > 0)
   {
   /* Assign argument values to local variables in this
      loop.*/
   }
   /* Close the buffer file, userdemo.usr, after reading
      the argument values*/
fclose(fp);
   /* Re-open the buffer file for function output*/
fp = fopen("userdemo.usr","w");
```

```
    /*********************************************/
    /* This would be the body of your function with  */
    /* the result written to the buffer file. Here we*/
    /* simply write 5.0 into the buffer file         */
    /*********************************************/
fprintf(fp,"5.0");
    /* Close the buffer file so SIGMA can read the
       result.*/
fclose(fp);
}
```

A simple prototype of a USER variable is provided on the SIGMA disk as the C program USERDEMO.C. This function is called as a USER variable in the SIGMA model USERDEMO.MOD. The SIGMA model USERDEMO.MOD is a single-event "simulation" that reads data from a file and executes the program USERDEMO.EXE, which has been compiled from USERDEMO.C. USERDEMO.MOD (randomly) reads input data from a disk file named USERDEMO.DAT (illustrates generating random variables from a discrete empirical probability function). USERDEMO.MOD also executes the program USERDEMO.EXE on your default disk, passing arguments through the file USERDEMO.USR. The program USERDEMO.C reads in three argument values that were written by SIGMA into a file it created called USERDEMO.USR. Then USERDEMO.C always returns the constant value 5 to SIGMA through the same buffer, USERDEMO.USR.

USERDEMO.EXE could have just as easily been written and compiled in Pascal, FORTRAN, or another language that creates a valid DOS executable file. As long as the conventions presented here are followed, linking USER variable functions to SIGMA is not necessary. You also need not worry about calling sequences for passing parameter values. This makes USER variables very easy to write and incorporate into your SIGMA models.

SIGMA USER variables have not been included in the translations to C or Pascal code. However, SIGMA USER type variables are simply calls to executable files on your default disk. The compiled object code (.OBJ file) for the called program can be linked with SIGMA-generated source code. Each time the corresponding USER type variable appears in an expression in the SIGMA-generated code, it is replaced with a standard C function call. If you have a USER function that is written in a language that cannot be compiled and linked with object files created by the compiler you use for SIGMA-generated source code, you can sometimes use the C function, system(), which is slower than linking the programs together before execution.

12.6 Eliminating Event Scheduling

By using preemptive vertex execution (delay times = *) it is sometimes possible to run a model without scheduling events. The model NOLIST.MOD on your

Figure 12.9: Event Graph without Scheduled Events

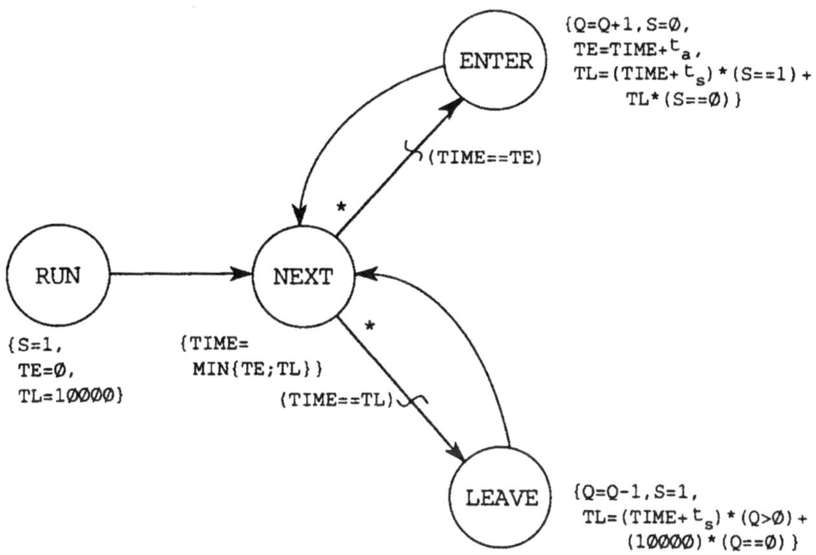

SIGMA disk does this for a single server queue. The graph for this model is given in Figure 12.9. In this model, the times of the next events are computed as state changes and the simulated virtual time (normally kept by SIGMA in the variable, CLK) is updated in the vertex, NEXT. The simulation generated from this model runs very fast but is difficult to modify. For readers interested in the more theoretical aspects of event graph modeling, the graph for this version of a single server queueing system is related to the geometric dual of the event graph of our earlier model of a single server queue, CARWASH.MOD.

12.7 Exercises

12.7.1 Multidimensional Arrays

Write an expression that will translate a point (w,x,y,z) in a four-dimensional array P with dimensions I by J by K by L into a one-dimensional array q.

13

Modeling Complex Systems

In this chapter, several models of complex systems are presented in detail. The first is a model with multiple types of jobs and multiple classes of workers. Next, a system with a network of queues is introduced. Starting with a simple model with one type of job, enrichments are made until the model simulates a queueing network with multiple job types. Finally, transient entities are introduced into the model to collect customer waiting times. This last model is considerably simpler than the other models since it makes use of the SIGMA `PUT{}` and `GET{}` queue management functions. However, it will execute somewhat more slowly.

13.1 Multiple Types of Jobs and Multiple Classes of Workers

To keep the ideas simple, here we will model a system with two types of jobs (short jobs and long jobs, indexed as job types `0` and `1`) and two classes of workers (trainees and experienced technicians, indexed as technical classes `0` and `1`). We will assume that 30% of the jobs are long jobs. When a job arrives, it is randomly assigned by a shop foreman to a technical worker class. We assume that 80% of the long jobs and 30% of the short jobs are assigned to experienced technicians. The job assignment rule is summarized in Table 13.1.

Table 13.1: Probability of Worker Assignment by Job Type

	Job Type 0	Job Type 1	Probability
Worker Class 0	0.7	0.2	0.55
Worker Class 1	0.3	0.8	0.45
Probability	0.7	0.3	1.0

Figure 13.1: Verbal Event Graph for Model with Two Job Types and Two Worker Types

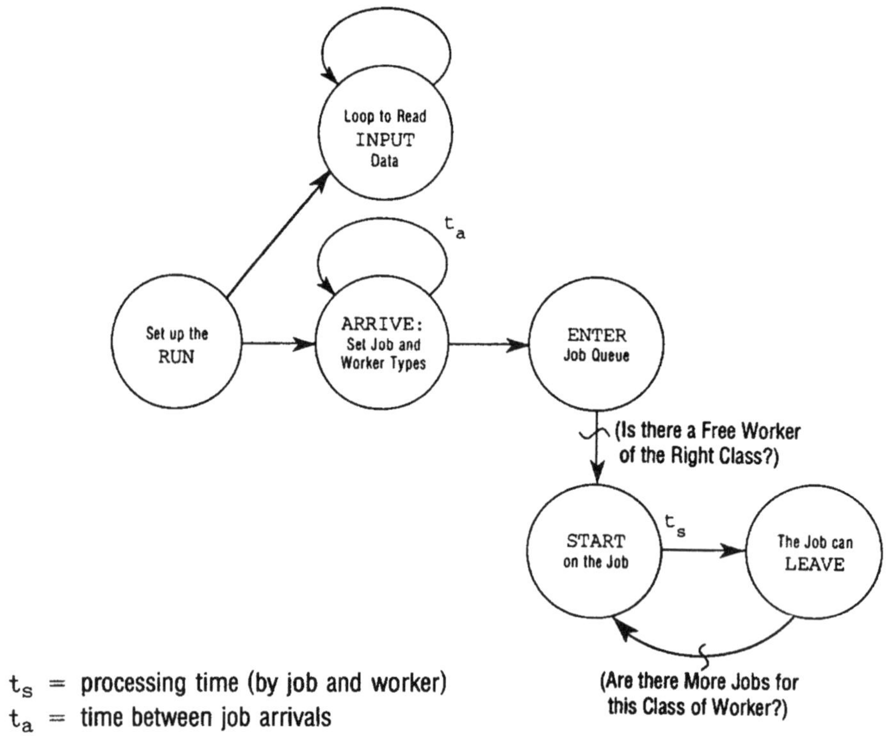

We will store the data for this model, including the assignment probabilities, in an easily changed data file. This will allow us to use our simulation to study the effects of staffing different numbers of each class of worker, making different assignments of jobs to worker classes, and having different service time distributions.

We will begin by developing a verbal event graph for this system like that given in Figure 13.1. We see from the edge conditions in Figure 13.1 that we need to define state variables that allow us to test if a worker is free in each technical class and if there are jobs waiting for each class of worker. Therefore, we will define the following state variables:

`FREE[0]` and `FREE[1]`: The number of idle technicians of each class.

Table 13.2: Queues by Tech Class and Job Type

	Job Type 0	Job Type 1
Tech Class 0	Queue[0]	Queue[1]
Tech Class 1	Queue[2]	Queue[3]

QUEUE[0],...,QUEUE[3]: The number of jobs waiting, categorized by the four different worker class-job type combinations.

The particular assignment of waiting lines for jobs is given in Table 13.2. We also need to know the type of job and the technical class of the worker involved in each event; so we define the indices as follows:

TYPE: Index for the type of job (0 = short, 1 = long).

TECH: Index for the class of technician (0 = trainee, 1 = experienced).

Finally, since there are different mean processing times for each type of job and technical class of worker, we will define

TIME[0;0],...,TIME[1;1]: A table of the mean processing times for each job type and worker technical class.

The queue for each TYPE of job and TECH class of worker is QUEUE[TYPE+2*TECH]. This illustrates how to use the 1-dimensional array, QUEUE, to represent a table. (Section 12.4 shows how to use arrays of any dimension.)

Of course, we could use the SIGMA PUT{} and GET{} functions to place the jobs in queues. We could then directly collect waiting times for the different types of jobs. While using PUT{} and GET{} might be easier to follow, it would tend to make the simulation run more slowly than using simple resident entity variables and estimating customer waiting times with Little's Law (see Section 5.7).

An event graph model for this system is given in Figure 13.2. The simulation TWOTYPES.MOD on your SIGMA disk is an implementation of our model for this system. You should open this model and follow along with this discussion by clicking on each vertex and its exiting edges as we discuss the model details.

We will assume that jobs arrive at random intervals with an exponential (Erlang{1}) distribution with a mean of 4. Job service times are also distributed according to an exponential distribution with means given by the TIME

Figure 13.2: An Event Graph for Multiple Job Types and Multiple Worker Types

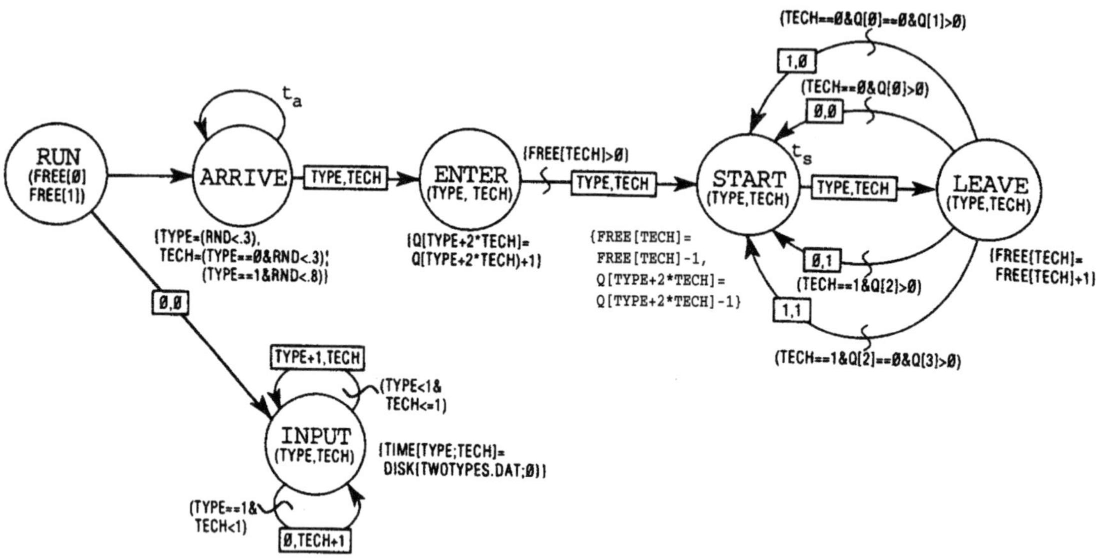

table. The values for the `TIME` table are in the data file `TWOTYPES.DAT` according to the layout in Table 13.3.

The `RUN` event initializes the run. Initial values for the number of free technicians of each type, `FREE[0]` and `FREE[1]`, must be specified at the start of each run in the **Run Options** dialog box.

After every occurrence of the `RUN` event, unconditionally initiate the first job arrival by scheduling the `ARRIVE` event to occur without delay. Also, the data `INPUT` event is scheduled unconditionally to occur without delay, using the attribute values `0,0`.

Table 13.3: Data Layout for `TWOTYPES.DAT`

	Job Type 0	Job Type 1
Tech Class 0	Time[0;0]	Time[0;1]
Tech Class 1	Time[1;0]	Time[1;1]

The INPUT event is simply a loop indexed by TYPE and TECH that reads in the TIME[TYPE;TECH] table from the file TWOTYPES.DAT. The INPUT vertex has a higher execution priority than the ARRIVE event so that all of the data gets read in before the first arrival occurs.

The ARRIVE event models the arrival of a job. This event assigns the type of job using a randomly valued Boolean expression, TYPE=(RND<.3). The probability that the value returned by the RND function is less than 0.3 is equal to 0.3; therefore, the condition on the right-hand side of this statement will be 1 (true) with probability 0.3 and 0 otherwise. This will make the TYPE of the arriving job 1 (long) with the correct probability of 0.3 and 0 (short) with a probability of 0.7, as we desire.

Next, we assign this job to one of the worker TECH classes. This can be done with the compound Boolean "or" (¦) statement:

```
TECH=(RND<.3 & TYPE==0)¦(RND<.8 & TYPE==1).
```

To see how this works, note that we have just determined the TYPE of job with the correct probability. We can now assign this job to a worker TECH class conditioned on job TYPE. Each of the two conditional probabilities comes from the second row of Table 13.1 and corresponds to one of the Boolean variables that we connected with a logical "or" (¦).

After every occurrence of the ARRIVE event, we unconditionally schedule the next arrival in 4*ERL{1} minutes (exponential with a mean of 4). This ARRIVE vertex will have a lower execution priority than any START event that might be scheduled by a LEAVE event in order to avoid the creation of a "phantom" worker if there is a time tie between the ARRIVE and LEAVE events (see Section 5.1.3 for an example of a phantom server). Also, whenever the ARRIVE event occurs, the ENTER event will be unconditionally scheduled to occur without delay, passing the attribute values of the job TYPE and worker TECH class to the ENTER vertex.

The ENTER event is where the job joins the proper waiting queue with parameters that give the job TYPE and worker TECH class involved. The waiting queue is incremented with the state change

```
QUEUE[TYPE+2*TECH]=QUEUE[TYPE+2*TECH]+1
```

If (FREE[TECH]>0), there is a free worker of the proper TECH class, and the entering job will schedule a START event with the free technician without delay. The values of the job TYPE and TECH class are passed to the START vertex. The START event, if scheduled by an ENTER event, has a higher execution priority than any of the other events in case of a time tie.

The START vertex has parameters specifying the job TYPE and worker TECH class that are involved. This event makes an additional worker busy with the following state change: FREE[TECH]=FREE[TECH]-1. Also, the state change

QUEUE[TYPE+2*TECH]=QUEUE[TYPE+2*TECH]-1

will remove a job from the queue for this job TYPE and worker TECH class. After every occurrence of the START event, a LEAVE event for this job TYPE and worker TECH class is scheduled to occur after the exponential (ERL{1}) service time with mean of TIME[TYPE;TECH].

The LEAVE event models the end of service with parameters for this job TYPE and worker TECH class. One additional worker is now freed by the state change

FREE[TECH]=FREE[TECH]+1

There are four edges from the LEAVE event to the START event, one for each combination of worker TECH class and job TYPE.

If TECH==0 and QUEUE[0]>0, then service the waiting job; that is, schedule the START event to occur without delay using the parameter value(s) of (TYPE,TECH)=(0,0).

If TECH==0 and QUEUE[0]==0 and QUEUE[1]>0, then service the waiting job; that is, schedule the START event to occur without delay using the parameter value(s) of (TYPE,TECH)=(1,0).

If TECH==1 and QUEUE[2]>0, then service the waiting job; that is, schedule the START event to occur without delay using the parameter value(s) of (TYPE,TECH)=(0,1).

If TECH==1 and QUEUE[2]==0 and QUEUE[3]>0, then service the waiting job; that is, schedule the START event to occur without delay using the parameter value(s) of (TYPE,TECH)=(1,1).

The first pair of conditions apply for workers of TECH class 0 and the last pair for workers of TECH class 1. Looking at each pair of conditions, we see that short jobs are given priority over long jobs since we do not START with a long job (type 1) unless there are no short jobs waiting in QUEUE[0] for TECH=0 or in QUEUE[2] for TECH=1.

13.2 A Network of Queues

Manufacturing and service systems that are composed of different processing centers where customers or jobs move from one processing center to another can be modeled effectively as networks of queues. Such systems are very common. In fact, several commercial simulation languages have been developed primarily to model queueing networks. In this section, we will start building our own queueing network simulator. The enrichments suggested by the exercises at the end of this chapter, if done correctly and efficiently, could result in a modeling tool that is as good as or better than many commercial simulators. The key difference is that you will have complete control over your simulation program, so you can change or enrich it as you see fit.

In the material that follows, we will refer to jobs passing through different machine groups. For other applications (e.g., hospitals), substitute the appropriate transient entities (patients) and resident entities (departments) in the model description.

A common example of a queueing network is a production system called a *jobshop.* A jobshop has several different processing centers with one or more identical machines at each center. Often the machine centers are located in the same area. Different types of jobs have different routings through the jobshop. In this section, we will use a jobshop as our example of a queueing network. While we develop our model, keep in mind any changes you might want to make to simulate other types of queueing networks, such as patient flow in a health care system, baggage flow in an airport, or information flow through a bank. A good jobshop simulation can come close to being a general "all purpose" discrete event system simulator.

Here we will develop a fairly general jobshop model. The models in this section are constructed to illustrate different aspects of event graph model building. Specifically, we will use multidimensional and circular arrays, `DISK` input, nested loops, branching, and event parameter passing. These models are more complicated than those we have seen previously and may be a bit intimidating at first. Remember that event graphs allow us to concentrate only on one vertex or edge at a time. We will start simply and enrich our model in small pieces.

To make our model specific, we will consider a jobshop with five groups of different types of machines and identify each machine group with a particular value of the index, `G`. This jobshop will process three types of jobs. Each type of job will have a different routing and a different processing time. We will indicate the type of job with the index, `TYPE`. In this system, the resident entities are the machines and queues associated with each machine group. The transient entities are the jobs flowing through the system.

We want to simulate systems with up to `MAXG` different machine groups. `MAXG=5` in our example, and we will number the machine groups `0` to `4`. A

Table 13.4: Number of Idle Machines in Each Processing Group

Group (G)	S[G]
0	3
1	2
2	4
3	3
4	1
5 (exit)	0

dummy sixth machine group (group 5) is used to indicate that a job has left the shop. We will denote the number of idle machines in group G as S[G]. There will be 3 machines in group 0, 2 machines in group 1, 4 machines in group 2, 3 machines in group 3, and 1 machine in group 4. Initially, we will set all machines idle according to Table 13.4.

Job processing times are modeled with an Erlang distribution with different means depending on machine group and job type involved. This jobshop is the most advanced system modeled in Law and Kelton (1991).

To make it easier to change input when running experiments, most of the specifications for our models will be read from disk files. Data driven models are much easier to use than models that must be updated each time a change is desired. Data input files sometimes are called experiment files or experimental "frames." Section 11.8 explains how you can easily conduct large simulation experiments with many runs that use different input and output data files.

13.2.1 A Single Type of Job

To begin, we will consider only one type of job, which we designate as job type 0. With only one type of job in the system, we can get by with a model that includes only resident entities (the queues and machines). For each machine group, all machines are identical; therefore, we only need to keep track of the number of jobs waiting and the number of machines that are idle. As we know from our earlier models, pure resident entity models tend to be much faster and easier to understand than models that include transient entities. If we were not intending to enrich this model considerably, we could model a single job type much more easily (see FLOWSHOP.MOD on your SIGMA disk for an example).

> *Comment:* It is important that the same machine group not be on the route more than once. A process where a job returns to the same machine group is called a *re-entrant* flow. Re-entrant flow occurs where production involves building up layers of material, as in

Table 13.5: Job Type 0 Routing

TASK	Machine Group	Mean Processing Time
0	2	0.250
1	0	0.300
2	1	0.425
3	4	0.250
4	5 (exit)	-99

automobile painting or semiconductor manufacturing. If we allow multiple visits to the same machine group, all waiting jobs might not be identical. (Some are first-timers; others have been there before.) Re-entrant flow will be allowed later when we add transient entities to our jobshop model.

The successive steps in processing a job are called *tasks;* the integer, `TASK`, will be the position that a job is on its route. The routing for job type `0` is shown in Table 13.5. We use a mean processing time of -99 time units for pseudo-machine group 5 to make any error of using this group obvious. In order to read the disk file containing our routing and timing data, we will need to know the maximum number of tasks on any of the routes for all of the jobs; we will call this variable `MAXT`.

Although it is not necessary for this model, when we enrich our model we will need to know which task corresponds to a particular machine group. We will keep this information in an array, `TASKLIST[G]`, indexed by the machine group `G`. That is, the value of `TASKLIST[G]` will be the `TASK` performed by machine group `G` on the job's routing. Our state variable definitions are summarized in Table 13.6.

Table 13.6: State Variables for Jobshop with One Type of Job

`MAXG`	Maximum number of machine groups
`MAXT`	Maximum number of tasks on all routes
`G`	Index identifying each machine group
`S[G]`	Number of idle machines in each group
`Q[G]`	Number of jobs waiting for each group
`TASKLIST[G]`	Task number for each machine group
`TASK`	Current position of a job on its route
`ROUTE[TASK]`	Machine group needed for each task
`MTIME[TASK]`	Mean processing time for each task
`OUTPUT`	Count of the number of finished jobs

Figure 13.3: Event Graph for NETWORK1.MOD with Only Job Type 0

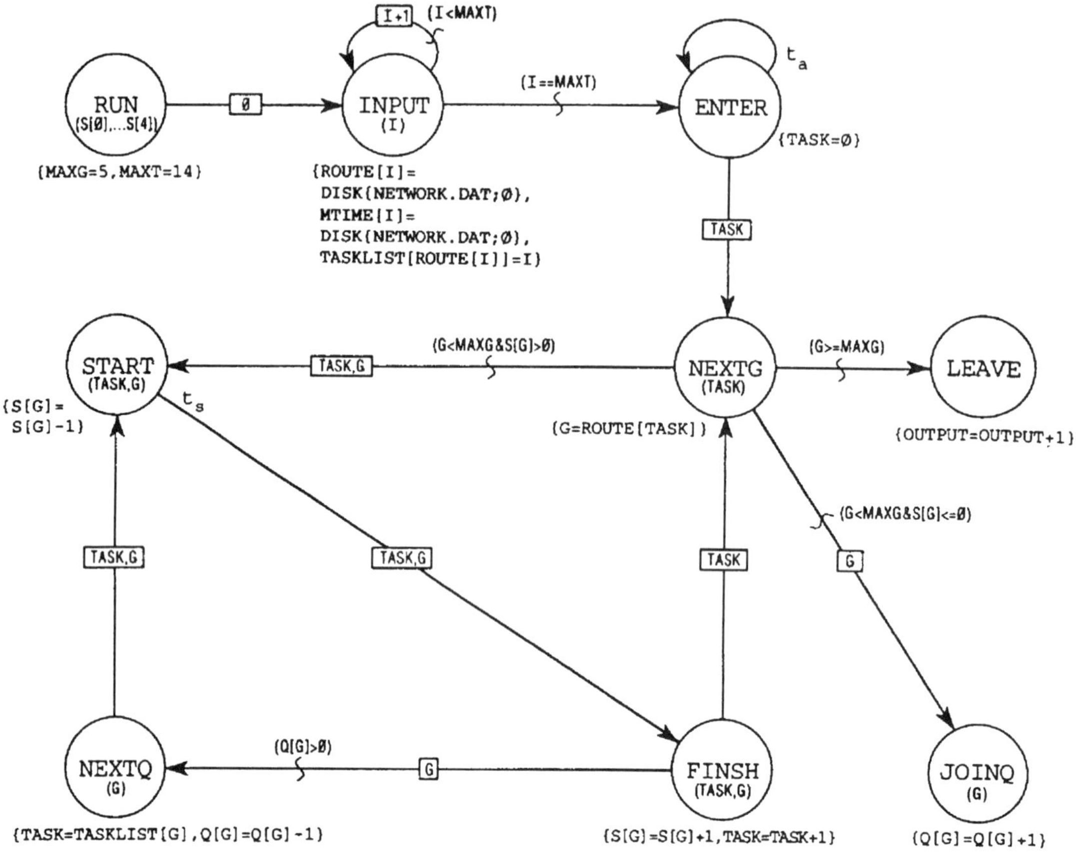

Our jobshop model with a single job type is given in Figure 13.3. This event graph model can be read in the usual way, by sequentially looking at each vertex and its exiting edges. The event descriptions in Figure 13.3 should clarify how this model works. Also refer to the model NETWORK1.MOD on your SIGMA disk. The data for this model and its subsequent enrichments are on your SIGMA disk in the file called NETWORK.DAT. You might want to print a copy of the input data file, NETWORK.DAT, so you can see what data is read into our model.

> In the RUN vertex, we will read initial values for some system constants and start our run. It is possible from the input data file, NETWORK.DAT, to read the maximum number of machine groups, the maximum number of tasks for any job routes, and the initial

values for the numbers of machines in each machine group. After the RUN event, data for the routes will be read in the INPUT loop.

The INPUT vertex reads the routing and timing data for our job. For I equal to each task, the machine group and average processing time are read from successive lines of the NETWORK.DAT file. Also, the task number for each machine group is set. There are two edges exiting the INPUT vertex:

> If I<MAXT, we have not read in all of the task data, so we loop to repeat the INPUT vertex for I+1.
>
> If I==MAXT, all of the input data has been read, and the first job can ENTER the system.

The ENTER vertex is where a new job arrives. This vertex sets TASK=0, indicating that the job is at the beginning of its route. After every occurrence of the ENTER event, we loop to schedule the next job to ENTER. We also schedule the NEXTG event to determine the machine group that is first on the job's routing.

The NEXTG vertex determines the next machine group on a job's route from the job's TASK number with the state change, G=ROUTE[TASK]. The job will take one of three possible exiting edges from the NEXTG vertex:

> If G>=MAXG, the job is finished and can leave the network, so we execute the LEAVE event.
>
> If G<MAXG and S[G]<=0, the job is not done but all the machines in the next group on its route are busy. This job must join the queue for machine group G; this is done by passing the value of the machine group as a parameter to the JOINQ vertex.
>
> If G<MAXG and S[G]>0, the job is not done and there is an idle machine in the next group on its route. Therefore, this job can immediately START processing with this task number and the machine group.

The START vertex models the start of a task at a particular machine group. The state change for this vertex is simply to have one less idle machine in group G. After every occurrence of the START event, we must schedule the job to finish processing with the same task and machine group. We do this by scheduling the FINSH vertex to occur after a processing delay with the current values of TASK and G passed as edge attributes to the parameter variables, TASK and G, for the FINSH vertex.

The FINSH vertex models the event where a task is finished at a particular machine group. This event causes another machine in group G to become idle and the task counter for the job to increment by one. After every occurrence of the FINSH event, we determine the next machine group on the job's route in the NEXTG vertex by passing the current value of the task number. Also, after the FINSH vertex, if Q[G]>0, jobs are waiting in the queue for the newly idle machine in this group, and we schedule the NEXTQ vertex where we select the next job waiting in the queue.

The NEXTQ vertex determines the task of the next job waiting in the queue for machine group G and removes it from the queue. This vertex determines the task number from the TASKLIST and decrements the number of jobs waiting in Q[G]. The determination of the TASK is not really necessary for this model, but it will be necessary when we add more job types. After the NEXTQ event, we START processing the current TASK at machine center G.

The JOINQ vertex models the event of a job joining the queue for a particular machine group. This event simply increases the number of jobs waiting in line for this machine group.

At the LEAVE vertex, a job leaves the system. Here we simply count the output from the jobshop.

The event execution priorities to break time ties in events are given in the model NETWORK1.MOD on your SIGMA disk. Basically these execution priorities are intended to ensure that when two jobs want a machine at the same time only one of them will get it.

13.2.2 Multiple Job Types

We will next enrich our model by adding multiple types of jobs. Each job type will have its own set of routings through the network and a different processing time at each machine group.

To keep the discussion specific but still relatively simple, we will add only two additional types of jobs. The number of job types can be increased without making the model any more complicated. Our two additional jobs will have the routings and mean processing times indicated in Tables 13.7 and 13.8. In our example, we have job types arrive according to the following probability distribution:

Probability {Type=0} = 0.3,
Probability {Type=1} = 0.5, and
Probability {Type=2} = 0.2.

Table 13.7: Job Type 1 Routing

Task	Machine Group	Mean Processing Time
0	3	0.550
1	0	0.400
2	2	0.375
3	5 (exit)	-99

Since the jobs waiting in a queue are no longer identical, we must keep track of the order that tasks are waiting in each line. However, we still do not have to introduce transient entities into our model. For model flexibility and efficiency, it is good practice to avoid using transient entities as long as possible; this can often be done by not drawing unnecessary distinctions between the jobs.

By stacking all of the routing data into one table, we can concatenate our three job types into a long `ROUTE` array that allows us to keep track of all of the information we need to know about each job. This is shown in Table 13.9.

If we know the current `TASK` of a job, we will know everything we need to know about the job to model our system. Knowing the `TASK` for a job tells not only its machine group and processing times but also the job type. To illustrate, `TASK=7` in our concatenated routing table refers to the third processing step for a job of type 1; `TASK=12` refers to what was task 3 of job type 2. (Look at the earlier routing table for job type 2 and see that machine group 3 with mean processing time of 0.450 is the correct data for this task.)

To have the jobs flow along their proper routes, we simply start each type of job at its appropriate task number (`TASK=0` for job type 0, `TASK=5` for job type 1, and `TASK=9` for job type 2). We then increase the `TASK` after each process until the job reaches dummy machine group `5=MAXG`, where the job leaves the network. `TASK`s where different types of jobs enter and leave the jobshop are indicated by the arrows in the last column of Table 13.9. For exam-

Table 13.8: Job Type 2 Routing

Task	Machine Group	Mean Processing Time
0	1	0.600
1	4	0.125
2	0	0.350
3	3	0.450
4	2	0.500
5	5 (exit)	-99

Table 13.9: Routing Data for Three Job Types

TASK	Machine Group (G)	Mean Processing Time (MTIME)	ENTER/LEAVE
0	2	0.250	⇐Type 0 ENTER
1	0	0.300	
2	1	0.425	
3	4	0.250	
4	5 (exit)	-99	⇒Type 0 LEAVE
5	3	0.550	⇐Type 1 ENTER
6	0	0.400	
7	2	0.375	
8	5 (exit)	-99	⇒Type 1 LEAVE
9	1	0.600	⇐Type 2 ENTER
10	4	0.125	
11	0	0.350	
12	3	0.450	
13	2	0.500	
14	5 (exit)	-99	⇒Type 2 LEAVE

ple, jobs of type 1 will start with `TASK=5`, proceed through `TASK=6` and `7`, and leave when they get to `TASK=8`. The entry `TASK` for a job can be determined by the state changes

```
R=RND,
TASK=5*(R>.3)+4*(R>.8)
```

To see how this works, recall that Boolean variables like `(R>P)` are set equal to `1` when they are true and to `0` whenever the condition is false. Assuming that `RND` is a true random number, the condition `RND>.3` will be false 30% of the time and both Boolean variables will be zero, making the `TASK=5*0+4*0=0`. This causes 30% of our jobs to be type `0`, which start their route with `TASK=0` as we desired. Similarly, `(.3<RND<.8)` is true 50% of the time, making `(RND>.3)=1` and `(RND>.8)=0`. Thus, `TASK=5*1+4*0=5` for 50% of the newly entering jobs, making these type `1` jobs, which will start with `TASK=5`. Finally, `(RND>.8)` will be true 20% of the time, making both Boolean conditions true. Thus, `TASK=5*1+4*1=9`, which are type `2` jobs, start their processing with `TASK=9`, as it should be. What we are doing here is generating random job types and mapping them into the corresponding initial `TASK` values.

We will keep the order that `TASK`s are waiting for each machine group in a two-dimensional table called `QUE[G;I]`. The rows of the `QUE` array represent the lines for each machine group and are independent of each other. For each machine group, G, there will be a row in the QUE array. The Ith column in row G will contain the value of the TASK that is Ith in line for machine group G.

When we refer to placing a job in the queue for machine group G we will mean placing its current TASK number in the last open column in row G of the QUE array. We will set a maximum length for any one line in our system equal to MAXQ. Since we are not trying to model limited waiting space, we need to set this maximum queue size large enough so that it is not exceeded during our runs.

The array FIRST[G] will be the column of QUE for the task that is currently first in line at machine group G. When a job is serviced at machine group G we simply add one to the value of FIRST[G]. To illustrate how this works, assume that TASKs were placed in the queue for machine group 4 in the following order: 3,2,11,2,6,3,2. The fourth row of the QUE array would now look like the following:

```
I            0  1  2   3  4  5  6  7  8   ...  MAXQ
QUE[4;I]     3  2  11  2  6  3  2  0  0   ...   0
             ↑                     ↑
             FIRST[4]=0            LAST=FIRST[G]+Q[G]=7
```

Now suppose that some time later, tasks 3 and 2 at the front of the queue have been processed and task 11 is now at the front of the line. After we processed tasks 3 and 2, we incremented the pointer, FIRST[4], twice. Now FIRST[4]=2, indicating that the task in column 2 (task 11) is now first in line. When task 11 is served, FIRST[4] is again incremented from 2 to 3 so that the task in column 3 (task 2) is now first in line.

We also have a variable, LAST, which is the column in the QUE array where the next job to arrive for service at machine group G will be placed. Since Q[G] is the total number of tasks in queue G, the value of LAST can be computed when needed as FIRST[G]+Q[G] for any of the machine groups.

To conserve space, we will use a circular index for the columns of the QUE array. When the column index reaches MAXQ, it wraps around and starts over at zero. This is done by expressing all column indices for QUE modulo (MAXQ) using the MOD{} function. For example, instead of adding 1 to FIRST[G] to increment the location of the first TASK in QUE, we use the expression

```
FIRST[G]=MOD{FIRST[G]+1;MAXQ}
```

When FIRST[G] reaches MAXQ it will start over at zero. Circular arrays are easily implemented by referring to column number I in QUE as column number MOD{I;MAXQ}.

Table 13.10: Additional State Variables for Multiple Jobs

MAXQ	Maximum length of any line
QUE[G;]	List of tasks in line G
FIRST[ ]	Location of the first task in line G
LAST	Last position in the current line
R	Random number used to determine job type

The additional variables for our model are summarized in Table 13.10. The enriched simulation discussed in this section is on your SIGMA disk as NETWORKR.MOD, and the model is given in Figure 13.4.

Figure 13.4: Event Graph for NETWORKR.MOD

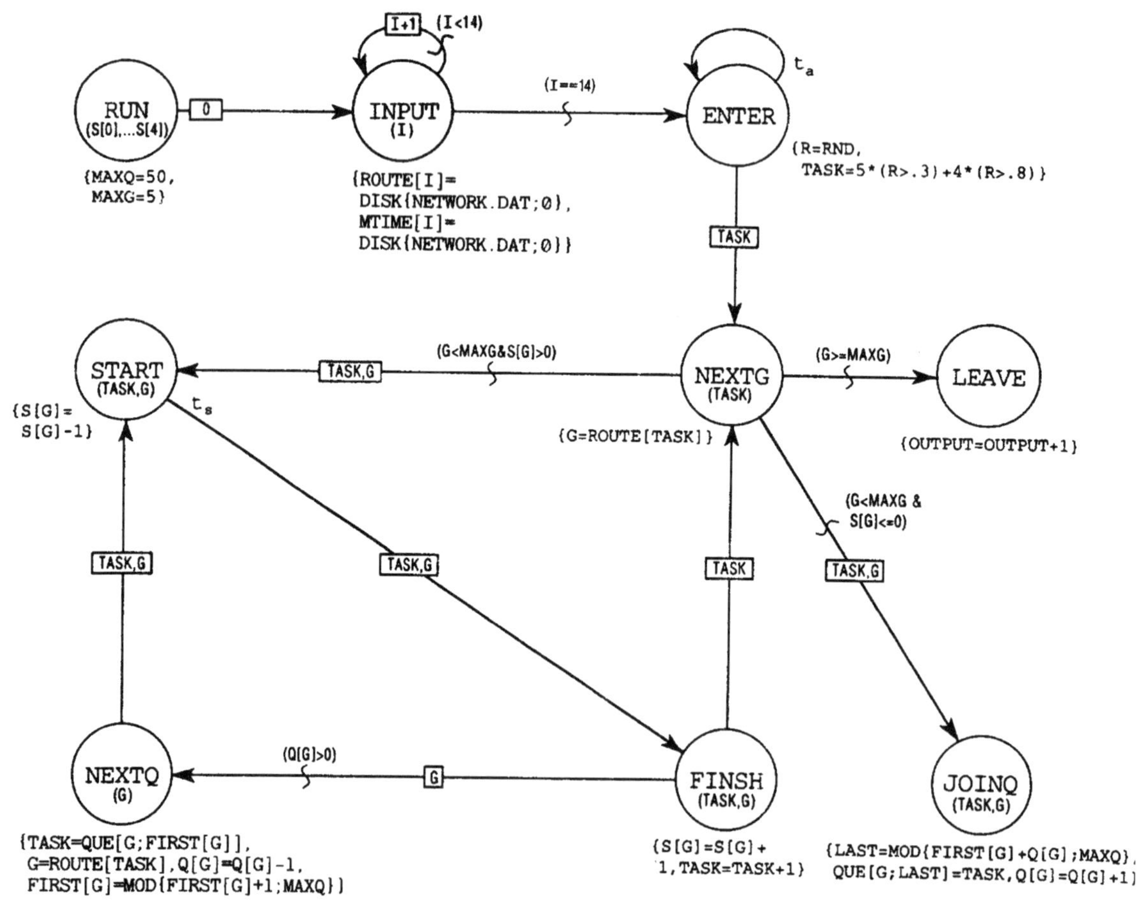

By ignoring the details and taking a high-level view of the event graph, we can see basically what is going on. The most distinctive feature of this graph includes the two triangles in the center area, where two "activity" cycles can be seen. One cycle (NEXTG, START, FINSH, and back to NEXTG) is followed by each job as it proceeds through the tasks on its routing. The job's task is incremented in the FINSH vertex and the machine group G changes whenever the job enters the next group vertex, NEXTG.

The other activity cycle (START, FINSH, NEXTQ, and back to START) is the busy/idle cycle of each machine in a particular machine group. Around this cycle the machine group G does not change. The TASK changes each time the machine selects the next job in its queue at the NEXTQ vertex. Therefore, the upper cycle can be viewed as the activity of a transient entity (a job) moving between resident entities (from machine group to machine group). The lower cycle is the activity of a resident entity (machine group) processing successive transient entities (jobs). We still do not identify particular jobs except by the TASK they are on, so this is basically a resident entity model.

We will read the graph in Figure 13.4 as before, by looking at each vertex and its exiting edges in succession. The START, FINSH, and LEAVE vertices along with their exiting edges are exactly like those in the model for a single job type in the previous section. The RUN and INPUT vertices are also very similar to our earlier model. The big differences are in the JOINQ vertex, where TASKs are placed in the queues, the NEXTQ vertex, where tasks are removed from the queues, and the ENTER vertex, where task types are generated.

> The RUN vertex reads initial values for some system constants and starts our simulation, just like the RUN vertex of the previous section. In addition, we also specify the limit on maximum queue length, MAXQ.
>
> The ENTER vertex is where a new job arrives. Here we also implicitly determine the job type by randomly generating the first TASK for the new job with the statements

```
R=RND,
TASK=5*(R>.3)+4*(R>.8)
```

> The exiting edges of the ENTER vertex are exactly like the model in the previous section.
>
> The JOINQ vertex models the job joining the queue for a machine group. This event causes the TASK to be placed LAST in the queue for machine group G.

```
LAST=MOD{FIRST[G]+Q[G];MAXQ},
QUE[G;LAST]=TASK,
Q[G]=Q[G]+1
```

The NEXTQ vertex models the selection of the next job in the queue. This removes the TASK that is FIRST in the queue for machine group G.

```
TASK=QUE[G;FIRST[G]],
G=ROUTE[TASK],
Q[G]=Q[G]-1,
FIRST[G]=MOD{FIRST[G]+1;MAXQ}
```

The exiting edges of the NEXTQ vertex are identical to those in the previous section.

Execution priorities for the events (to break time ties) are again set to ensure that when two jobs want a single idle machine, only one of them will get it. Such time ties occur when a new job arrives at the same time that another job finishes or when two jobs finish processing at the same time. The model NETWORKR.MOD on your SIGMA disk has execution priorities set with this intent.

This example is a good test of your comprehension of simulation modeling. Do not let the complexity of the graph discourage you; focus on one vertex at a time. As before, successively interpret each vertex and all its exiting edges. The graph keeps everything tied together. This is a rather complicated model; however, reading an event graph is much easier than understanding the simulation source code. It may help to think of the edges as belonging in one of three categories:

1. Edges for the flow path of the transient entities (jobs).
2. Edges in the cycle for the resident entities (machine groups).
3. Edges that update the queues.

The two central cycles in the graph are where all the action occurs. The rest of the graph merely reads in data, computes waiting times, and maintains the queues. You can think of the job cycle and the machine cycle as being two "activities" that interact where they share a common edge (i.e., during processing). After a little practice, you should find that looking at the paths of temporary entities or the activity cycles of permanent entities on an event graph can tell you, pictorially, a great deal about how the system works.

13.2.3 Adding Transient Entities

We might want to collect job waiting times directly rather then use Little's Law (introduced in Section 5.7). This is done by adding transient entities to our model using the PUT{} and GET{} functions to manage the queues. The ENT[] array will serve as a buffer for the attributes of jobs that we wish to put into and get from the queues. We will define elements of this array as follows:

ENT[4] = type of job,
ENT[5] = next task for the job, and
ENT[6] = time the job entered the shop.

The other elements of the ENT array can be used for other job attributes. If we want to give some jobs priority over other jobs, we can set the values of the ranking job attribute with the RNK[] array and have priority ranking of the queue by job type or arrival time.

The transient entity model for our jobshop is NETWORKT.MOD on your SIGMA disk. The event graph for this model is in Figure 13.5. To save space on the event graph, we will shorten our notation and replace the variable TASK

Figure 13.5: Event Graph for NETWORKT.MOD

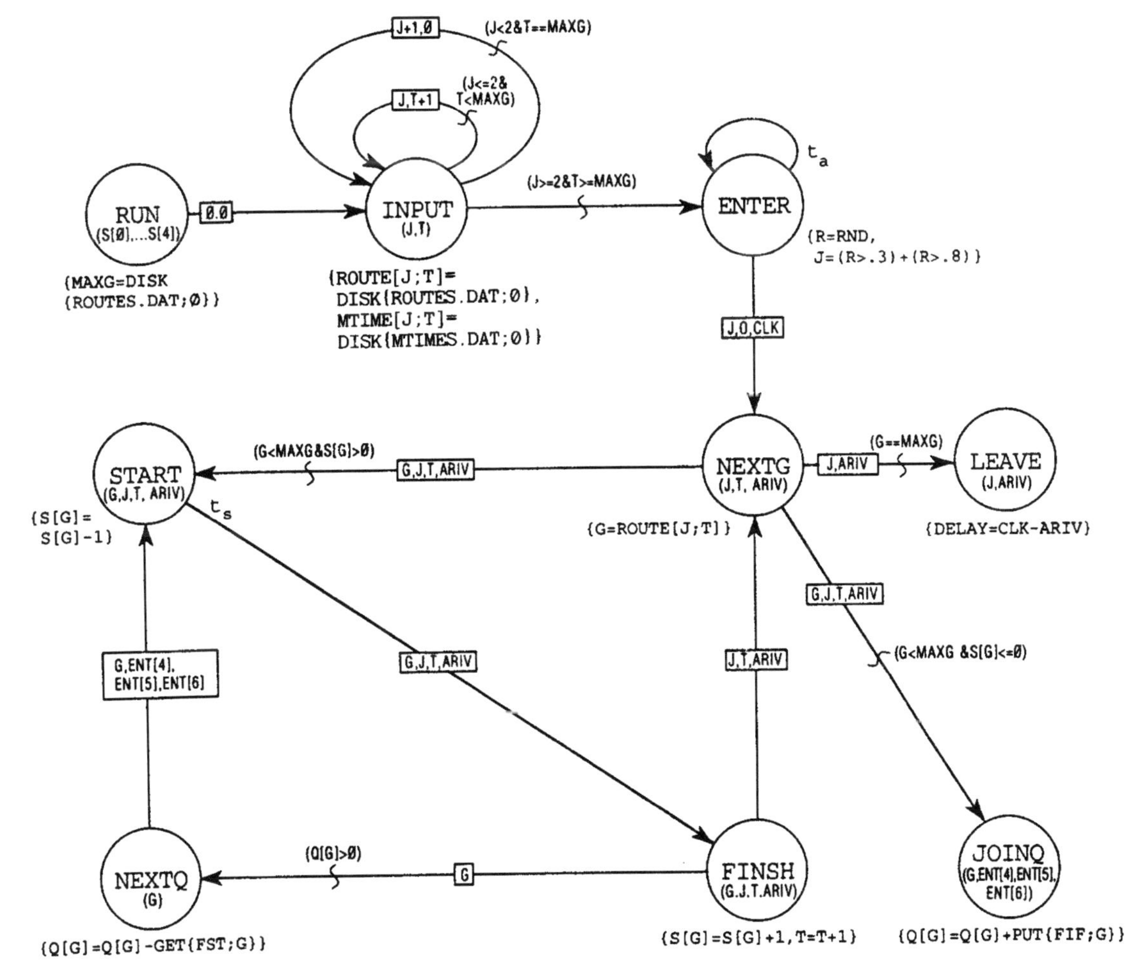

with the variable T to designate task numbers. We explicitly designate the job type with the variable J. Job routings and timings are kept in two-dimensional tables. The tables ROUTE[J;T] and MTIME[J;T] hold the machine groups and the mean processing times for each of the tasks, T, involved in processing each type of job, J.

The total time spent in the system will be collected in an output variable called DELAY. When a new job arrives, we mark its entry time with the variable ARIV. Look at the simulation NETWORKT.MOD in SIGMA while we discuss this model. Besides the use of the PUT{} and GET{} functions to manage queues, the major difference in this model is that the type of job, J, its current task, T, and the time the job arrived, ARIV, are passed along the edges. The event vertices and the exiting edges for the new model are discussed below.

> The INPUT vertex now is a two-dimensional nested loop reading in the ROUTE and MTIME tables by job TYPE and TASK. The data for these tables are in the disk files ROUTES.DAT and MTIMES.DAT.
>
> The ENTER vertex has the same state changes as the model in the previous section; however, it passes the current clock time, CLK, into the variable, ARIV, along the edge to the NEXTG vertex. This sets the time that the job arrives in the system and will be used to compute how long it took to process.
>
> Like our previous models, the NEXTG vertex models the determination of the next machine group on the job's route. However, here we do this by looking up the machine group, G, in the ROUTE table, G=ROUTE[J;T]. If there are no idle machines in the next machine group, the job will join the queue in the JOINQ event by passing the type of job, J, the current task, T, and the job's arrival time, ARIV, into elements 4, 5, and 6 of the ENT[] array, where they will be PUT into queue G.
>
> The START vertex is essentially the same as for our previous models. The job arrival time, stored in the variable ARIV, is merely passed through this vertex to the next vertex.
>
> The FINSH vertex is also essentially the same as in our earlier model.
>
> The JOINQ vertex models a job joining a queue. This vertex has as its parameters G, ENT[4], ENT[5], and ENT[6], which receive the values of G, J, T, and ARIV that were passed to it from the NEXTG vertex. The single state change, Q[G]=Q[G]+PUT{FIF;G}, places these values for this job first in queue G and increments the value of Q[G] by the value 1 returned from the PUT function.
>
> The NEXTQ vertex models the selection of the next customer in queue G. The single state change, Q[G]=Q[G]-GET{FST;G}, removes

the data for the next customer and places it in elements 4, 5, and 6 of the ENT array and subtracts 1 (the value returned by the GET function) from the number of jobs waiting in Q[G]. The values of these elements of the ENT array are passed as edge attributes into the parameters J, T, and ARIV of the START vertex along with the machine group G.

The LEAVE vertex computes the total time that the job spent in the system by subtracting its arrival time from the current clock time, CLK, with the state change, DELAY=CLK-ARIV.

13.3 Exercises

The models referred to in these exercises are on your SIGMA *disk. Exercises identified as mini projects are more extensive and may take considerably longer than the typical exercise.*

13.3.1 Condensing Events

Use pre-emptive vertex execution (edge delays equal to * to "condense" several event vertices into a single event) to make the simulation NETWORKR.MOD run as fast as possible without changing the output. Be careful about using * too often and causing a stack overflow, as explained in the text.

13.3.2 Worker Assignment Problem

In the model TWOQUEUE.MOD on your SIGMA disk, there are 2 servers assigned to a constant time setup operation followed by 6 workers assigned to a random time processing operation. Is this a good assignment of the 8 workers? Experiment with the model to determine an optimal allocation of the 8 workers, assuming that all of the workers are equally skilled and paid the same amount. Justify your answer (how do you define "optimal" and why?) as well as the way you designed your experiment.

13.3.3 Execution Priorities

Look at the model TWOQUEUE.MOD on your SIGMA disk. This is a model of two multiple-server queues in a series, where a constant time setup operation is followed by a random duration processing operation. The first set of servers has a constant service time of 5 minutes. The second set of servers has a random service time with an Erlang(1) (i.e., exponential) distribution with a mean of 4 minutes.

(a) Click on the double edge between the STRT1 and LEAV1 vertices. Change the execution priority on the edge from the LEAV1 vertex to the

STRT1 vertex from 3 to 5. Notice that QUEUE[1] goes negative before time 60. Why?

(b) Change the execution priority on the self-scheduling edge from STRT1 to STRT1 from 1 to 6. Notice that the number of idle servers for queue 0 goes negative right away. Why?

13.3.4 Welding Line (Mini Simulation Project)

The following system is used to weld hoods to automobiles. There are several parallel welding robots. The cars pass by the robots on conveyor lines. Transfers between lines are done using cranes that run north and south on fixed tracks. A schematic of the system for four welding robots is given below.

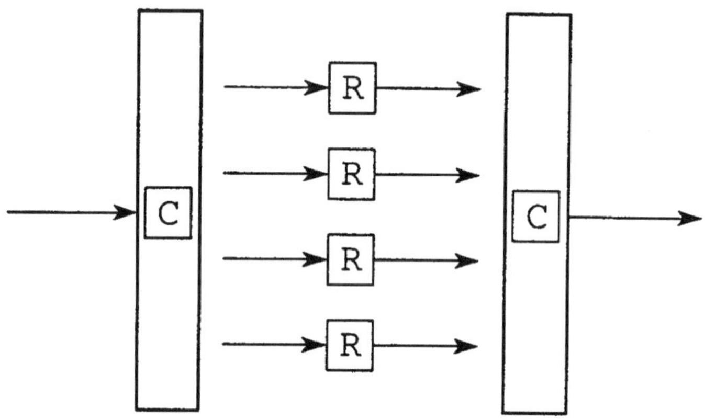

Type	Percent	Average Weld Times
A	31%	50 (sec.)
B	16	63
C	16	25
D	16	41
E	12	155
F	9	155

The input rate is 93 jobs per hour. There are six types of automobiles produced at this plant. The average welding time and percentage for each type of car are given below the figure. The time it takes for the crane to pick up a car or release a car is 8 seconds. For simplicity we consider only an approximation to the effects of crane acceleration. The first section of track traveled takes 9 seconds and every additional section traveled without stopping takes 6.5 seconds. A section of track is between each of the loading or unloading points on a crane track. For example, the crane takes 15.5 seconds to travel two sections of the track without stopping.

Cars must leave the welding operation in the same order that they enter it, since components added later on in the assembly process must be for the right car. Setup times for some of these later operations are very large, thus requiring that setups start before cars arrive. The last crane in the schematic above sorts the cars as they come out of the hood welding operation.

Write a simulation program for this system. For now, consider each of the times to be deterministic. Your model should allow up to three cranes per track and up to six parallel robots. You may use any computer language that you wish for this assignment. Flesh out your model and translate it to C or Pascal to fill in the details (see Chapter 11). Use "entities" and the `PUT` and `GET` functions.

In the automobile production subsystem simulation model, add 33 seconds to each of the average welding times given. Now make the welding times uniformly distributed with a range of 20% of the mean. All confidence intervals are to be at the 90% level.

(a) Run the simulation of the automobile production system five times for 200 cars each. Use independently selected pseudo-random number generator seeds for each replication. Compute a confidence interval for the mean throughput rate of the system (rate that cars exit).

(b) Run the simulation for one run of 1000 automobiles. Compute confidence intervals for the mean throughput rate using the batched means method with 5 batches.

(c) Comment on the above experiment, including identification of possible sources of error.

(d) Given that there is space for 15 automobiles in the system, decide how these 15 buffer spaces should be allocated. Justify your design and give confidence intervals for the throughput rate.

13.3.5 A Barge Unloading System (Mini Simulation Project)

River barges arrive at a warehouse carrying "piggyback" truck trailers mounted on flatcars. These flatcars are to be unloaded and mounted on railroad flatcars that will be taken away by trains. There are 4 trailers on each barge. The time between barge arrivals has a uniform distribution between 3 and 5 hours. A barge must wait for a single berth before it can dock. A single crane is used to move the trailers from the barge to the warehouse and from the warehouse to the flatcars. After being unloaded from the barges and mounted on flatcars, the trailers are taken to a large rail yard where they are assigned to trains according to their destination.

Once a barge has docked, 4 spaces in a warehouse must be free in order for unloading to start. There are 20 trailer spaces in the warehouse. The time to unload a barge is uniformly distributed between 1 and 3 hours. A train arrives at the warehouse to collect the waiting trailers. The time between train arrivals has a uniform distribution between 3 and 7 hours. The train has between 6 and 12 empty flatcars when it arrives. It takes 30 minutes to load each trailer onto a flatcar.

(a) Develop a resident entity simulation model that will keep track of the lengths of all important queues and utilizations of the warehouse space, berths, and crane. Clearly state any assumptions you make in your model. Run this model for a time of 20 (hours) and trace the number of trucks unloaded. Run the model for 100 hours in **High Speed** mode and use the output file to see how many trucks were unloaded from the barges. What is the major bottleneck: the berth, number of available flatcars, warehouse space, the crane?

(b) Consider the purchase of an automatic crane that cuts the barge unloading time by 50%. Model this (reduce the delay time between the start unload event and the end unload event). Run the new model for 100 time units and observe (from the output trace) the number of trucks unloaded. Do not create any new state variables.

(c) Add the necessary (two) event vertices that permit the crane to shut down every 10 hours for 1 hour of preventive inspection/maintenance. The crane will finish what it is doing before undergoing inspection.

(d) Eliminate the inspection/maintenance procedure and have the automatic crane break down every 8 to 12 hours (uniformly distributed). Have the repair time be uniformly distributed between 0.5 and 1.5 hours. If the crane is busy when it breaks, the current unloading operation must be restarted from scratch (use a cancelling edge). Run the simulation for 100 hours and compare with the systems in parts (a), (b), and (c). (This problem was suggested by G. Samorodnitsky.)

13.3.6 Buffer Capacities

In the model `NETWORKR.MOD`, assume that each machine group has a finite capacity queue. For machine group `G`, no more than `B[G]` jobs can be waiting. If the next queue for a job is filled, that job does not free its machine; it is blocked. Enrich your model to include this constraint. Be careful not to send two parts to a queue that only has space for one; when the second part arrives, it will find the queue full! (Hint: Reserve space in the next queue before freeing the current machine.) Assume that `B[G]` is 4 for all machine groups, and run at least 20 jobs through your model. Debug your model.

13.3.7 A Layout (Mini Simulation Project)

Using `NETWORKR.MOD` as a starting place, include the transit times between the various machines. Assume the job transit data is deterministic (conveyors?)

and is provided in an array called `TRANS(I,J)`, which is the time it takes to travel from machine group `I` to machine group `J`. The transit times are proportional to the distance between machine groups (state assumptions you are making). What data structures in C or Pascal could be used effectively in this model? (Hint: The `ENTITY` structure.) Tell how the structures will be used. How is your model improved with these structures (if at all)?

(a) Translate your model to C or Pascal. Use this simulation (or your model) to help determine an efficient high-level layout for a jobshop (i.e., the shapes, sizes, and locations for the different machine groups). Each machine takes 16 square yards of space (including space for the job being processed and aisle space). Each job waiting in the queue takes 4 square yards of space. Transit between machine groups is by overhead crane, so travel is rectilinear, not line-of-sight. Transit time between machine groups is 5 seconds per yard traveled between the head of each input queue. Write a report that explains and sells your design.

(b) Assume that you will make $10 for each type `1` job completed, $20 for each type `2` job completed, and $30 for each type `3` job completed. You may sequence the jobs in each queue in any manner you see fit. With the machines specified in the text, lay out the factory to maximize the rate that income is generated and minimize the size of the factory.

(c) To help solve this problem, design and run experiments to decide how to allocate waiting space for work-in-process (be creative). Explain the rationale for your experimental strategies: How did you initialize the system? Determine run lengths? Use variance reduction techniques? Compute confidence intervals?

13.3.8 Processing Priorities

Assume in `NETWORKT.MOD` that completed type `1` jobs are worth twice as much money as type `2` jobs, which in turn are worth three times as much money as type `3` jobs. It has been suggested that the jobshop operate by priority. The obvious scheme is to process waiting type `1` jobs before waiting type `2` jobs, with waiting type `3` jobs to be processed last. Make the necessary adjustments to your model for priority job processing. (Use the `PUT` and `GET` functions in SIGMA.)

(a) Make 5 runs of 8 hours each with the priority service rule and 5 runs of 8 hours with the current FIFO rule (a total of 10 one-day runs). Use independent streams for each run and estimate a confidence interval for the difference in total income for the day.

(b) Repeat this experiment using common seeds for each pair of runs (with and without the priority rule). Use independent seeds for different pairs of runs. Again estimate a confidence interval for the difference in total income for the 8-hour day.

(c) Comment on the differences between parts (a) and (b). What might be wrong with this experiment? Do you recommend the priority processing rule? Do you know a better one?

13.3.9 Motor Vehicles Department (Mini Simulation Project)

A State Motor Vehicles office has three clerks on duty. The office opens at 10:00 A.M. and closes its doors at 5:00 P.M. Customers already inside the office after closing are served. Between the hours of 10 and 12 (noon), walk-in customers arrive according to a Poisson process at a rate of $\lambda(t\text{-}10)$ customers per minute, where t denotes time in hours. Between the hours of 12 and 13 (i.e., over the noon hour), customers arrive at a constant rate of 2λ. Finally, between times 13 (1:00 P.M.) and 17 (5:00 P.M.), the arrival rate is $\lambda(17 - t)/2$.

Clerks process customers according to a uniform distribution between 0.5 and 2 minutes per customer. Occasionally a customer will call on the telephone and one of the clerks will take the call (possibly interrupting service for a customer). The time between phone calls is distributed as an exponential random variable with a mean of 5 minutes. It typically takes half the time to serve a call as to serve a walk-in customer. Every 20 minutes, one of the clerks is due for a 10-minute break on a rotating basis (one break per hour for each clerk).

(a) With at most 10 runs of the model, give an estimate of the capacity of the system as a function of the demand constant λ. Use whatever system performance measures you think are reasonable and justify them. Make and carefully state any additional assumptions about the system that you need; be sure to offer some justification for each assumption. A run is for a single day of operation. Carefully plan your experiment and give the rationale for your experimental design.

(b) As an aid in contract negotiations, consider the effect of adding an additional clerk or cutting the amount of break time taken by each clerk.

There is a plan to add a drive-up window to the office. This window is to be serviced by the same clerks that serve walk-in customers. Drive-in customers arrive according to the same pattern as walk-in customers. Drive-in customers will balk if there are 3 or more cars waiting for service at the drive-in window. Of these balking drive-in customers, 80% will try to park their cars in the parking lot and walk inside for service. Once a former drive-in customer parks and walks inside, s/he will not balk unless the line has more than 10 customers in it. The parking lot has space for 10 cars. Customers desiring parking in a full lot will wait only 30 seconds before balking. Assume that it takes between 2 and 3 minutes (uniformly) for a customer to travel from the lot to the office and vice versa (including time to park).

Enrich your simulation to include the possible drive-in window. Use the model to advise the state as to what it should do (hire more clerks? build the drive-up window? increase the size of the parking lot? etc.).

13.3.10 A Turnpike Gas Station

A toll road gas station has 2 pumps in tandem but only 1 access lane. Cars arrive only from the left at intervals that are spaced T minutes apart. Pumping gas and paying takes P minutes. If both pumps in a lane are free when a customer arrives, the customer will use the "down stream" pump. A car at pump 1 cannot pass a car at the pump in front of it even if it has finished.

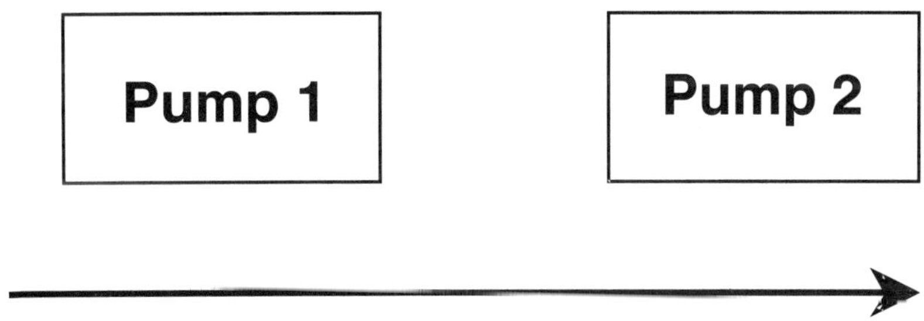

(a) What are the resident entities in this system? What are their attributes? What are the transient entities and their attributes? Describe, in words, the resident entity cycles and transient entity path(s). List any additional assumptions you are making about this system. Give an event graph model for the resident entities in this system. At a minimum, your graph could be used to measure the utilization of each pump.

(b) Create a SIGMA model of the turnpike gas station. Modify the problem so that if there are 4 or more cars in line when a customer arrives, the customer will go on to another station. Run your model until 20 cars have been served and analyze the queue size and utilization of each pump (charts, numbers, intuition, etc.). Start the system empty. Assume that car interarrival times are uniformly distributed between 1 and 5 minutes and service times are between 1 and 7 minutes.

13.3.11 A Turnpike Gas Station (continued) (Mini Simulation Project)

Enrich the preceding turnpike gas station model to include two access lanes, one on either side of the pumps. Potential customers arrive from the right and left at intervals that are randomly spaced. Assume that customer interarrival times are uniformly distributed between 2 and 6 minutes when coming from the left and uniformly spaced between 2 and 4 minutes when coming from the right. Service times are between 3 and 5 minutes at each pump.

(a) Customers cannot pass cars in front of them even if they have finished. Each pump can pump to only one car at a time in either lane and cars cannot drive around to change lanes. If there are more than four cars waiting in a lane, customers arriving from that direction will not stop. Draw an event graph of this system that can be used to study the resident entities (pumps and queues). Carefully justify your event graph model; do not just tell what you did and how, include why!

(b) Create a SIGMA model of your graph and print the English translation (`*.ENG`) and the event graph for your model. Run your model and discuss the output. (What kinds of questions can you answer with your model?)

(c) Using the `PUT` and `GET` functions, collect waiting time data for customers in each lane. Present and discuss histograms and time plots of the waiting time data.

(d) Using event parameters, tell us how you would enrich your model to include several service islands.

(e) Consider two service options: "full" service where service times are between 3.5 and 4.5 minutes at each pump and "self" service where service times are uniformly between 1 and 7 minutes at each pump. If both pumps are free when a customer arrives, that customer will use the "down stream" pump only half the time unless there is a "full" service attendant on duty. Create a SIGMA model of this system that can be used to study these two alternatives. Run your model under each alternative for 1 simulated hour. Write up your experiment and recommendations in less than five pages. How much can you afford to pay the extra attendant needed for the full service option (in terms of profit from lost sales)?

13.3.12 Parts Assembly

In an assembly operation, machines `A`, `B`, and `C` make parts that are joined together by machine `D`. It takes 3 parts from machine `A`, 2 parts from `B`, and 1 part from `C` for each assembly operation at machine `D`. All processing times have exponential (Erlang{1}) distributions. The mean processing times are input to the simulation as parameters of the first vertex. Build a simulation model of this simple assembly operation. Run your model for 10 complete assembly operations where the mean processing times for machines `A`, `B`, `C`, and `D` are `0.1`, `0.2`, `0.3`, and `0.4`. Which machine appears to be the bottleneck machine in this operation? What if machine `D`'s processing time were reduced to 0.05 minutes? Translate your model to C or Pascal and run it until 1000 assemblies are finished. Does your bottleneck machine change once the system has warmed up?

13.3.13 The Texas Ferry Service (Mini Simulation Project)

Along the Texas coast, an east-west four-lane highway was built to promote the tourist trade to the Padre Islands. Unfortunately, this highway must cross a wide channel used by large oil tankers. Providing free automobile ferry service is considered to be an alternative to building a bridge. There is room for up to 6 loading/unloading berths on each side of the channel. Whenever a tanker comes through the channel, the ferries have to wait until it passes. Evaluate the ferry option. Do a sensitivity analysis to various levels of demand. (How much can we spend on a bridge? How bad can it be?) Hint: Consider modeling aggregate arrival processes (e.g, ferry loads/hour for the different size ferries).

Relevant data are as follows: Each berth costs $2,500,000 to build. There are three sizes of ferries that can use the berths:

Type 0 holds 25 cars and costs $1,500,000.
Type 1 holds 50 cars and costs $3,250,000.
Type 2 holds 100 cars and costs $5,500,000.

On Friday afternoons during a two-hour peak period, it is estimated that cars will arrive roughly according to a Poisson process with a rate of 20 per minute from the east (Corpus Christi toward the Padre Islands). The time between arrivals is thus `20*ERL{1}`. On Sunday afternoon over a four-hour period, roughly the same number of cars will return to Corpus Christi. At other times (during the tourist season) traffic in both directions is expected to arrive at a rate of about 6 cars per minute.

The ferries take between 12 and 18 minutes to cross the channel (depending on the tides). Tankers come by according to a Poisson process at a rate of 1 every half-hour, and it takes 8 minutes for a tanker to pass the ferry lanes. Cars can be loaded onto a ferry at a rate of 3 per minute and unloaded at a rate of 5 per minute.

Note: It was decided to use ferries instead of building the bridge. Five berths on each side were built and 6 medium-sized ferries operate during the peak periods. Do you think this was a good decision? What factors, in addi tion to cost, might have guided the decision?

APPENDIX

A

Event Execution Sequence

In SIGMA, a mathematical expression can be used almost anywhere a variable can be used. This includes vertex state changes, edge delay times, and edge attribute values. In fact, SIGMA allows the execution order of simultaneous events to be state dependent through the use of mathematical expressions to model dynamic edge priorities. This gives SIGMA additional modeling power and allows rather complex applications where state-dependent event sequencing is important. In SIGMA the order of execution for an event vertex is as follows:

1. Set the vector of parameters for this vertex to the values of the edge attribute expressions placed on the future events list when this vertex was scheduled.
2. Make the state changes specified for this vertex.
3. Evaluate the edge conditions for *every* edge exiting this vertex.
4. For each exiting edge with a true edge condition:
   a. If the edge is a vertex scheduling edge,
      i. Evaluate each of the edge attribute expressions.
      ii. Compute the edge delay time.
      iii. If the delay is equal to a *, immediately execute the destination vertex and go to the next event; otherwise, compute the edge execution priority and schedule the destination vertex for this edge onto the future events list.
   b. If the edge is a vertex cancelling edge,
      i. If the edge attribute is equal to a *, cancel all scheduled vertices that are the same type as the destination vertex, regardless of the values of their attributes.

ii. If the edge attributes are left blank, cancel only the next scheduled vertex that is the same type as the destination vertex, regardless of the values of its attributes.

iii. If the edge attributes are not blank and not equal to a *, cancel any vertices that are of the same type as the destination vertex with the exact same attribute values as this cancelling edge.

Most of the time you will never have to think about execution order; however, you should be aware of it. The intuitive notion of an "event" would be a subgraph with zero-delay times on all of the edges in this subgraph. Event graphs are merely pictures that decompose events into manageable logical components.

APPENDIX

B

Reading SIGMA-Generated C Programs

This appendix is intended to help persons not familiar with the C programming language understand the C simulation programs generated by SIGMA; it is not intended to be a comprehensive introduction to C. You should look at the C simulation, `CARWASH.C`, to find examples of C program elements discussed here. Consult a good reference on C (Kernighan and Ritchie, 1988) for correct definitions and details on the C language. SIGMA-generated C programs also run under C++, which includes objects with the C language as a subset.

There are several powerful features of C that are not used in the simulations generated by SIGMA. These include structures, pointers, "do-while," etc. Learning C or C++ is strongly encouraged as it will allow you to greatly improve the efficiency of your simulations. The library of simulation functions, `CSIGLIB.C`, makes more extensive use of the C language than do the simulations generated by SIGMA. The source code in this library is extensively documented, so you should be able to tell what is going on by reading the comments embedded in the code.

B.1 Functions

C programs have a simple and elegant structure. They are composed of *functions*—that is, subprograms that return a single value when called by another function. Functions are identified by function names followed by parentheses, `()`. The parentheses following a function name contain the parameters for the function; these are the names of any variables whose values the function will need. Every C program has a master function, called `main()`, where execution starts. The `main()` function typically does little else except initialize variables and call other functions. The functions in a C program should be defined at the top of the program or in a file (called a header file) that will be included in the program before it is compiled.

B.2 Parameters

Parameters for functions have only their values passed to the function, not the variables themselves. Therefore, the values of the parameters passed to a function are not changed in the program that calls the function (unlike some implementations of FORTRAN).

B.3 Comments

Comments to increase understanding can be included anywhere in the code; they are ignored by the compiler. Comments begin with the delimiter `/*` and end with the delimiter `*/`; they cannot be nested. In C++, the delimiter `//` denotes a comment that ends at the end of the line. The code generated by SIGMA has extensive commenting, with most comments being the descriptions you entered when defining the variables, vertices, and edges in your event graph model.

B.4 Variables

All variables and functions must be *declared* by giving them a *type* and a *name.* Variable and function names are sequences of letters or digits starting with an underscore, _, or letter. These identifiers may be of any length; however, some compilers only distinguish as few as the first six characters. Case is important—e.g., the variable `TimeOfDay` is entirely different than the variable `timeofday`. The code you created in your SIGMA model as well as SIGMA key words will appear in the C translation in upper-case letters. All other C code generated by SIGMA is in lower-case. This way you can tell instantly the C code you created that is specific to your simulation from the generic C code needed to run your program.

> ➢ **Important:** *Code that you created that is specific to your* SIGMA *simulation will appear in upper-case characters. Generic C code is in lower-case.*

Variable definitions consist of the variable type followed by one or more variable names. Examples of C variable type definitions used by SIGMA include the following:

```
int i, J;            /* i and J are defined to be short
                     integers */

long k;              /* k is defined to be a long integer
                     (with more significant digits)*/

float g,f[6];        /* the variable, g, and array, f with 6
                     elements, are defined to be real (floating
                     point) numbers with decimals */

double h;            /* the variable, h, is defined to be a
                     double-precision floating point number */

char target[10],     /* target and date are defined
       date[100];    to be strings of characters of the
                     specified lengths, the size of the string
                     should allow for the final null string
                     termination character, '/0'. Indices of n
                     element array are 0 to n-1.  */

int *p;              /* the variable p is a pointer to the
                     address of an integer */
```

The last example is a pointer that will have as its value the memory address of an integer variable. To find the value of the memory address of a variable, place `&` in front of the variable name.

Using only upper-case characters for SIGMA expressions to avoid confusion with lower-case reserved words used by ANSI Standard C is not foolproof. For example, it is acceptable in SIGMA to name an event vertex `EXIT` or `exit`. However, if you use a Microsoft C (Version 5.1) compiler, these words have special meaning. This seems to cause no problems if you use other compilers. Of course, these other compilers also have functions added to their libraries, and you must avoid their function names.

B.5 Statements

Simple statements in C can be made, as in most other languages, with a variable being set equal (=) to an expression. C statements are grouped into related blocks of code delimited by braces, `{}`. These blocks of code determine the ranges of variable definitions as well as the range of iterations (loops) and sequencing (branching) statements. A statement ends with a semicolon (`;`) but is otherwise free-form, starting and ending in any column.

The C arithmetic operators used by SIGMA include addition (+), subtraction (−), multiplication (`*`), and division (`/`). C has a shorthand notation that is popular but redundant. In this notation, the statement `X=X+7` might be written `X+=7` and the statement `X=X+1` might be written simply as `X++`. This shorthand is irritating to people new to C, but in general people like it once it is familiar. The power operator (^) used in SIGMA does not exist in C; the function `pow()` is used instead. Relational operators for comparing two expressions include greater than (>), less than (<), greater than or equal to (>=), less than or equal to (<=), equal to (==), and not equal to (!=). Boolean logical operators in C are "&&" (and) and "¦ ¦" (or).

As in SIGMA, there are "side effects" to using functions to test edge conditions. For compound edge conditions using Boolean "and" operators, many C compilers will evaluate only until the first false condition is found. SIGMA, on the other hand, will evaluate all conditions before *and*ing. For example, if you have an edge condition (`Q>0&PUT{LINE;FST}`) in SIGMA, the `PUT` function will always be executed. This condition translates to C as (`Q>0&&PUT(LINE,FST)`), and the `PUT` function may only be executed if `Q>0`, depending on which C compiler you use.

C has bit operators that are not used by SIGMA. Note that in SIGMA, Boolean "and" and "or" operators are & and ¦ , respectively, which are bitwise operators in C. In C, ^ denotes the "exclusive or" bitwise operator.

B.6 Directives

Lines that start with a pound sign (#) are called directives. Some examples of directives are the following:

```
#include csiglib.h  /*insert the code in the header file,
                       csiglib.h, in your default
                       directory*/

#include <stdio.h> /*insert the file stdio.h from the
                      include subdirectory of your C
                      compiler*/

#define TRUE 1 */define the constant TRUE to be equal to
                  the integer 1*/

#if defined MSDOS /*if there is an environment variable
                     called MSDOS defined execute the code
                     until an #endif directive is reached*/

#define SIN(a) (sin(a)) /*define the upper-case function
                           SIN(a) to be equivalent to the
                           standard C function sin(a) with
                           the same argument*/
```

Substitutions indicated by directives are executed in the first phase of compilation. Directive statements do not end in semicolons.

B.7 Sequencing or Branching

The sequence of statement execution can be controlled in several ways. The most common is the `if-else` construct, which has the following format:

```
if(condition)
   {
   /* execute this block of code if the condition is true
      (not equal to zero)*/
   comments, statements and function calls
   }
else
   {
   /* execute this block of code if the condition is false
      (equal to zero)*/
   block of code
   }
```

It is common to nest `if-else` statements within other `if` and `else` blocks of code. Another common flow control statement is the `switch-case` with the following format:

```
switch(expression)
   {
   case 1:
      block of code
      break;
   case 2:
      block of code
      break;
   ...
   case constant_expression:
      block of code
      break;
   default:
      block of code
      break;
   }
```

The block of code following the `case` equal to the `switch` argument is executed until a `break` is hit. For example, if the expression in the `switch` evaluates to the integer 6, only the code following `case 6:` is executed. The key word, `break`, prevents the execution of statements following the next case. C also has the `goto` statement, but this is very rarely used.

B.8 Iteration (Looping)

To iterate a block of code several times, C provides the `for` and the `do-while` constructs. The `for` construct looks like this:

```
for(starting_expression; ending_condition; looping_expression)
     {
     block of code
     }
```

This will execute the block of code if the condition expression is true, beginning with the execution of the starting expression and executing the looping expression each time until the condition expression is false. For example, the statement

```
for(index=1;  index<6; index=index+1)
     {block of code}
```

will execute the block of code starting with index equal to 1 and increase the index by 1 for each loop as long as the index is less than 6. (The loop is not executed with index equal to 6.)

The forms of `while` and `do-while` statements are

```
while (expression) {block of code}
```

and

```
do {block of code} while (expression)
```

In each case if the expression is true, the block of code continues to be executed (unless a `break` is hit). In the `while` format, the expression is tested before the block of code is executed, and in the `do-while` format the expression is tested after the block of code is executed. In each case, a `break;` will exit the loop and a `continue;` will pass control to the next iteration.

B.9 Organization

The typical main C program skeleton is as follows:

```
directives (lines beginning with #).
global variable declarations
function definitions
main()
   {
   local variable declarations, comments, statements, and
   function calls
...
   }
```

Typical C functions have the following skeletons:

```
function_return_type  function name (list of parameters)
   parameter declarations
```

```
{
declarations, comments, statements and function calls
}
```

The default type of value returned by a function is an integer. (A "void" type function does not return any value.)

B.10 Input and Output

In C, output is commonly done with a standard C function, such as,

```
printf("format control string", list of variables);
```

This will cause the variables in the list to be printed in the default output device (typically the screen). The format control string dictates how the variables are to be printed.

The control string may contain ordinary characters and conversion specifications (preceded by a percent sign, `%`). Common conversion specifications are as follows:

`%s` - print as a character string
`%f` - print as a floating point number
`%d` - print as a decimal integer

Optional field specifications can also be included: `%20.10s` indicates that the field should be at least 20 characters wide, and 10 characters should be printed with right justification. `%-20.10s` will also print 10 characters in a field at least 20 characters wide but with left justification. Printing control characters can also be placed in the format control string, such as `\n` (end of line) and `\t` (tab). To illustrate, if `val` is a floating point number currently at 6.57643, `i` is an integer with a value of 3, and `name` is a string with value "profit," the statement

```
printf("The %s for quarter, %d, = $%-5.2f\n", name,i,val);
```

should result in the line

```
The profit for quarter, 3, = $6.57
```

being printed on the default output device.

Data are typically input into a C program using a standard library function such as

```
scanf("format conversion string", pointers to addresses of
variables)
```

The format conversion string is similar to the `printf` statement. Since function arguments in C are passed by value, not reference, it is important that the values of pointers to the addresses of variables being read in are given, not the names of the variables themselves;

```
scanf("%d",i);
```

would not read in a value for the variable, `i`; however,

```
scanf(%d, &i);
```

would. Placing the character & in front of a variable name indicates that we mean a pointer to the address of the variable. Examples of the `printf` and `scanf` functions can be seen when prompts for input are given in the simulation `CARWASH.C` on your SIGMA disk.

B.11 Referencing Disk Files

Files on your disk can be read from and written to using file pointers with standard C library functions. You need to define the special data type `FILE` and assign pointers to files of this type. For example:

```
FILE *i_file, *o_file;   /*pointers to files */
```

Files also need to be opened and closed using the `fopen` and `fclose` statements, like

```
i_file = fopen("input.dat","r"); /* open input.dat to read */
o_file = fopen("output.dat","w"); /* opens output.dat to
write */
```

and

```
fclose(i_file);
fclose(o_file);
```

An example of a function that reads data from a disk file, `ROUTES.DAT`, and echoes to the screen is the following `INPUT` function:

```
/*** READING ROUTES FROM DISK ***/
void INPUT()
{
FILE *fp; /* declare a file pointer for DISK input */
int i, route[18]; /* index for reading data and the route */

/*open the DISK file in read-only mode */
fp = fopen("routes.dat","r");
/* loop to read 17 values from the disk file */
   for(i=0; i<17; i++)
     {
     fscanf(fp,"%d",&route[i]);   /* read the data */
     printf("route[%d]=%d\n",i,route[i]);/ *echo to screen */
     }
```

```
fclose(fp); /*close the DISK file */
}
```

B.12 Redefining Standard Input or Output Devices

When a C program is executed, the default input and output devices (the screen and keyboard) can be changed to any devices you want by using the < and > conventions. This is best illustrated with an example. You have an executable C program, `TEST.EXE`, on your A: drive whose input usually comes from the keyboard and whose output usually goes to the screen. To run this program with these default input and output devices you simply enter a:test.

Now suppose that you want to read the input from a disk file named `INPUT.DAT` on your C: drive and you want the output to be written to the file `OUTPUT.DAT` on your C: drive. You execute the program by entering

```
a:test    <c:input.dat    >c:output.dat
```

The < indicates where the keyboard input will be coming from and the > indicates where the screen output will be written. This is useful in batching runs of a simulation where different input data and output files are desired for each replication. Be careful about redirecting the input; if the program needs information not in the specified file, you may have to reboot to use the keyboard.

B.13 Arrays, Pointers, and Data Structures

C has several features that are not exploited by SIGMA, including data structures and pointers. Pointers are variables whose values are the addresses in memory where data are located. The type of pointer (`int`, `char`, etc.) tells you how many bytes in memory are in the block of memory to which the pointer is pointing. A pointer is identified by having an asterisk (`*`) before the variable name. The operator `&` gives the address in memory of an object. If your program has the following declarations:

```
int var; /* var is some integer variable */
int *p;  /* p is a pointer to the address of an integer */
```

To have "`p` point to `a`" you can write

```
p = &var; /* assigns the address of var to the pointer p */
```

and you can increase the value of `var` by 5 with either

```
var = var + 5;
```

or

```
*p = *p + 5
```

Pointers are particularly useful in simulations when they are used to point to structures.

This brief introduction is intended not to give you a complete background on the use of structures and pointers but merely to give you some indication of their power. Hopefully, you will be encouraged to learn more about structures and pointers and use them in your models. Structures are used extensively in the Pascal and C library functions, `PSIGLIB.PAS` and `CSIGLIB.C`. A data structure can be thought of as the complement of a data array. Where an array gives you the value of a single variable when you specify one or more indices, a structure gives you one or more values for variables when you specify a single index (in the form of a pointer). An array can be used to represent many-to-one relationship and structures to represent one-to-many relationship.

Data structures can be used in simulations as records of information that pertain to a particular entity (school records for a group of students). Setting up data structures is useful when you need to keep track of many characteristics of an entity in your simulation model. Suppose you are simulating a factory and you want to keep track of each job's type, current task, location, start time, routing, and time the job will take on each of several machines. If you assign a unique job identification number to each job in the system, you might use several arrays as we did in the SIGMA queueing network models discussed earlier. For each job, you could keep its type, current task, *x-y* coordinates of its location, and the time it was started in a collection of arrays like `TYPE[JOB]`, `TASK[JOB]`, `LOCATION[JOB;2]`, and `START_TIME[JOB]`. You could also have numbers representing the machine needed for each processing task for each job type in a table represented by the nested arrays, `ROUTE[TASK[JOB];TYPE[JOB]]`. The two-dimensional array `ROUTE[]` is an example of a two-to-one relationship; you specify two values, `TASK` and `TYPE`, and get one value of the machine number.

What we really want is to access many items of information about a single job, a one-to-many relationship. This is what a data structure does. A data structure set up to contain the relevant information for each job might look like the following in C:

```
struct tag {
   int   type;
   int   task;
   float        x_location;
   float        y_location;
   float        start_time;
   int          *route;
   }job;
```

You can also use structures within other structures. To reference an element of a structure, you use a period—e.g., `if(job.task==2)` would test if the current task of a specific job was equal to 2.

Then an array of pointers to job records could be set up as

```
struct tag *job;
```

If we want to assign to the variable `t` the time of job 8 and `x` and `y` to its location, we could use the statements

```
struct tag *job;
t=job[8]->type;
x=job[8]->x_location;
y=job[8]->y_location;
```

A general-purpose structure called an `Entity` is defined in `CSIGLIB.H`. This is an array of pointers to linked lists of arrays; it is used to model transient entities, queues, etc. Memory for new entities is dynamically allocated as the entities are created. Memory is freed when entities are removed from lists. The `Entity` structure is defined as follows in C:

```
/* The Entity data type is a double-linked list */
/* S_MAXLIST lists have S_MAXATRIB elements in each entry */

typedef struct entity{
struct entity
   *prev, /* pointer to previous entity on list */
   *next; /* pointer to next entity on list */
float attrib[S_MAXATRIB]; /* attribute list for this
entity */
} Entity;

/* Set up Arrays of Pointers to Linked Lists of attribs */
Entity *head[S_MAXLISTS], *tail[S_MAXLISTS];
```

You do not need to know about the `Entity` structure to use SIGMA, but it is useful if you understand it. This structure is a reasonable test of your comprehension of C. A schematic of this structure is shown in Figure B.1.

The last `Entity` is the queue of events on the future events list. The attributes of an entry on the future events list are `attrib [0]`, the scheduled time of the event occurrence, `attrib [1]`, the type of event, and `attrib [2]`, the execution priority; the remaining attributes are used to pass parameter values to the scheduled event. The `CSIGLIB` function, `c_file(S_EVNT, S_EVNTLST)`, schedules events onto the future events list. The function, `c_timing()`, finds the next scheduled event on this list and advances the clock to the time for that event occurrence.

Figure B.1: Schematic of the `Entity` Structure

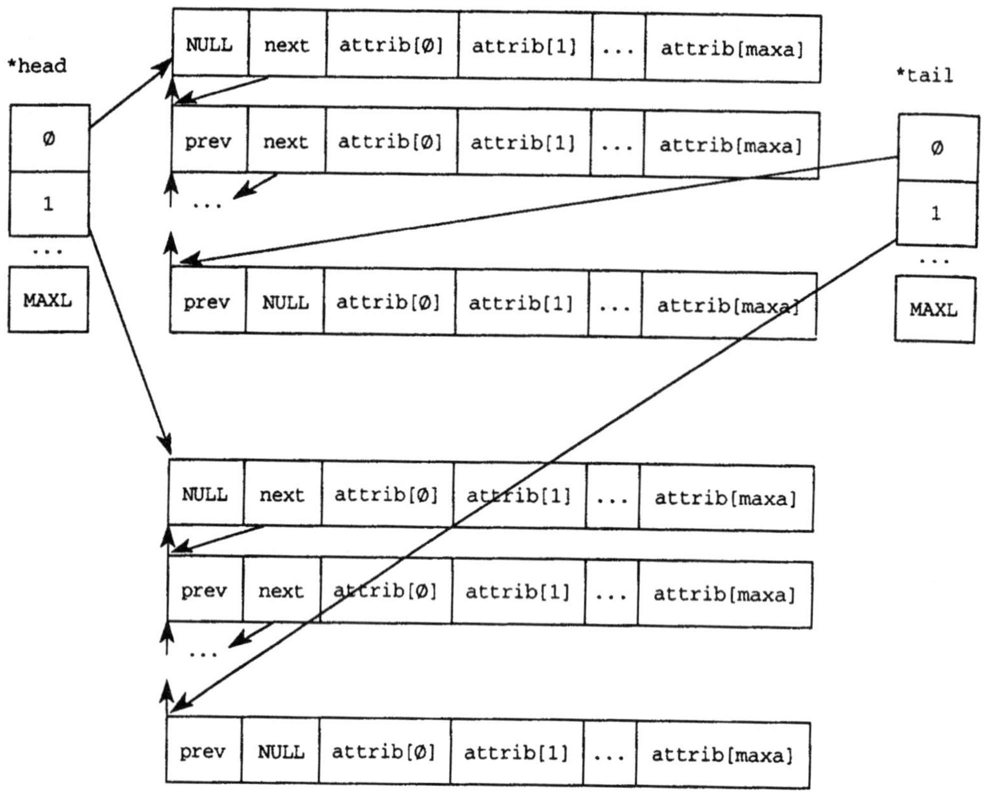

B.14 Incompatibilities Between C and SIGMA

The general SIGMA `USER` variable/function typically requires a workstation and has no counterpart in C. Also, the SIGMA power operator (^) does not exist in C. (In C, ^ is one of several bitwise operators that are not used directly in SIGMA simulations but appear in some of the `CSIGLIB.C` library routines that support SIGMA.) Your C compiler probably has a power function in its library, called `pow(x,y)`, which you can use to replace `x^y`. Finally, the indexed access of the SIGMA `DISK` function is not standard (a Microsoft `fseek()` function is used in `CSIGLIB.C`). You will probably use the standard C library input functions that are discussed in this appendix anyway.

REFERENCES

Banks, J., and J. Carson II (1984). *Discrete Event System Simulation.* Prentice Hall: Englewood Cliffs, NJ.

Berg, S. (1992). Private communication.

Bratley, P., B. Fox, and L. Schrage (1987). *A Guide to Simulation,* 2nd edition. Springer-Verlag: New York.

Brockwell, P. J., and R. A. Davis (1987). *Time Series: Theory and Methods.* Springer-Verlag: New York.

Chen, B., and R. G. Sargent (1984). Confidence Interval Estimation for the Difference Between Two Stochastic Processes Using Standardized Time Series. Working paper 84-004, Dept. of IE and OR, Syracuse University.

Cheng, R. C. H. (1978). Generating Beta Variates with Non Integral Shape Parameters. *Comm. Assoc. Comp. Mach.,* 21, 317-322.

Devroye, L. (1986). *Non-Uniform Random Variate Generation.* Springer-Verlag: New York.

Duersch, R., and L. Schruben (1986). An Interactive Run Length Control for Simulations on PCs. *Proceedings of the 1986 Winter Simulation Conference.*

Goldsman, D. (1983). Ranking and Selection in Simulation. *Proceedings of the 1983 Winter Simulation Conference,* 387-393.

Goldsman, D., and L. Schruben (1984). Asymptotic Properties of Some Confidence Interval Estimators for Simulation Output. *Management Science,* 30, 1217-1225.

Goldsman, D., and L. Schruben (1990). New Confidence Interval Estimators Using Standardized Time Series. *Management Science,* 36, 393-397.

Heidelberger, P., and P. Welch (1983). Simulation Run Length Control in the Presence of an Initial Transient. *Operations Research,* 31, 1109-1144.

Hoover, S., and R. Perry (1989). *Simulation: A Problem Solving Approach.* Addison-Wesley: New York.

Johnson, M. E. (1987). *Multivariate Statistical Simulation.* John Wiley: New York.

Kernighan, B. W., and B. M. Ritchie (1988). *The C Programming Language,* 2nd edition. Prentice Hall: Englewood Cliffs, NJ.

Law, A. M., and W. D. Kelton (1991). *Simulation Modeling and Analysis,* 2nd edition. McGraw-Hill: New York.

Leemis, L. (1986). Relationships Between Common Probability Distributions. *Amer. Statistician,* 40, 2.

Lewis, P. A. W. (1981). Simple Multivariate Time Series for Simulations of Complex Systems. *Proceedings of the 1981 Winter Simulation Conference.*

Lewis, P. A. W., A. S. Goodman, and J. M. Miller (1969). A Pseudo-random Number Generator for the System 360. *IBM Systems Journal,* 8, 136-146.

Lewis, P. A. W., and E. J. Orav (1989). *Simulation Methodology for Statisticians, Operations Analysts, and Engineers: Vol 1.* Wadsworth & Brooks/Cole: Pacific Grove, CA.

Lewis, P. A. W., and G. S. Shedler (1979). Simulation of Nonhomogeneous Poisson Processes by Thinning. *Nav. Logist. Res. Quart.,* 26, 403-413.

McKenzie, E. (1985). Some Simple Models for Discrete Variate Time Series. *Water Res. Bulletin,* 21(4).

Nozari, A. (1985). Confidence Intervals Based on Steady-State Continuous-Time Statistics. *Operations Research Letters,* 4, 213-220.

Pegden, C. D. (1987). Introduction to SIMAN. Systems Modeling Corp.: Sewickley, PA.

Pritsker, A. A. B. (1986). *Introduction to Simulation and SLAM II.* John Wiley: New York.

Ramberg, J. S., P. R. Tadikamalla, E. J. Dudewicz, and E. F. Mykytka (1979). A Probability Distribution and Its Uses in Fitting Data. *Technometrics,* 21, 201-214.

Schmeiser, B. W. (1983). Batch Size Effects in the Analysis of Simulation Output. *Operations Research,* 30, 565-568.

Schruben, L. W. (1980). Establishing the Credibility of Simulations. *Simulation,* 34, 101-105.

Schruben, L. (1982). Detecting Initialization Bias in Simulation Output. *Operations Research,* 30, 569-590.

Schruben, L. (1983). Confidence Interval Estimation Using Standardized Time Series. *Operations Research,* 31, 1090-1107.

Schruben, L. (1983). Simulation Modeling with Event Graphs. *Communications of the A. C. M.,* 26, 957-963.

Schruben, L. (1985). Standardized Time Series: An Overview. *Proceedings of the 1985 Winter Simulation Conference.*

Schruben, L., H. Singh, and L. Tierney (1983). Optimal Tests for Initialization Bias in Simulation Output. *Operations Research,* 31, 1167-1178.

Wagner, H. M. (1988). Operations Research: A Global Language for Business Strategy. *Operations Research,* 36, 797-803.

INDEX

Arithmetic, Test, & Boolean Operators				
Function	SIGMA	C	Pascal	FORTRAN
Assignment	=	=	:=	=
Addition	+	+	+	+
Subtraction	-	-	-	-
Multiplication	*	*	*	*
Division	/	/	/	/
Exponentiation	^	pow()	^	*
Test for equality	==	==	==	.EQ
Test for inequality	!=	!=	<>	.NE
Test for greater than	>	>	>	.GT
Test for less than	<	<	<	.LT
Logical *and*	&	&&	and	.AND
Logical *or*	¦	¦¦	or	.OR
True (affirmation test)	[*Value*] > 0	[*Value*] > 0	True	
False (negation test)	[*Value*] = 0	[*Value*] = 0	False	

A

C

D

E

N

T